Words of Praise for *Ruth*

"If there was ever a woman that exemplified her bitter weakness, it is mother-in-law Naomi. If there was a woman who exemplified her ultimate loyalty, it's daughter-in-law Ruth. Diana has written a revealing, sobering, instructional love story that will encourage you to evaluate yourself, help break the bonds of intimidation, cause you to want to study the Word, and give you a greater appreciation for the character and characters in the Book of Ruth in the Holy Bible.

Once you've captured these eye-opening pages in your heart, your strength can increase, and your burdens of fear can decrease."

—THELMA WELLS

President, A Woman of God Ministries
Founder/President, Daughters of Zion Leadership Mentoring Program
Speaker, Women of Faith Conferences
Professor, Master's Divinity School and Graduate School
Author, *The Buzz—7 Power Packed Scriptures to Energize Your Life*

"What a refreshing, powerful, passionate, and clear teaching of the book of Ruth. In this book Diana takes you deep into God's truth, and walks you through descriptive Biblical explanation of how our covenant-keeping God will use the good, bad and the ugly in our lives to bring about restoration, hope and blessing. We are reminded again through this beautiful story of Ruth's life of how faithful and deliberate God is to define His love for us in accomplishing His will and plan for our lives. He truly is a covenant-keeping God."

—LOIS EVANS

Senior Vice President of The Urban Alternative
President of Global Pastor's Wives Network

Thank you, Diana, for writing *Ruth: the Romance of Redemption*. I had heard you teaching on it on TV briefly and I felt compelled to purchase it. There are two areas of my life that I struggle with: rejection and worthiness. I recently had to let go of a relationship that was unhealthy for me, but I thought it was the best that I could get. Your book has helped me see myself as the Heavenly Father sees me. Your book has taught me that I don't need to settle for being second in anyone's life. I am redeemed by the Blood of Jesus, and He loves me, and His love is enough. Your book has given me hope. In God's perfect time He will send me my earthly husband who will put me first and love and protect me—and I am worthy of that.

I have only been a Christian for less than two years and have heard that Jesus wants to be my husband, but I never really understood what that meant. Your book has helped clarify that in my heart and my mind.

In the 18 months since my conversion, I have read many books from recognized and anointed people. I have a deep desire to know Him more and more. This book is an answer to my prayers! You have made the Bible come alive to me in a way no one else has. Now when I read the Bible, I think about the circumstances and the environments surrounding the people God has chosen to reveal Himself through. Thank you so very much.

—MARY FAHEY

DIANA HAGEE

Best-selling Author of *The King's Daughter*

Ruth

the

ROMANCE

of

REDEMPTION

A LOVE STORY

NELSON BOOKS
A Division of Thomas Nelson Publishers
Since 1798
www.thomasnelson.com

Published in Nashville, Tennessee, by Thomas Nelson, Inc.

Nelson Books titles may be purchased in bulk for educational, business, fundraising, or sales promotional use. For information, please email SpecialMarkets@ThomasNelson.com.

All Scripture quotations, unless otherwise indicated, are taken from the New King James Version®. Copyright © 1982 by Thomas Nelson, Inc. Used by permission. All rights reserved. The specific edition used is *The Life Plan™ Study Bible,* Copyright © 2004 by Thomas Nelson, Inc.

Scripture quotations noted KJV are from The Holy Bible, KING JAMES VERSION.

Scripture quotations noted AMP are from THE AMPLIFIED BIBLE: Old Testament. Copyright © 1962, 1964 by Zondervan Publishing House (used by permission); and from THE AMPLIFIED NEW TESTAMENT. Copyright © 1958 by the Lockman Foundation (used by permission).

Scripture quotations noted NIV are from the HOLY BIBLE, NEW INTERNATIONAL VERSION®. Copyright © 1973, 1978, 1984 by International Bible Society. Used by permission of Zondervan Bible Publishing House. All rights reserved.

The "NIV" and "New International Version" trademarks are registered in the United States Patent and Trademark Office by International Bible Society. Use of either trademark requires the permission of International Bible Society.

Library of Congress Cataloging-in-Publication Data

Hagee, Diana.
    Ruth : the romance of redemption : a love story / Diana Hagee.
        p. cm.
    Includes bibliographical references.
    ISBN 0-7852-0866-6 (pbk.)
    1. Bible. O.T. Ruth—Criticism, interpretation, etc. 2. Christian women—Religious life.
I. Title.
    BS1315.52.H34 2005
    222'.3506—dc22

                                                                            2005020282

Printed in the United States of America

06 07 08 09 VG 6 5 4 3 2

To my Naomi—
Vada Swick Hagee

"Your God shall be my God!"

ACKNOWLEDGMENTS

Heartfelt thanks to my husband, Pastor John C. Hagee, and our dear friend Rabbi Arnold Scheinberg, whose knowledge and love of God's Word directed me through this beautiful journey.

CONTENTS

CONFESSIONS OF A PASTOR'S WIFE

For years the Word of God intimidated me. I was afraid to open its pages for fear I would not understand its message. As a pastor's wife I knew I would be expected to interpret the words of this sacred Book to others, and the weight of this charge was too heavy to carry. I was overwhelmed. What if I made a mistake? What if I led people astray? It was a risk I could not take. So I did nothing.

Slowly, at the prodding of my ever-thoughtful husband, I began to search the Word for answers. I searched its infinite wisdom for direction. I combed its pages for comfort and, as time passed, the Word became a great and inseparable friend.

The first book of the Bible I read in its entirety was the Book of Ruth. I chose Ruth for two reasons. First, it was short, and I felt secure in that. Second, it was about a woman. This fact amazed me. Why would the God who created the universe and formed man with His own hands dedicate an entire book of His consecrated Word to a woman?

Each time I opened the Book of Ruth, my prayer was always the same: *Teach me, Father, to hear from Your precious Word. Be patient with me, for I know so little. Show me what You would have me learn from Your sacred Scripture.* He always heard my prayer and always answered. Now I want to share some of the beautiful truths I have found in this remarkable love story, one of the greatest ever told.

The word *love* is revealed in every page of this book, yet never used within the text. Today's society habitually uses the word *love*, and consequently we no longer remember its true meaning. We promise to love until death, yet one out of two marriages ends in divorce. We say we love our children, but abuse is at epidemic proportions. We desire "free love" and, as a result, more than 43 million babies have been aborted. Therefore, I ask the question, what is love? Hopefully we will have a better understanding of the profound significance of the word *love* by the end of our journey.

The Book of Ruth is a story of tragedy that leads to triumph—a story of loneliness exchanged for romance—a story of heartache that explodes into rejoicing—a story of hopelessness transformed by redemption.

In order to make our journey into the Book of Ruth more enjoyable and easier to grasp, I have divided it into eighteen vignettes. Each vignette begins with a window into Naomi's heart as she shares her life with you. I want you to envision this remarkable love story in the theatre of your mind.

The next section will be the actual study of the Book of Ruth, where I often dissect each verse to better understand Jewish culture and the historical surroundings of Judah at the time the book was written.

I have used both Christian and Jewish sources in my research. I have consulted my husband, Pastor John Hagee, a biblical scholar in his own right, and Rabbi Arnold Scheinberg, a dear friend and Orthodox theologian, to help me communicate the extraordinary message of this vibrant story surrounding one of God's remarkable gifts: redemption. The Scripture will be taken from *The Life Plan Study Bible.*

From time to time I will mention Jewish sources, and I wish to define some of these terms. The *Torah* means "instruction" and refers specifically to the five books of Moses. The *Tenakh* is an acronym for the Jewish Bible made of three parts—*Torah (Ta)*, which is the Pentateuch or the Law; *Nevi'im (Na)* refers to the writings of the Prophets; and *Ketuvim (Kh)* are the wisdom writings beginning with Psalms. The *Tenakh* is the Old Testament to Christians. The *Midrash* means "to inquire" and is defined as the exposition of Scripture. *Mishnah* means "teaching" and is the recommended "oral law" established by authoritative Rabbinical teachers. *Talmud* is Hebrew for "study or learning" and is a compilation of the discussions of the *Midrash* by Rabbinic scholars. And finally, *gematria,* which is an interpretive device in Rabbinic Judaism focusing on the numerical value of each word.

It is hard to conceive that God has ordained me to write about the Book of Ruth. Diana—who was intimidated by His Word? Diana—who felt so unworthy? Diana—who knew so little about Scripture? This act in itself shows His goodness and mercy toward me.

My desire is for you to understand this book so clearly that it will shatter any intimidation you may have about studying the Word of God, the same intimidation that cursed my life for years. I want you to have a passion for the Word of the Living God. I want you to read it. I want you to hunger for the study of it. I want you to share the Word with those you love so they too may be blessed by its powerful message. For once you have been redeemed, it is your obligation to lead others to redemption!

God also wants us to learn about His Word for He knows the power His Word possesses and the destruction that comes to those who do not know it:

> *My people are destroyed for lack of knowledge. Because you have rejected knowledge, I also will reject you from being priest for Me; because you have forgotten the law of your God, I also will forget your children.* (HOSEA 4:6)

I do not want to be destroyed for lack of knowledge. I do not want to be rejected by God, and I certainly do not want Him to forget my children. Instead I want His blessings, and I want my children to be blessed!

The final part of each section will be called Life Lessons. Christ applied the Word to the lives of those He taught, and we must apply it to our lives as well, so we may benefit from its infinite riches. The Word of God is the Bread of Life, but His Word will not profit us, no matter how spiritually nourishing it is, until we consume it.

The Word of God is the protoplasm of life—dynamic and in constant motion. The Word of God will transform itself and become whatever I need, whenever I need it. The Word of God will restore my soul, whatever my condition.

When I have lack, the Word of God is my abundance. When I am weak, the Word of God is my strength. When I am hungry, the Word of God is my nourishment, for His Word is milk for spiritual babes and meat for the mature. When I am confused, the Word of God is my compass. When I am discouraged, the Word of God is my joy. When I lack knowledge, the Word of God is my wisdom. When I am lonely, the Word of God is my companion, for He promises to be closer to me than a brother. When I need protection, He is my shelter from the storm. The Word of God is whatever I need, whenever I need it. The Word of the living God is everything to me, and I will draw from its riches for the rest of my life.

My desire is for the King's daughters to grow to a new spiritual dimension and to receive all our Father has for us. You and I are about to take a journey into the pages of an incredible book about two women and their Redeemer. This journey will change our lives forever.

Let's begin with a window into Naomi's heart . . .

Chapter One

THE ROMANCE OF REDEMPTION

Naomi's husband, Elimelech, told her to do something she thought she would never have to do. He asked her to close the doors of her home and pack their belongings for a long journey, perhaps the longest journey of their lives. It was difficult for her to understand her husband's reasoning, but she knew she must follow him to Moab.

Naomi's palatial home had been a great joy to her and her family for decades. She gave birth to her adored sons in this home. Fond memories of precious days of laughter lingered within the walls of her lovely sanctuary. As she folded her clothing into large trunks, she found herself crying for the good times. Oh, how she missed them.

She carefully packed away a beautiful linen robe made with trim of red silk and gold thread; it was the robe she wore the day of her betrothal to her beloved husband. The town envied her beauty that day. What a fine day that was! Never had she seen Bethlehem so joyful and Elimelech so handsome. He had always been a man of striking features and strong will—two qualities she admired in him.

Today will be the most difficult of days. Today Naomi will remove the final remembrances of her family from her home. Today she will bid her friends goodbye.

A famine had plagued Israel for years, but Naomi had always kept a secret supply of flour and honey for her renowned honey cakes. She faithfully thanked Jehovah for the blessings of provision and favor that followed her family.

Tears streamed down her face as she began to prepare tea for her cherished guests. She had known them for as long as she could remember. They shared the good times and the sad moments of each other's lives. It was time to say goodbye to a lifetime of beautiful memories and treasured friendships. What would she say?

THE BIBLE STUDY

In order to better understand the Book of Ruth I asked questions of the Lord before I began to study the first verse. Questions such as: Why did the Holy Spirit choose this remarkable work from so many inspirational writings to be included in His divine library called the Holy Scriptures? Why did the prophet Samuel feel he should author this amazing manuscript? How did a gentile woman enter the genealogy of Christ? The answers to these questions helped me to unveil some of the mysteries within the pages of the Book of Ruth.

Many liberal interpretations of Scripture teach that the Bible is degrading in its portrayal of women. This could not be further from the truth. Just think, out of the sixty-six books of the Bible, two are completely devoted to women. The first, the Book of Esther, is a book about a Jewish maiden who marries a gentile and saves her people from annihilation. This book is known as the Romance of Providence.

The second is the Book of Ruth, a book about a Gentile girl who marries an Israelite and is grafted into the root of David. This book is known as the Romance of Redemption.[1]

The Jews read five books, called the Megilloth, in their synagogues during the Feasts. These feasts celebrate past events that have greatly impacted the Jewish people. The Book of Esther is read during the Feast of Purim, which celebrates the deliverance of the Jews from death at the hand of Haman.

The Book of Ruth is read during *Shavout,* or the Feast of Pentecost. Why is this book read during Pentecost? For the Jew, there are three reasons. First, the book of Ruth begins with the barley harvest and ends with the wheat harvest (from Passover to Pentecost). During this season of anticipation, Ruth went to Boaz on the threshing floor, and their meeting became part of a series of events which led to their marriage and eventual birth of their son Obed. Second, the book of Ruth centers on the personality of King David's grandmother, and it is believed that David was born and died during *Shavout.* And third, *Shavout* is also recorded as the time when God revealed the *Torah* to Moses on Mount Sinai, reminding every Jew that they too were once converts to Judaism just as Ruth, who is the consummate paradigm of converts.[2] It was at this moment in time that all of God's chosen had the opportunity to accept the great challenge, responsibility, and destiny of becoming a Jew.

To the Christian, Pentecost is the birthday of the church. Pentecost is the Bethlehem of the Holy Spirit—its birthplace—for He came on that day to be made flesh. Scripture says:

> **Know ye not that your body is the temple of the Holy Ghost, which is in you?** (I CORINTHIANS 6:19 KJV)

J. Vernon McGee states that "Pentecost is the line of demarcation between Law and grace. It marks the ending of the age of Law and the beginning of the age of grace."[3]

Oh, how we as children of the living God depend on His mercy and His grace! Grace is the main component throughout this precious book. I know this is one of the reasons I love it so, for what would have become of my life without my portion of grace?

Samuel is said to have written Ruth during the reign of David (1000–961 BC), yet the actual setting takes place during the period of the judges' rule over Israel, sometime between 1150 and 1100 BC. During this time in Israel's history the judgment of God was upon His people because of their adulterous relationships with other gods. Israel reaped the consequences of their disobedience through the famine God sent to the land.

Yet in even the darkest of days, we see a loving God working out His purposes in the lives of individuals who are rightly related to Him by covenant. In Hebrew, two terms denote *people* within Scripture. One is *am* and the other is *goi*. *Am* refers to a people with a shared cohesion of values—a people of covenant. God calls Israel His *ami* or "My people." The word *goi* or *goyim* is a word that refers to a nation of people in terms of politics or geography. As history has evolved, *goyim* has become linked to those people or nations outside of God's chosen. Scripture attests that God, our Father, is always interested in the affairs of His children.[4]

I used to refer to myself as a *goi* when speaking to Rabbi Scheinberg because I was a non-Jew; however, after researching the Hebrew I realized I was grafted into the root of Jesse by the death of my Savior at the cross. I am God's *ami,* part of His people—of His covenant. I was not God's child by birth; I became God's child through adoption. Hallelujah!

Jewish scholars believe the prophet Samuel wrote the Book of Ruth in honor of David to justify his royalty. The crown of kingship is placed on David's head as well as on the regal household of the Messiah because of the lineage included in this historical book. In essence the Book of Ruth establishes the "Scarlet Thread" of genealogy within Scripture.

In 1 Samuel we see the story of a disobedient Israel, an Israel that demanded a king from the Lord. At this time, God was Israel's king. He raised judges for her and guided them to lead her. Through these judges He protected her and He provided for her:

> *And when the LORD raised up judges for them, the LORD was with the judge and delivered them out of the hand of their enemies.*
> (JUDGES 2:18)

This was not enough for God's people, and they went their own way. God brought judgment to them by lifting His protection and allowing other nations to suppress them:

> *Then the anger of the LORD was hot against Israel; and He said, "Because this nation has transgressed My covenant which I commanded their fathers, and has not heeded My voice, I also will no longer drive out before them any of the nations which Joshua left when he died." (JUDGES 2:20–21)*

However, the Israelites did not know the heart of God, and they believed their oppression was brought on because they did not have a king to lead them in battle. They demanded a king, and therefore, rejected the Lord God of Israel:

> *And the LORD said to Samuel, "Heed the voice of the people in all that they say to you; for they have not rejected you, but they have rejected Me, that I should not reign over them." (1 SAMUEL 8:7)*

This was a time of spiritual confusion for Israel, marked by compromise and apostasy. Israel's desire for a king was not the dilemma—Israel's impure *motive* for wanting a king was the problem. They wanted to be like other nations; they wanted someone else's supervision other than God's. They did not want to be a people set apart to the one and only true God of Abraham, Isaac, and Jacob:

> *Nevertheless the people refused to obey the voice of Samuel; and they said, "No, but we will have a king over us, that we also may be like all the nations, and that our king may judge us and go out before us and fight our battles." (1 SAMUEL 8:19–20)*

Even though Samuel was displeased with Israel's disobedience and was reluctant to appoint a king over her, he obeyed the voice of the Lord and anointed Saul as commander over the people:

> *Then Samuel took a flask of oil and poured it on his head, and kissed him and said: "Is it not because the* LORD *has anointed you commander over His inheritance?"* (1 SAMUEL 10:1)

Samuel anointed Saul. Samuel kissed Saul on the forehead. Samuel spoke of Saul before the nation of Israel. As time passed Samuel grew to love Saul; through the Lord's guidance, Samuel discipled Saul and taught him to fear the Holy One of Israel.

After serving as leader over Israel, Saul, too, became disobedient. He sought the advice of a witch and obeyed the voice of the people instead of the God who anointed him commander. The kingdom was taken from Saul by the Lord and given to another, and Samuel was heartbroken. Always obeying the voice of God, Samuel went to Bethlehem in search of the new king that the Holy One of Israel had selected. Yet Samuel searched with a grieving spirit:

> *Now the* LORD *said to Samuel, "How long will you mourn for Saul, seeing I have rejected him from reigning over Israel? Fill your horn with oil, and go; I am sending you to Jesse the Bethlehemite. For I have provided Myself a king among his sons."* (1 SAMUEL 16:1)

Samuel lamented so deeply over the loss of Saul that he did not recognize God's anointed. The Lord rebuked Samuel when David stood before him, and He instructed His prophet to anoint His chosen king:

> *Then Samuel took the horn of oil and anointed him in the midst of his brothers; and the Spirit of the* LORD *came upon David from that day forward.* (1 SAMUEL 16:13)

The Lord had instructed Samuel to anoint Saul using a flask of oil, which signified a temporary kingdom, but David was anointed with a horn of oil, which represented a kingdom that would last for eternity.[6] Saul was appointed "commander" over the Lord's inheritance while David was declared "king" over Israel.[7]

Saul was a commoner who became a commander. David was a commoner who became a king, prophet, poet, and a man after God's own heart. Out of David's loins would come a kingdom without end, a kingdom where Shiloh would have dominion forevermore:

He shall build a house for My name, and I will establish the throne of his kingdom forever. (2 SAMUEL 7:13)

In crowning David king, God was doing a separate and sovereign work that would affect the future of mankind and eternity.

Many Christian scholars, such as J. Vernon McGee, believe one of the main purposes of the Old Testament is to furnish a reliable genealogy of the Lord Jesus Christ.

The Book of Ruth is the only book in the Old Testament that presents the family tree of David, proving to be the most vital link from Abraham to the coming Messiah. The genealogical table in Ruth is duplicated, in part, in the New Testament in the Gospel of Matthew from Perez to David, with a few unique details added to the lineage in Matthew.

Four names are added to the genealogy of Christ in the Gospel of Matthew, and they are not the names of men. These names are of four women, unique in itself because women were omitted from genealogy according to the practice of the times.[8] One of these women is Ruth. We will follow the trail of Ruth and the other chosen Gentile women in our journey as we uncover some of the beautiful lessons the Word of God has for us.

Samuel fulfilled his destiny when he wrote this book about a Moabitess portraying her as she really was, a woman of beauty and humility who took refuge under the wing of her Redeemer. The Book of Ruth is infused with hidden love for her grandson, David, and from this book Samuel's purpose is accomplished—a crown is placed on the royal house of the Messiah.[9]

Thus the story begins.

Chapter Two

THE VISITATION

C ome, come into my home! I'm honored you would come and allow me to bid you goodbye. Please have a seat. Would you care for a cup of hot tea?" Naomi asked her dear friends as they settled into the room.

Naomi was nervous for the first time in a very long time. Hospitality came so effortlessly to her, but today was sadly different. She poured everyone a cup of tea and with childish excitement announced her extraordinary treat. "I have something more for you. I have saved back from our rations so I could surprise you with honey cake! I hope you will bless me and partake of my table."

The eyes of the women in the room opened wide and their mouths began to water with anticipation for the morsels of confection. Honey cake! How long it had been since they had tasted this sweet delicacy! The famine had prevented them from using flour for anything but bread, and as for honey, well . . . no one had honey. It was just like Naomi to make their visit in her home so special. Eagerly they all took of her love offering and slowly savored every bite.

After exchanging pleasantries and updating each other on the condition of their families, Naomi knew it was time to tell them what they all came to hear. "When you were at the city gates, I am sure you heard rumors about our leaving Bethlehem. Instead, I want you to hear it from me," she nervously began to explain.

"Well, it's true. Elimelech has decided to take us away for a time . . . Where will we go, you ask? Well, we leave for Moab . . . I know, I know. We have been taught not to even pass through Moab, but what can I say? Elimelech has decided . . .

"The famine? The famine has been in Judah for too long. We must leave or lose all we have. My husband has been generous to a fault. He has given so much to . . . to . . . well, to everyone. Now he says it's time to go while we still have livestock, servants, and sufficient wealth to begin anew."

Naomi was especially uncomfortable now. Many of the families they had helped during the long famine were represented by the women in her home. She did not want to offend them. Her heart began to pound in her chest so loudly that she could not hear what was being asked of her.

"What was that? What is that you want to know? . . . How long will we be gone? I don't know. I have thought of that often. Elimelech says it will only be for a season. To be honest, I simply don't know."

Tears began to well up in her eyes. She had promised herself she would not cry, but now it was too late. All the emotion she had held within her for the last several weeks swiftly flowed from her like a rushing stream whose dam had burst. As she cried the women surrounded her with care and concern.

"I have cried until my bed clothes are soaked, for I know I will miss you and Bethlehem dearly." Naomi held them closely and felt their genuine compassion. Oh, how she loved them!

"Enough, I must stop crying. My husband has decided. We leave for Moab at daylight."

Regaining her composure, Naomi stood and hugged each one of them tightly and handed them the parting gifts she had prepared for them. She was a wealthy woman and owned many beautiful things. Naomi wanted her friends to remember her kindly, so she gave each of them a robe or a scarf or some adornment they had admired through their years of friendship. To each she also handed honey cakes wrapped in muslin cloth to take to their families, a gift she knew they would enjoy during this time of famine.

"Now I bid you all good-bye and pray that the God of Abraham, Isaac, and Jacob will one day bring me back to my beautiful home and to you, my cherished friends. But for now I say *Shalom*."

One by one they left. She closed the door behind them and continued to weep.

THE BIBLE STUDY

Now it came to pass, in the days when the judges ruled, that there was a famine in the land. And a certain man of Bethlehem, Judah, went to dwell in the country of Moab, he and his wife and his two sons.

The name of the man was Elimelech, the name of his wife was Naomi, and the names of his two sons were Mahlon and Chilion— Ephrathites of Bethlehem, Judah. And they went to the country of Moab and remained there.

Then Elimelech, Naomi's husband, died; and she was left, and her two sons. Now they took wives of the women of Moab: the name of the one was Orpah, and the name of the other Ruth. And they dwelt there about ten years.

Then both Mahlon and Chilion also died; so the woman survived her two sons and her husband. (RUTH 1:1–5)

When the Judges ruled. The time of judges was marked by spiritual adultery and moral decay. This is a time known by Jewish scholars as when "God Judged the Judges." In the actual Hebrew, verse one of chapter one is translated as "the days of the Judgment of the Judges.[1]

Famine. God often brought famine upon His chosen people during times of disobedience. Famine came to Israel during Abraham's time (GEN. 12:10), Isaac's time (GEN. 26:1), and during the life of Elisha (2 KINGS 8:1). The famine during the time of Judges came in two forms: one was for lack of bread, and the other was famine for the Torah—for the sacred Word of the living God.[2] The famine in Bethlehem was a direct consequence of Israel's rebellion against God.

Bethlehem, Judah. Why was it necessary to mention Judah? The reason was twofold: first, to distinguish this village from other villages in provinces with the same name; and second, because Elimelech decided to leave both his home and his Jewish homeland, for Judah was the Promised Land.[3]

The first time we have mention of Bethlehem is the birth of Benjamin and the death of Rachel. Jacob would never forget the town of Bethlehem because of the death of his beloved wife, Rachel. The world would never forget this same town because of a birth—the birth of our beloved Savior.[4]

The family of Elimelech came from Bethlehem. Naomi and Ruth returned to Bethlehem. Ruth met and married Boaz in Bethlehem. Obed, their son, was born in Bethlehem. This brought the lineage and eventual birth of David, son of Jesse, to the little town of Bethlehem.

Naomi's and Ruth's return from Moab made the coming of Christ to Bethlehem possible! The beautiful "Scarlet Thread" of genealogy can be traced through Bethlehem—the "house of bread":

> *But you, Bethlehem Ephrathah, though you are little among the thousands of Judah, yet out of you shall come forth to Me the One to be Ruler in Israel, whose goings forth are from of old, from everlasting.* (MICAH 5:2)

The Book of Ruth rescues the town of Bethlehem from oblivion.

Moab. In contrast to Bethlehem, we have the city of Moab, a city born out of incest. There was a distant blood relationship between the land of Moab and Israel. Moab, the man for whom the city was named, was the son of Lot, Abraham's nephew. The birth of Moab came about through an incestuous relationship between Lot and his eldest daughter after the destruction of Sodom and Gomorrah (GEN. 19:30–37).

After the account of his birth, Moab was not mentioned again until the children of Israel, on their way through the wilderness to the Promised Land, encountered his descendants. Scripture is only concerned with a country when it touches the chosen nation of Israel.[5]

By the time the Israelites reached the land of Moab, the Amorites had conquered the territory. When the Israelites overcame the Amorites in battle, Balak, the king of Moab, became terrified of Israel. He called on the prophet Balaam to curse God's chosen. Instead, God put a curse upon Moab and its descendants:

> *An Ammonite or Moabite shall not enter the assembly of the LORD; even to the tenth generation none of his descendants shall enter the assembly of the LORD forever, because they did not meet you with bread and water on the road when you came out of Egypt, and because they hired against you Balaam . . . to curse you.*
> **(DEUTERONOMY 23:3–4)**

Two cities are introduced in the first verse of Ruth: Bethlehem, the house of bread and peace, and Moab, the nation born of incest, a land King David would call his "wash pot."[6]

Elimelech. His name means "My God is King," but he did not measure up to its meaning for he took his family from the place of bread to the place condemned by the God he served. Hebrew law stated that a Jew was not permitted to leave the Promised Land during famine unless it was impossible to find anything to sell or buy. Elimelech left anyway.[7]

Hebrew genealogy says that both Elimelech and his wife came from notable ancestors and should have acted righteously since they were the outstanding leaders of their generation.[8]

The *Torah* teaches that *tzedaka* or charity starts at home. First and foremost, we have a responsibility to the members of our immediate family, followed by our extended family, then to our community and the community of mankind.[9]

Elimelech, a man of wealth, separated himself from his extended family and his community when he could have helped them through the famine. Instead of encouraging them through times of trial, he caused them to lose heart. When he left, he not only took with him silver and gold, but also opportunities for work that would have provided for those in Bethlehem.[10]

Elimelech rationalized that he would take his family and "sojourn" in Moab; the Hebrew for *sojourn* is *gur* and means "for a season as a stranger among other people; to have temporary resident status." Elimelech's plan was to escape the famine and maintain his wealth while in the far country, then return to Bethlehem when the famine was over. In desperation, Elimelech created a plan and in the process of executing his plan he took his family to the far country, a place away from the covering, protection, and purpose of God.

Naomi. In the history of Scripture, the wife of Elimelech is known as the "mother-in-law." Yet there is so much more to this incredible woman. She was a submissive wife, for she followed her husband into the far country. She was an exceptional mother and mother-in-law, for she was dedicated to her children and influenced her daughters-in-law so profoundly they wanted to follow her, leaving mother, father, and country.

Her name described her character quite accurately; Naomi name means "pleasant, delightful, and lovely."[11] She was a woman called back to the Land of Promise by the Spirit of the living God. She was forgiven, restored, and rewarded as she became part of the "Scarlet Thread" leading to King David and our beloved Messiah.

Mahlon. The eldest son of Elimelech and Naomi. His name means "weak and sickly."[12] Mahlon was married to Ruth.

Chilion. The second son to Elimelech and Naomi. His name means "destruction or blotted out."[13] Chilion was married to Orpah.

And remained there. Instead of staying in the far country for a season, Elimelech and his family stayed in Moab permanently. When contemplating the "far country," we rationalize the "pig sty" as a place where we will only dwell for a season. But Elimelech's family is a sad example of the far country becoming a permanent residence.

Elimelech "enjoyed the swill of the sty more than the house of bread, because of his 'rebellion.'"[14] He forgot that the house of bread is better in a time of famine than the land of Moab in a time of plenty.

Elimelech . . . died. When the family chose to leave Judah, they also chose to walk away from the covering of their God. When you look at the Scripture more closely, you see that the family remained in Moab for several years. Jewish sources say that before Elimelech died, his horses, his donkeys, and his camels died.[15] The family was prosperous in Bethlehem, yet became destitute in Moab.

They experienced hard times in a land that did not have a famine. Elimelech could have taken his family back to Bethlehem on a road called repentance, back to the Promised Land, back under the covering of the God of his fathers. Instead Elimelech chose to remain in the far country, and that is where he died, outside of the will of God.

And she was left. Naomi was left alone with her two sons. No longer did she have her beloved Elimelech with whom to share her life. Naomi felt completely cut off from the God she loved so much.

Women of Moab. Choosing not to go back, Mahlon and Chilion became comfortable enough in Moab to marry Moabite women, which was contrary to Mosaic Law:

Nor shall you make marriages with them. You shall not give your daughter to their son, nor take their daughter for your son. For they will turn your sons away from following Me, to serve other gods; so the anger of the LORD will be aroused against you and destroy you suddenly. (DEUTERONOMY 7:3–4)

God did not want Naomi's sons to be unequally yoked. He does not want His children to be paired with one who will take them from following after Him. Naomi's sons did not choose Moabite women as wives until the death of Elimelech; such marriages were something he most likely forbade.

Elimelech knew the benefits of having a godly woman as a wife, a woman of covenant; he was married to Naomi. However, either Naomi made no objection to these marriages because of her resignation of never returning to her home country, or her grief was so great over the loss of her husband that she no longer cared. Nonetheless, the longer the family remained in Moab, the more their transgressions multiplied.

Jewish scholars feel that the sons of Elimelech took on the attitude of self-centeredness, which prevailed in Moab. This spirit of disobedience and self-interest is the same spirit that caused Moab not to provide bread and water for God's people when they passed through the wilderness. This attitude caused Naomi's sons to marry outside their faith and remain in the far country.

Ingratitude is the antithesis of kindness. To be kind is to go beyond the requirements of the Law. To be kind and compassionate is to live by grace and be motivated by mercy, traits that can only be inspired by the Holy Spirit of the living God. When Elimelech left Bethlehem to preserve his family's wealth, he took the covering of *Hashem* from his family and chose to live under the judgment of His Word.

Allow me to clarify the word *Hashem*. Out of reverence, the Jews often refer to God as *Hashem*, which is two words in Hebrew: *Ha* meaning "the," and *Shem* meaning "name." The Lord is often referred to as "The Name" so as not to offend Him by using His holy name in vain. When writing the name of God, observant Jews will write the name of God as G-d, again so as not to offend the One who is holy.[16]

Disobedience offends God, and without His covering, wayward servants are left to judgment and destruction. Think of Elimelech and what became of his life when you read Psalm 109:8–18.

Orpah. One translation of the name is "fawn" or "young doe." A fawn or doe flees at the first sign of adversity. Another root meaning of *Orpah* is "double-minded" or "nape of the neck," meaning stiff-necked or stubborn.

Jewish tradition suggests Orpah was a descendant of the royal line of the king of Moab.[17] She loved her mother-in-law. But when Naomi pointed out all the possible consequences of following her to Bethlehem, Orpah wavered in her choice and returned to the gods of her country. She could have been grafted into the root of Jesse, but instead she chose comfort and security, and because of her choice she went into scriptural obscurity. With her return to Moab, she vanished from the pages of biblical history.[18]

Ruth. The Hebrew meaning of *Ruth* is "friend" or "beauty as in something worth seeing."[19] In the Hebrew language, names are more than tags that distinguish one person from another; they reflect and describe the nature of an individual.

The words *friend* and *beautiful* certainly describe Ruth. She extended the kind of love and friendship to Naomi that transcends every meaning of the words. Her beauty is referred to several times within the book. Ruth was so beautiful to look at that she immediately caught the attention of Boaz in the field. Ruth also possessed an inward beauty, which set her apart from all other women.

Jewish tradition suggests Ruth was also a daughter of King Eglon of Moab, and the granddaughter of Balak, the Moabite king who paid to have the Israelites cursed as they were on their way to the land of Israel. Ruth had a

Divine destiny. Her destiny did not begin when she was born. It did not begin when she married Mahlon, nor did it begin when Mahlon died. Her destiny began before creation, because *Hashem* called forth her destiny in His heart.

Mahlon and Chilion also died. During the years Naomi lived in Moab, she was torn between the love of her family and the love of her people. Now, after the death of her husband and her sons, she was left alone, a remnant—a remnant linked to Zion's future triumph.[20]

Why had she survived? With her husband gone, why couldn't she have died instead of her sons? Why couldn't they be part of the remnant and produce heirs to further Elimelech's name? Why? Why? Why?

Naomi did not know—and could scarcely even imagine—what her beloved *Hashem* had planned for her:

> *"In that day," says the* LORD, *"I will assemble the lame, I will gather the outcast and those whom I have afflicted; I will make the lame a remnant and the outcast a strong nation."* (MICAH 4:6–7)

She had been chosen through the kindness and compassion of her God, the Righteous Judge, to remain as the spark of life of Elimelech's family in order to inherit the line of passage to the Messiah.[21]

LIFE LESSONS

LIFE LESSON ONE:
REPENTANCE YIELDS GOD'S MERCY

Just as in the time of the judges, so are we today in North America and many places around the globe. Everyone, including our leaders, is doing what is right in their own eyes. We have allowed ourselves to be led by corrupt judges who have hijacked our nation with their liberal interpretation of the law. Furthermore, many of the pulpits of today's churches are led by pastors who in the name of inclusiveness have interpreted God's Word in a "feel good" manner, ignoring the power and the purpose of the Cross of Jesus Christ.

In the name of choice, federal judges decide for the murder of innocent children within the wombs of their mothers. In the name of art, these same judges rule in favor of child pornography. And in the name of love, these unrighteous judges decree in favor of same-sex marriage. All the while men and women of faith selectively ignore the message of the Word of God and the consequences of sin in fear of offending the masses. Many Christian leaders remain silent when they should warn the sheep of God's pasture of imminent danger:

> *All you beasts of the field, come to devour, all you beasts in the forest. His watchmen are blind, they are all ignorant; they are all dumb dogs, they cannot bark; sleeping, lying down, loving to slumber. . . . And they are shepherds who cannot understand; they all look to their own way, every one for his own gain, from his own territory.* **(ISAIAH 56:9–11)**

We, like Bethlehem, suffer from a spiritual famine. One of every two marriages within the church ends in divorce. Our children are led by gangs in the street because of absentee fathers and are a target of a deviant world that has emerged from the aftermath of pornography. We are in economic reversal, not because the elderly are living longer and are taking away the social security benefits of the next generation, but because the next generation that was to replenish social security has been destroyed by more than *43 million abortions since 1973!*[22] Our borders are no longer protected from those who seek to destroy us; therefore our young men and women must shed their blood on foreign lands in defense of our freedom.

It is time to turn away from the ways of the world and turn to the God of our fathers—the God of Abraham, Isaac, and Jacob. It is time to repent at the cross of Christ and begin anew:

> *If My people who are called by My name will humble themselves, and pray and seek My face, and turn from their wicked ways, then I will hear from heaven, and will forgive their sin and heal their land.* (2 CHRONICLES 7:14)

Only when we repent will we be under the covering of the Lord God of Israel and benefit from His infinite mercy and grace:

> *O Israel, hope in the LORD; for with the LORD there is mercy, and with Him is abundant redemption.* (PSALM 130:7)

LIFE LESSON TWO:
JESUS IS CALLING AND WAITING

At one time or another in our lives, we have all made choices for the far country. Just as we choose to *go* into the far country, we can choose to *leave* the far country. This one thing I know: The longer we decide to stay in the far country, the more comfortable we will become comfortable with its ways.

The "far country" can be defined as anyplace where God is not. You could live in your home but bring the far country into your life through pornography. You could live in your home and practice manipulation and intimidation, refusing to do what the Word of God asks of you; you are in a distant place, away from God's blessings and protection.

You may have had an abortion, and you have yet to ask forgiveness or have not forgiven yourself for the sin you have committed. You feel guilty and unworthy. You may be ravaged by the sin of homosexuality or be a wayward spouse, locked in the sin of an affair. Hear the Spirit of the living God calling you to come home.

The longer you wait, the fainter His voice will become. You may first walk with the ungodly, but soon you will stand with them, and before long you will sit with them.

You will no longer want the things of God.

Yet a loving God who forgives all our transgressions and promises to never remember them again is waiting for you to come home:

> *I have blotted out, like a thick cloud, your transgressions, and like a cloud, your sins. Return to Me, for I have redeemed you.* (ISAIAH 44:22)

Just stop for a moment and think about what the Lord is saying to you! Have you ever been in a deep fog where you cannot see beyond a few feet? Put your sins in that deep cloud—hidden and seen by no one. When the brilliance of the sunshine burns away the fog and brings clear vision to your eyes, your sins are no longer there. Your transgressions are forever lost—never to be remembered. What a gift He has given us! All we must do is repent of our sins and receive His forgiveness:

> *For I will forgive their iniquity, and their sin I will remember no more.* (JEREMIAH 31:34)

I encourage you to come home. I encourage you to come from the spiritual "pig sty" into the arms of a loving Father who is patiently waiting for your return. I ask that you begin to delight in His love, for His love is good. The time is now.

LIFE LESSON THREE:
TRUST GOD IN TIMES OF ADVERSITY

No one can dare imagine the pain associated with the death of a child, much less two. What grief Naomi must have experienced! I have shared with you the death of my sister Rosie in my book *The King's Daughter* and how I witness an ever-present memorial to her passing in the eyes of my parents, even at times of laughter.

Naomi was convinced that her sin was far greater than that of her husband and her sons, which is why she was destined to live in guilt and grief for the rest of her life. She believed that God was dealing with her according to the sins and iniquities of her family. She did not consider God's goodness and compassion for her, His chosen:

> *Bless the* LORD, *O my soul; and all that is within me, bless His holy name! Bless the* LORD, *O my soul, and forget not all His benefits: who forgives all your iniquities, who heals all your diseases, who redeems your life from destruction, who crowns you with lovingkindness and tender mercies, who satisfies your mouth with good things, so that your youth is renewed like the eagle's.* (PSALM 103:1–5)

When we are grieving, it is difficult to see the hand of God.

Many years ago, the most magnificent diamond in the world's history was found in an African mine. The stone was sent to Amsterdam to be cut by one of the finest diamond cutters in the industry. The diamond expert took the diamond and put a notch in the unblemished surface. Then he struck a hard blow with his instrument, and instantly the precious stone lay in the cleft of his hands in two pieces!

The question arises: Did the diamond cutter do this out of recklessness, wastefulness, and criminal carelessness? Absolutely not! For days and weeks he had studied and planned that critical blow. Drawings and models had all been calculated with minutest care. The man to whom this stone was entrusted was one of the most skillful diamond cutters in the world.

Was that blow a mistake? No! Instead this was the climax of the diamond cutter's skill. When he struck that blow, he did the one thing that would bring that gem to its most perfect shapeliness, radiance, and jeweled splendor. That blow, which seemed to ruin the superb precious stone, was, in fact, its perfect redemption! From those two halves were wrought the two magnificent gems that the skilled eye of the diamond cutter saw hidden in the rough, uncut stone.

Sometimes God executes a stinging blow upon our lives. The blood spurts. The nerves wince. The soul cries out in agony. The pain is unbearable. The blow seems to be an appalling mistake or penance for some great transgression. But it is not, for we are the most priceless jewels in the world of our Savior. He is the most skillful diamond cutter in the entire universe. We must trust in Him. No matter what our circumstances, we are His and He keeps us in the cleft of His hands, ever to be cared for and loved. He has many wonderful plans for our future, which we know not:[23]

For I know the thoughts that I think toward you, says the LORD, thoughts of peace and not of evil, to give you a future and a hope. (**JEREMIAH 29:11**)

Trust Him!

Chapter Three

THE ROAD TO REPENTANCE

Naomi had grown weary of grieving. Her official time of mourning had come to an end, but she knew she could never fully remove the sackcloth draped over her heart. As she walked toward the graves of her husband and sons, it seemed as if her inconsolable sorrow would be with her for the rest of her life. The pain she felt within her soul was so deep it almost brought with it a strange sedation for the reality of life.

It felt like it was only yesterday that her two sons stood beside her at the grave of her husband, Elimelech. Today, she stood at the graves of Mahlon and Chilion with her two daughters-in-law. The dreadful question pounded within her head again and again: *What could I have done to merit such judgment from the God I love so much?*

Orpah and Ruth stood stoically by Naomi's side as she informed them, "Today will be the last visit to our husbands' resting place. Tomorrow, I will begin my journey back to Bethlehem."

For the last several weeks, Naomi had awakened in the middle of the night with the same dream. The dream was of Bethlehem. Bethlehem seemed to be beckoning her home. Naomi loved Bethlehem. Oh, how she missed the place of her birth! She longed for her home. But how could she dare think of returning to Judah? She had asked that question of herself for days. Could it be that the God she cherished so much would allow her to return? Had He forgotten her because of her sin, or had He remembered her as He remembered His people? Could it be that the great *Hashem* would forgive her transgression?

As the three widows stood at the graves of the men they loved, Ruth and Orpah held Naomi closely between them. The women wept quietly.

Composed enough to speak, Naomi instructed the only loved ones she had left on this earth. "My dear little ones, we must be home before nightfall. Remember we have no men to watch over us. We are alone now . . . What is it you ask?" Naomi secured her soaked kerchief under the sleeve of her cloak as she glanced at Ruth to confirm the question she was asking.

"Yes, of course, my precious Ruth, we do have each other; we thank the great Jehovah for that. Orpah, you ask if we will return to their graves once more . . . I know in my spirit I will never return to Moab. I must go back to my people. I have had this urgency in my spirit, a longing you might say, to go back to Bethlehem. You have seen and heard the peddlers in the streets of Moab sell their produce and speak of Jehovah's blessing on Judah. The famine is over, and *Hashem* has remembered Judah. Maybe, just maybe, He will remember me . . . Yes . . . Ruth, I love you, too, and the two of you have been more than I could ask for. You have loved my sons in life and in death. I want the best for you and for your days to come." Naomi reached out to the two women and kissed them on the forehead.

"Come. Come now, my beautiful birds, we must be ready to leave by early morning if you intend to go with me to the outskirts of the city." With that, the women said farewell to their dead and left in silence.

THE BIBLE STUDY

Then she arose with her daughters-in-law that she might return from the country of Moab, for she had heard in the country of Moab that the LORD had visited His people by giving them bread. Therefore she went out from the place where she was, and her two daughters-in-law with her; and they went on the way to return to the land of Judah. (RUTH 1:6–7)

Then she arose. Naomi did not suddenly wake one morning and decide to return to her people. Her time of mourning was over.[1] Naomi had been compelled to leave Moab and return to Bethlehem for quite some time. Jewish scholars describe Naomi's obsession to leave the far country as the Holy Spirit's compelling her to return to the land of her fathers. She was moved by prophetic forces much greater than her own.

Even though Naomi was called back to Judah, she still had to choose to go back. One Jewish source interprets the word *arose* in a spiritual sense as "fallen down, she lifted herself by returning to *Eretz Israel.*"[2] *Eretz* in Hebrew means "the Land." Naomi was going home to the land of Israel, the place of her birth, the place of her purpose.

The country of Moab. In the Hebrew, the word *country* is translated as "field."[3] Therefore Naomi had "heard in the field of Moab." The fields signify a temporary place, a place of mobility and lack of stability. Naomi was leaving the transient field and going back to the "house of bread."

The LORD had visited His people. The word *visited* is the Hebrew word for *remembered.* The Lord had remembered His *ami,* His people, with bread. The famine was over. Naomi had seen Jewish merchants peddling the produce of Israel in Moab. From them she had heard that *Hashem* had blessed Bethlehem and lifted His judgment.[4]

Yet this was not the sole reason for her desire to return. She had lived in Moab well over ten years, and Moab had not experienced a famine. Food was not the reason for Naomi's desire to return to Judah; she was called to come home by the Spirit of the God who lived within her.

The Lord always remembers His people:

For the LORD will not cast off His people, nor will He forsake His inheritance. (PSALM 94:14)

Could Naomi's God possibly remember her as He had remembered her people? Could she dare hope? She longed for her home, her people, and her God.

And her two daughters-in-law. In Hebrew custom it is presumed that there is natural antagonism between daughters-in-law and mothers-in-law; therefore they cannot testify against one another.[5] What made these two women love their mother-in-law so much that they would desire to leave their country and their people and follow her to an unknown land?

The passionate devotion these two women had for their mother-in-law provides a glimpse into the life they must have shared together. Jewish scholars believe Orpah and Ruth were drawn to "Naomi like the planets gravitate toward the sun."[6]

Orpah and Ruth had learned from Naomi. They were nurtured by her in a Jewish household. She taught them the traditions of her people and transformed her teachings into bonds of love. These bonds of love between the three women created a desire for Orpah and Ruth to join Naomi's people and a longing to know Naomi's God.[7] Naomi had planted precious seed in the lives of these two women, and she was about to partake of her harvest.

LIFE LESSONS

LIFE LESSON ONE:
YOUR TIME OF MOURNING IS OVER

Many of you taking this journey with me are in mourning, and you have been in this state for too long. There is a season for grieving and a season for rejoicing, both of which have their rightful place. God does not want you to be stoic at the passing of a loved one or even the death of a marriage.

Stoicism is a pagan philosophy practiced by the Greeks.[8] This philosophy espoused no emotion—no crying or laughing. God is our Father. He created us in His image. He is our King, and we are His children. God knows the pain of the passing of a loved one, and He understands our grief. Remember, He witnessed the death of His own Son.

When Israel lost Moses, God permitted the Israelites thirty days of mourning before they continued on their journey to the Promised Land (DEUT. 34:8).

No matter how deep your mourning, there is a Name for God that fits that darkness. When you are walking in the valley of grief, try to focus on the God who is the Author of life—the God who promises a new tomorrow. He will hear your cry, and He will help you. He has great plans for your future. He is waiting for you to allow Him to work in your life for your good:

His favor is for life; weeping may endure for a night, but joy comes in the morning. (PSALM 30:5)

LIFE LESSON TWO:
REPENTANCE IS THE DOOR TO FREEDOM

After I was saved and began to read God's Word, I could not comprehend many of the Bible's teachings. I grew up with a concept of "big sins" and "little sins," each sin carrying within it a level of atonement equivalent to its level of severity. With this concept in mind, I could not understand why Saul, who had visited a witch and had done what the people wanted instead of heeding the voice of God, merited more severe consequences than David, a man who had committed adultery and premeditated murder. Why did the Spirit of God depart from Saul (1 SAM. 13:14; 16:14), yet David was a man after God's own heart (ACTS 13:22)? I could not understand God.

I went to my husband and asked him to explain the difference in their sins. First, he pointed out: Saul committed spiritual adultery when he consulted the witch of Endor, whereas David committed physical adultery with Bathsheba. Our God is a jealous God. He tells us this over and over again in Scripture:

For the LORD your God is a consuming fire, a jealous God. (DEUTERONOMY 4:24)

When Saul consulted the witch of Endor, he was telling God, "I do not need Your wisdom to lead Israel. I can find guidance from a source other than the Almighty."

The second reason David remained "a man after God's own heart" was David's willingness to repent. Repentance is the lifeline to the Lord, our Father. Without repentance we have nothing and are nothing.

We have been taught that Adam and Eve were banished from the Garden of Eden because of their disobedience. Disobedience was certainly the sin that began the course of events leading to their expulsion, but I believe there was another contributing element. Even though Adam and Eve disobeyed the Lord and took of the tree of knowledge of good and evil, we cannot believe God—the all knowing, all powerful God we serve—was unaware of the sin committed by the man and woman He created. He knew of their sin just as He knows about ours.

God did not expel them from the Garden until after He had a conversation with both Adam and Eve, so obviously something must have taken place in their exchange that ultimately caused their eviction.

In Genesis 3, God asked Adam a question: "Where are you?" Yet our omnipotent God knew exactly where Adam was: He had gone into hiding after his sin—just as we do. Know this fact: When God asks a question, He is not looking for the answer. He knows the answer—He knows everything—and He is giving us the opportunity to return to righteousness, the opportunity to repent. Why would the God who later gave His only Son to die on the cross to rectify the sins of mankind not give Adam and Eve the opportunity to repent and begin anew?

Adam refused to take responsibility and blamed the woman God gave him for his actions. How this must have grieved our loving Creator! After Adam's refusal to repent, the Father of mankind went to the woman and gave her an equal opportunity to confess her sin and rectify the wrong she had committed. Instead, Eve blamed her actions on the snake. She, too, refused to take responsibility.

Adam and Eve disobeyed God, and He, in His infinite mercy and grace, gave both of them the opportunity to repent—as He gives every one of His children—and they refused. God had no choice but to banish Adam and Eve from the beautiful place He had created for all of mankind.

In contrast, when confronted with his sin, King David acknowledged his transgressions, made no excuses or rationalizations, repented before God, and asked Him to forgive him:

> *Have mercy upon me, O God, according to Your lovingkindness; according to the multitude of Your tender mercies, blot out my transgressions. Wash me thoroughly from my iniquity, and cleanse me from my sin. For I acknowledge my transgressions, and my sin is always before me. Against You, You only, have I sinned, and done this evil in Your sight—that You may be found just when You speak, and blameless when You judge.* (PSALM 51:1–4)

Our merciful God heard David's plea and forgave him, just as He will forgive us if we repent.

When we committed our transgressions, our God was there. When we tried to hide our sin, our God was aware. He is waiting for us to come to Him in a spirit of repentance and contriteness.

Don't allow Satan to hold you hostage to your sin. God already knows of your sin. He is waiting for repentance. God doesn't need a reason to restore you; it's His nature to do so. He is waiting to forgive you. He is waiting to give you a fresh beginning, free of the past and the sin it holds. Experience a freedom from sin, which only God can give and no one can duplicate or immolate. I ask that you repeat this prayer of repentance and be free from the sin of your past:

> *Father, I come to You with my sins. I have grieved Your Holy Spirit and ask You to forgive me. As David, I have sinned before You and You alone. As David, I want to be loved by You and be a child after Your own heart. Thank You, Father, for Your promise to forgive all my iniquities and remember them no more. Thank You for the opportunity to begin anew, as if I never sinned. I love You, Lord, and I depend on Your tender mercies. Amen.*

Chapter Four

THE CONVERSION

Naomi pleaded with her daughter-in-law as they stood on the road to Judah, "Ruth, I beg of you, please follow Orpah back to Moab!" The two women watched Orpah as she slowly turned away and began her journey back to the land of her fathers and her gods. Naomi and Ruth gazed in silence until Orpah's silhouette disappeared into the horizon.

Naomi wept once more as she saw the last remnant of her son Chilion's life walk out of sight; he would be gone forever. Motionless, she caught her final glimpse of what now seemed only a shadowy image; it was almost as if Orpah had never existed. Suddenly, she felt Ruth cling tightly to her.

Naomi took Ruth's face in her hands and stared directly into her red, swollen eyes. "For the third time I entreat you, Ruth. Go back to your people! Please consider the consequences of your choice to travel with me to Judah!" Naomi raised her voice, hoping to convince her steadfast companion.

"There is no future for you in the land of my people. You will be an outcast. I have neither sons nor the ability to bear sons, so you have no hope for a husband in Bethlehem. You have no hope for children. I do not want you to go through life without the joy of motherhood. I beg of you . . . stay!"

Ruth shook her head no as she held Naomi even tighter.

"Are you sure, my sweet treasure?" Naomi took Ruth's face in her hands and once more looked deep into the window of Ruth's eyes until it seemed she could almost see Ruth's soul. "Yes . . . I see . . . you will not be moved by my arguments." It was confirmed within Naomi's heart: Ruth not only wanted to follow her to Bethlehem; she wanted to follow Naomi's God as well.

"Very well, it seems clear to me now that you want to know the God I serve, as your own . . . After I acquaint you with the laws of my faith, I will ask that you proclaim your vows."

Naomi took Ruth's hand and walked over to a large stone lying by the side of the road. The two women sat and held hands as Naomi explained the importance of the statements she was about to make so Ruth would carefully acknowledge their significance.

Naomi began to recite the laws of Jehovah God, which she had referred to many times in their years together. She issued seven declarations from the Word of God, pausing between each one to allow Ruth to speak.

"We are forbidden to walk more than 2,000 cubits out of town on the Sabbath." She waited for Ruth's positive response before she went further.

"We are not allowed to be secluded with a member of the opposite sex." Naomi paused, and Ruth responded, vowing to Naomi and Jehovah that she would lodge wherever Naomi lodged.

"We are obligated to 613 commandments." Tears streamed down Naomi's face as she witnessed this beautiful woman give her affirmation to the sacred Torah, Ruth's words issuing forth like some powerful, passionate melody resonating with love and utter devotion.

"We are prohibited from worshiping idols . . . The court is authorized to carry out four types of death penalty . . . The executed are buried in two different burial plots." After each law was spoken, Naomi paused, and Ruth responded with her vow.

Finally, Naomi heard Ruth commit to her conversion to Judaism and seal her vows with an oath. No longer a Gentile, Ruth was now part of Jehovah's *ami*. She would qualify for His forgiveness, His mercy, and His blessings. This so pleased Naomi that she felt joy in her heart, a sensation she had not felt in a long time.

The two women embraced. They looked into each other's eyes and shared a new kinship. Confirming their allegiance to each other and their God, the two women smiled. It seemed like a lifetime since they had last felt joy.

"I will not mention your past again, Ruth. You are one of my people. We will go forth from here, two women serving the same God, both relying on His goodness and His mercy. Jehovah will take care of us." Naomi took Ruth's arm, and together they continued on the road to Bethlehem, the beautiful road of repentance.

Soon Naomi's fear of returning home shook her from this precious moment into reality. Her thoughts turned to how she would be greeted by the friends she had left years before. Would they receive her precious Ruth? How would she and her daughter-in-law survive? Only Jehovah knew.

THE BIBLE STUDY

And Naomi said to her two daughters-in-law, "Go, return each to her mother's house. The LORD deal kindly with you, as you have dealt with the dead and with me. The LORD grant that you may find rest, each in the house of her husband." So she kissed them, and they lifted up their voices and wept.

And they said to her, "Surely we will return with you to your people."

But Naomi said, "Turn back, my daughters; why will you go with me? Are there still sons in my womb, that they may be your husbands? Turn back, my daughters, go—for I am too old to have a husband. If I should say I have hope, if I should have a husband tonight and should also bear sons, would you wait for them till they were grown? Would you restrain yourselves from having husbands? No, my daughters; for it grieves me very much for your sakes that the hand of the LORD has gone out against me!"

Then they lifted up their voices and wept again; and Orpah kissed her mother-in-law, but Ruth clung to her. And she said, "Look, your sister-in-law has gone back to her people and to her gods; return after your sister-in-law."

But Ruth said, "Entreat me not to leave you, or to turn back from following after you. For wherever you go, I will go. And wherever you lodge, I will lodge. Your people shall be my people, and your God, my God. Where you die, I will die, and there will I be buried. The LORD do so to me and more also, if anything but death parts you and me."

When she saw that she was determined to go with her, she stopped speaking to her. (RUTH 1:8–18)

"Go, return . . . The LORD deal kindly with you." According to Jewish law, Naomi was obligated to dissuade her daughters-in-law three times before conversion—this was her first attempt.[1] She also blessed her daughters-in-law, for they had not only dealt kindly with her but also with the bodies of her deceased sons.

Specific burial rituals must be followed under Jewish law. Among them, the body must be purified with water, prepared with oils, and wrapped in a shroud before burial.

Elimelech and his family were the only Jewish family living in Moab. And Naomi was the only Jew who remained. Orpah and Ruth helped Naomi do what was needed to give her sons a suitable Jewish burial. This was an act of pure love, for which Naomi would be eternally grateful.

"You may find rest." *Rest* in this verse implies security, the kind of security found in the marriage to a good husband. Naomi wanted Ruth and Orpah to find husbands who would give them children and would financially provide for their families. She wanted them to rebuild their lives in the midst of their own people.[2]

"Turn back . . . why will you go with me? . . . Would you restrain from having husbands?" At this point, Naomi got to the true core of the problem. She was too old to bear sons who could redeem her daughters-in-law. She explained what the Torah ordained when it came to widowhood:

> *If brothers dwell together, and one of them dies and has no son, the widow of the dead man shall not be married to a stranger outside the family; her husband's brother shall go in to her, take her as his wife, and perform the duty of a husband's brother to her. And it shall be that the firstborn son which she bears will succeed to the name of his dead brother, that his name may not be blotted out in Israel.*
> (DEUTERONOMY 25:5–6)

Naomi knew she could not ask Orpah and Ruth to never marry again; they were too young. They must turn back; they would find no redeemer in Israel. This was the second attempt Naomi made to convince Ruth and Oprah to walk away from conversion.

"The hand of the LORD has gone against me." Naomi believed the Lord was punishing her for her sin and the sins of her family. She feared she, too, would meet her demise if she lingered in Moab. Futhermore, if her daughters-in-law went with her to Bethlehem, they would be outcasts, and the three of them would have no future.

And wept again. Orpah's parting was marked with weeping. She heard all that Naomi had to say, and Orpah felt there would be no future for her in Bethlehem. Yet, the young widow loved Naomi and Ruth. They had become her family. She had laughed with them. She had cried with them. They had helped her bury her husband, Chilion.

Orpah had learned of Naomi's God at Naomi's side as she lit the Sabbath candles and prepared her house for Passover. Orpah had danced with Naomi as she taught the two young women about the feasts of the Lord. Time and time again, she had heard Naomi pray to her God, and time and time again, Naomi's God answered her prayer. Yet Orpah knew she had to think reasonably. She made her decision. She would return to Moab.

Orpha kissed. Orpah kissed Naomi in her parting. This is where the text begins to distinguish the difference in the character of these two daughters-in-law. Both Orpah and Ruth were from royal lineage, for biblical history assigned them to the first family of Moab; both women possessed good virtues and both felt love for their mother-in-law.[3]

Orpah was very emotional and ready to shower Naomi with kisses. However, she wavered with her decision to follow Naomi. Orpah demonstrated love through feelings.[4] She made a profession of her love for Naomi, but this profession was not sufficient to cause her to follow on the journey of repentance once she rationalized the circumstances. She demonstrated "reason faith," and her faith wavered when the moment of truth came.

Ruth clung. Unlike Orpah, on the other hand, Ruth possessed "revelation faith" and unconditional love for Naomi and the journey they were about to undertake. She decided to act beyond reason. Her spirit told her to stay the course. No matter what argument Naomi presented, Ruth clung to her decision and to the woman she loved. Ruth possessed genuine faith, which produced fruit and good works. She wanted to know the God of the Jews, and God acknowledged her expression of faith and rewarded her one-hundredfold. She received the promise of Deuteronomy 4:4:

> ***But you who clung fast to the Lord your God are alive, every one of you, this day.*** (AMP)

Such revelation faith could only come from God . . .[5]

For by grace you have been saved through faith, and that not of your- selves; it is the gift of God, not of works, lest anyone should boast. (EPHESIANS 2:8–9)

"Return after your sister-in-law." This is the third and last time Naomi tried to discourage Ruth from following after her. After Naomi's second attempt to discourage her daughters-in-law, Orpah made the choice to return to Moab, so there was reason for Naomi to think that Ruth would do the same.

Naomi put the argument for Ruth's return on two levels. One reason was for "your people," and the second, "to your gods." Being of royal lineage, the two young women could go back to a life of wealth and comfort, something they would not find in Bethlehem, for Naomi had nothing left to her name.

The two daughters-in-law were also sure to find husbands and bear chil- dren in Moab. Bethlehem would never afford them a husband and children, for they were considered outcasts (DEUTERONOMY 23:3–4)[6]

Finally, there was the choice between returning to "her gods" or deciding for the one and only Jehovah God. Why would Naomi use idolatry as the final attempt to persuade Ruth to return to Moab?

This was the ultimate test. Naomi wanted Ruth to make her decision based on her faith. Ruth had seen Naomi worship the God of Israel. She had heard of His wonderful works, His unconditional faithfulness and His boundless love. There had to be more than human affection to cause Ruth to leave her country and her people. Ultimately, there was her heart's relationship to the one true God, the God of Abraham, Isaac, and Jacob.

On this day, on a road called repentance, two women chose whom they would serve. This choice was the demarcation that was to separate them for eternity. Orpah went back to idolatry. Nothing more was mentioned of her name. Like Judas, she went to her *place.* Once her choice was made, her name was taken from Scripture; this silence, which is more eloquent than words, describes a life of sure tragedy. Orpah went on a path of darkness, paganism, superstition, and eventual obscurity. Orpah touched the hand of God and chose to walk away.

Ruth chose God, and He chose her, in the greatest plan of the ages. Through her, He *brought* the lineage of King David, which led to *bringing* Jesus Christ, our Savior, the Messiah into the world. At the crossroads of her life, Ruth chose for eternity, and she would never be faced with such a choice again. Because of her decision and God's unwavering sovereignty, Ruth will be forever remembered in history as the "Mother of Royalty."[7]

"Entreat me not to leave you." These next two verses are some of the most beautiful in all literary history. J. Vernon McGee states, "If a monument had been reared to Ruth, this certainly would have been its inscription."[8] Within these two verses are included seven vows that were never broken. Each vow progressed with the passion of Ruth's love for her mother-in-law and the God she chose to serve. Jewish scholars identify these beautiful words of prose as Ruth's conversion to Judaism.

First, Ruth asked Naomi not to entreat her to leave, for she was unwavering in her decision to stay her course.

Second, Ruth was determined to go wherever Naomi went.

Third, Ruth would stay wherever Naomi stayed, never again leaving her side.

Fourth, Ruth was leaving the people of Moab for good and choosing Naomi's people forever.

Fifth, Ruth was making a decision for Naomi's God. Ruth decided to leave her idolatrous past and serve only the God of Abraham, Isaac, and Jacob. This was the most important vow of all.

Sixth, she made her choice for a lifetime. She chose to be buried wherever Naomi was buried.

Her seventh statement—"The LORD do so to me and more also, if anything but death parts you and me"—was a seal to the previous vows that consummated the covenant in which God brought Ruth into the lineage of Jesus Christ.

Each one of Ruth's proclamations was a direct response to one made by Naomi, who was quoting a specific law found in the sacred Torah. From Ruth's responses, we can deduce which law Naomi was quoting.

The Book of Ruth cradles extensive narratives that tell a beautiful story. In its descriptive dialogue, we see two women and the remarkable bonds of love that meld them together. We have two races: one a Gentile, the other a Jew. We see two generations: one vibrant and in the prime of life, the other old and beyond childbearing years. Yet because of their love one for the other, their hearts are knit together in admiration and commitment. Because of their devotion to each other and the providential love for the God they both chose, these two women will be remembered for eternity. Because of this incomparable love, the Book of Ruth holds the title "The Crown Jewel of the Old Testament."[9]

She stopped speaking to her. Torah law states that once a person has converted to Judaism, one need not make any further effort to dissuade the convert.[10] Naomi simply stopped speaking to Ruth about her past.

Something more happened on the road called repentance than Ruth's conversion to Judaism; Naomi saw her life filled with meaning again; she had a glimmer of hope because of Ruth's acceptance of Jehovah God. She led her precious Ruth to a conversion that made her one of God's *ami*. Ruth was redeemed from obscurity. Naomi felt that maybe—just maybe—she might still be of value in the hands of God.

Naomi must have smiled when she knew that her precious Ruth, wife of her beloved Mahlon, would walk with her to Bethlehem as a believer in the one and only God. He would take care of Ruth when Naomi could not. Even though this was a small flicker of hope, it was the only light to guide Naomi's path back home.

LIFE LESSONS

LIFE LESSON ONE:
RIGHT CHOICES PRODUCE GOOD RESULTS

Naomi was returning to a land she never should have left, because Bethlehem was the place of her divine purpose.

Many of you have left God's appointed place for your life. You have made choices that have taken you from God's covering, and you have suffered the results of life without His guidance and protection. You have not led a separated life; instead you have tried to be friendly with the world at the same time you are friendly with Christ. Your compromise with good and evil has given you bitter fruit. Your marriage is failing; you and your spouse have lost passion for each other. Your finances are lacking. Your children are in the far country. Your health is poor. Ask yourself this question, "Am I suffering the consequences of wrong choices?"

Samson chose for Delilah, and he lived in blindness as a slave until his death. Saul chose for the witch of Endor, and the spirit of God departed from him. David chose for Bathsheba, and the sword did not depart from his house. The rich young ruler chose for his riches and walked away from eternity with Christ. Judas chose to betray Jesus and walked into eternal damnation.

Sin will take you further than you want to go, keep you longer than you want to stay, and make you pay a price greater than you can afford. You can either be enslaved to sin or bound to Christ—the choice is yours.

It's never too late to make the right choice. At this moment see yourself on the crossroads of your journey. You can choose to go back to your sin, a far place where God is not. Or you can choose the road called repentance and find Christ's appointed place for your life. He will walk this path with you. When you choose Christ, you will never walk alone again.

If you wish to walk the road to repentance, here is another opportunity to pray the prayer of repentance on page 32.

As you begin your new life in Christ, remember that not all adversity comes from the result of wrong choices. And not all adversity will produce defeat. Some of the world's greatest men and women have encountered disabilities and adversities yet have managed to overcome them.

Cripple a woman, and you have Joni Eareckson. Lock a man in prison, and you have the apostle Paul. Bury him in the snows of Valley Forge, and you have George Washington. Strike him down with infantile paralysis, and he becomes Franklin D. Roosevelt. Deafen a genius composer, and you have Ludwig von Beethoven. Have her become deaf, mute, and blind, and you have Helen Keller. Have them born black in a society filled with racial discrimination, and you have Booker T. Washington, George Washington Carver, and Condoleezza Rice. Have him born of parents who survived a Nazi concentration camp, paralyze him from the waist down when he is four, and you have Itzhak Perlman, an incomparable concert violinist. Call him a slow learner, mentally disabled, and write him off as uneducable, and you have Albert Einstein.[11]

Christ did not come to do away with suffering. He did not come to explain difficulty. He came to fill agony with His presence.[12]

LIFE LESSON TWO:
YOU MUST DO MORE THAN PROFESS YOUR FAITH;
YOU MUST POSSESS YOUR FAITH

Orpah and Ruth represent two kinds of members in the visible body of Christ—the professors and the possessors. Orpah made a profession of faith and failed when her faith was tested. Ruth possessed genuine faith and her faith endured.

The Book of Ruth is about love: the love of one woman for another, the love of one man for a woman, and the love of three women for God. Orpah loved the God of Naomi when it was reasonable. Naomi loved God, yet accused Him of dealing bitterly with her. Ruth loved Jehovah God unconditionally. She could believe in the sun when it didn't shine for her, she could believe in love when it was not shown, and she could believe in God even when He was silent.[13] Genuine faith believes in a dream only you and God can see.

Genuine faith caused Ruth to stay the course and desire Naomi's God. She did not merely profess her faith, which is often weakened by circumstances; she possessed her faith, and it possessed her. No matter what our circumstances, our faith in a faithful God will carry us through life. When we stop arguing with our faith, when we stop putting God on trial, then we can truly decide for Christ. Then we will be carried to levels of joy we can only imagine. This decision will not only carry us through life but keep us in His loving arms for eternity.

Helen Keller, handicapped in life without sight, speech, or hearing, is a prime example of a woman who possessed her faith in a miracle-working God. She said: "I believe that life is given us so we may grow in love, and I believe that God is in me as the sun is in the color and fragrance of a flower—He is the Light in my darkness, the Voice in my silence." [14]

Helen Keller had no sight, but she was full of vision. Helen Keller believed. Ruth believed. We too can believe in a God who never fails; a God who will take us to the mountaintop or walk with us in the valley of the shadow of death. He did not fail Helen. He did not fail Ruth. He will not fail you. He cannot. It's not His nature to do so.

When you accept Him as Savior, you become one of His *ami,* one of His own. He is the King, and you are the King's daughter, chosen by the Creator of the universe to inherit all He has ordained for you. Accept Him as your own. Possess Him in your heart. Your life will never be the same again!

LIFE LESSON THREE:
WHAT YOU ARE WILLING TO WALK AWAY FROM WILL
DETERMINE WHAT GOD CAN BRING TO YOU

Orpah was not willing to walk away from the far country, her people, or her gods. Consequently, she chose the path to oblivion.

Ruth walked away from Moab . . . and *Jehovah Rohi*, the Lord, her Shepherd, brought her to Israel. She walked away from paganism . . . and *Jehovah M'Kaddesh*, the Lord who sanctifies, brought her into His covenant. She walked away from darkness . . . and *Jehovah Tsidkenu*, the Lord her Righteousness, brought her to the Light of the world. Ruth walked away from the only life she ever knew . . . and *Jehovah Jireh,* the Lord her Provider, gave her a life of grandeur beyond what she could imagine.

Every one of us needs to walk away from something when we choose to take the road of repentance on the way to the Cross of Christ, just as my husband did. When John was a young man living at home with his mother, father, and three brothers, he wanted nothing to do with Christianity. Even though he lived in a pastor's home, he was completely turned off by the legalism of keeping man-made rules to obtain righteousness with God. He would tell his parents, "If heaven is filled with legalism, then hell won't be half bad!"

John Hagee had a passion to go to West Point. He was an accomplished student and athlete. After receiving an endorsement from his senator, Lyndon Baines Johnson, his dream came true: He received his appointment to this prestigious institution.

His mother, Vada Swick Hagee, wanted all of her four sons to know Christ. When she learned of my future husband's appointment, she became gravely concerned instead of rejoicing with him for his accomplishment. She knew in her heart that if her son left home before accepting Christ, he would never come to know Him as Savior.

She began to pray that John would not make the journey to West Point. Night and day, she spoke to her son about his decision. She pleaded with him not to go. Nothing she could say would change his mind.

Then something happened on the journey to his dreams. On the second Thursday night of the month of January in the year 1958, John sat on the back pew of his father's church, the First Assembly of God Church in Houston, Texas. This was a place he found to be a safe and quiet site to do homework as well as an easy out after the service because his pew was close to the exit.

At first, John sensed nothing different in this service to distinguish it from the thousands he had attended before. But then he heard a visiting evangelist give the altar call. To this day, he can't remember what the minister preached; he can only remember his desire to know Christ as Savior. I have often heard John describe that moment as one when he wanted Christ more than he wanted breath.

My mother-in-law says a revival broke out in the church the day John Hagee accepted Christ, for the parishioners knew a miracle had taken place in my husband's life. At that moment, he made his choice to turn from his dream and walk the path of God's providence.

Because of his choice to walk away from his ambition, John was given the opportunity to pastor Cornerstone Church, a church of thousands of believers. Because he walked away from his dream, God gave him the privilege to preach to America and the nations of the world by radio and television. Because he was willing to walk away from his passion, God gave him the blessing to disciple our son, Matthew, the sixth generation and the forty-eighth descendant of the Hagee family to preach the gospel since they arrived in America on a ship called *Spirit*.

What you are willing to walk away from will determine what God can lead you to. Ask yourself this question: "What do I need to walk away from to achieve my divine destiny?" God may have more in mind for you than you can ever imagine.

Chapter Five

THE HOMECOMING

The weight of Naomi's feet increased with every step. She walked slowly as she entered the city gates, looking downward with Ruth holding fast to her arm. For a moment Naomi saw herself in a memory of long ago, riding out of Bethlehem in her canopied carriage, adorned in the finest colored fabrics.

Blinking away the past, Naomi looked through her tears at her worn sandals and tattered clothing. *I left Judah clothed in glory, and now I return draped in shame,* she thought. She called on the name of Jehovah to bring her strength.

Naomi could hardly speak as she held back her tears and glanced onto Ruth's beautiful countenance, pale with hunger. "We are home now, my precious." Naomi smiled weakly, trying the best she could to assure her daughter-in-law.

Both women glanced at the faces of the townspeople gathered inside the gates. The two widows could see the crowd pointing at them as they witnessed their homecoming in disbelief. Naomi could hear their whispers. "Could this be Naomi?" someone asked. "Is this the woman who shared her clothing with us?" another queried. "Is this the same Naomi who gave us jewels and linen scarves? . . . Look at her now." Each woman spoke without thinking of the added disgrace their words brought to the prodigal returning home.

Naomi could hardly manage her entrance into her beloved Bethlehem. If the shame became any heavier, she knew she would collapse under its burden. Finally, she addressed the crowd.

"Don't call me Naomi; call me Mara, for the Almighty has dealt bitterly with me! I went out full, and the Lord has brought me home again empty." Naomi was all too sensitive to the stares cast her way, which pierced her heart and hurt her ever so deeply. "Why do you call me Naomi, since the Lord has testified against me, and the Almighty has afflicted me?"

When the women called out her name, they reminded Naomi of her former glory, making the pain of her present condition even worse. Then, suddenly, she stopped thinking of herself as the crowd's attention was drawn to Ruth.

Instantly, Naomi squared her shoulders and took Ruth's hand, holding it tightly to protect her from the accusing stares and inquisitive chatter. Naomi wanted Bethlehem to witness her unwavering support for her young companion.

Naomi gave another weak smile as she looked at Ruth, trying to encourage the precious young woman who had walked away from all she knew to accompany Naomi on her journey. "Jehovah will care for us, Ruth. Do not fret, my dear little bird. We will be fine." With that, Naomi held her head high and looked stoically forward as she walked beyond the city gate toward her home.

Naomi heard the words coming from her mouth, yet she could not completely believe them herself. Where would help come from? *Jehovah Jireh* had provided for Bethlehem, but Elimelech's fields had been left desolate with no one to till or plant them: They were barren. Naomi and Ruth had nothing.

Finally Naomi arrived at her empty home, which was devoid of servants, furnishings, and loved ones. Her once-palatial dwelling was now only filled with dust and faded memories.

Naomi wandered from room to room, recounting the wonderful times with her family from years before. *How sad life has become,* she thought. She came upon Ruth, who stood by the window, gazing into the horizon toward the city square.

Naomi looked at Ruth's pale, yet beautiful, face. *What could she be thinking, this Gentile daughter-in-law of mine, this princess of Moab? I pray she does not regret her decision.* The two women sat by the window of their desolate home and listened to the joyful sound of the harvesters who were celebrating their plentiful crops. Both of them wondered what tomorrow would bring.

THE BIBLE STUDY

Now the two of them went until they came to Bethlehem. And it happened, when they had come to Bethlehem, that all the city was excited because of them; and the women said, "Is this Naomi?"

But she said to them, "Do not call me Naomi; call me Mara, for the Almighty has dealt very bitterly with me. I went out full, and the LORD *has brought me home again empty. Why do you call me Naomi, since the* LORD *has testified against me, and the Almighty has afflicted me?"*

So Naomi returned, and Ruth the Moabitess her daughter-in-law with her, who returned from the country of Moab. Now they came to Bethlehem at the beginning of barley harvest. (RUTH 1:19–22)

Now the two of them went. Once Ruth made her commitment to Jehovah God, the Scriptures ranked her equal to Naomi and one who possessed the same resolve to go to Bethlehem.[1]

"Is this Naomi?" Jewish scholars believe the day Naomi and Ruth entered Bethlehem was a day of celebration. As a sacrifice of praise to the Lord, a measure of barley was offered on the second day of Passover by the grateful townspeople who had gathered at the city gate.[2]

In years past, Naomi was often seen going about the city walking with servants in tow. Now she walked into Bethlehem escorted by a lone Moabite girl, both of them hungry and tattered. What a pitiful sight they made! The afflicted woman who walked before the townspeople was once so radiant that many women were jealous of her beauty. Today was different. Naomi was so changed in appearance her friends could hardly recognize her. Without thinking they asked the question, "Is this Naomi?"

In essence, the townspeople were asking the question, "Was this curse sent after Naomi on the day her flight had become known—the flight that caused Israel to lose heart?"[3]

"Do not call me Naomi; call me Mara." Because the Hebrew text says, "Call me embittered one," scholars deduce that this is the utterance of a bitter woman submitting to her lot as she tried to justify it to those whom she had sinned against. Naomi was not only admitting her guilt, she was also pleading for the townspeople's forgiveness. She did not want the women who had been her friends in the days of her glory to think she came back without a repentant heart.[4]

"I went out full." The word *full* in the Hebrew has the same connotation as pregnant; therefore this word implies "pregnant with wealth and children." Naomi left Bethlehem "full" with a rebellious spirit and came back "empty"—widowed, childless, and poverty stricken, yet with a broken and repentant spirit.

"The Almighty has afflicted me." Naomi told her friends that God, had lifted His blessings and protection from her and her family. Now, on her return Naomi interprets that their leaving Israel was displeasing to God, and they had lost his blessing and protection.

Naomi . . . and Ruth . . . returned from the country of Moab. The Scripture indicates both women were returning to Bethlehem. Naomi was obviously returning to her birthplace, but what of Ruth? Ruth was entering Bethlehem for the first time. She was the first Moabite who repented and converted to Judaism.[5] Why, then, does Scripture identify both women as "returning"?

It is believed that Ruth entered *Eretz Israel* with the same burning desire as

Naomi. At the time of Ruth's conversion, the Lord had put within her the same passion He puts within every person who is born a Jew: a passion for the Promised Land!

The beginning of barley harvest. This time of year refers to the "Omer" harvest during Passover. This chronological detail not only serves as an introduction to the next chapter, it tells us that it was too late to plant new crops in Elimelech's fields.[6] Therefore, the two women were completely poverty stricken. *Jehovah Jireh,* The Lord our Provider, would be the only One who could help Naomi and Ruth. He and He alone would be their source.

LIFE LESSONS

LIFE LESSON ONE:
CHRIST PROMISES CHANGE

After leaving her beloved Bethlehem, Naomi often dreamed of her beautiful home. She missed her abundant lifestyle. She longed to go back. Naomi wanted everything to be the same, but it wasn't.

I have often heard people who have been away from God and suffered the consequences of their choices speak of their disappointment once they return home. After the brief time of reunion and rejoicing is over, they settle into reality and begin to recognize that life will never be the same again. They long for the good times. They desire to go back to "the way things were." They refuse to acknowledge that God doesn't want their lives to remain the same. He wants change. He demands change.

During one of the many wars in Biafra, the American Red Cross gathered supplies, medicine, clothing, and food for the suffering people of this poverty-stricken country. A letter was inside one of the boxes deposited at the collection site. The letter said, "We have recently accepted Christ, and because of our conversion we want to try to help. We won't ever need these again. Can you use them for something?"

Several Ku Klux Klan sheets were packed within the box. These sheets were then cut into strips and eventually used to bandage the wounds of black people in Africa. What precious symbolism! What remarkable transformation! The emblems of hatred became bandages of love! Christ had truly brought about His promised change in the lives of the people who wrote this letter[7]:

> *But now you yourselves are to put off . . . the old man with his deeds, and have put on the new man who is renewed in knowledge according to the image of Him who created him.* (COLOSSIANS 3:8–10)

Once we are in Christ, we should not want to return to our former lives. We should desire change. He has a new path for us to travel and a new level for us to reach. Christ promises change.

LIFE LESSON TWO:
CHOOSE TO BECOME BETTER, NOT BITTER

Naomi left Bethlehem blessed with her husband, sons, and abundance; she came back empty. Naomi became bitter for the condition she was in. However, she did pause to realize that her family's actions had caused them to suffer the consequences of their choices. Now was the time for her to trust in God for her future. Eventually, Naomi made her choice to become better.

My husband often teaches our congregation about choices. We have the liberty to accept Christ or the right to deny Him. We have the opportunity to choose for life or choose for death, to choose for blessings or for curses. We have the freedom to become bitter or better.

Forgiveness has much to do with these choices. Bitterness is unavoidable, and becoming better is impossible, *if we do not forgive ourselves or others who have caused us pain.* Forgiveness causes the root of bitterness to die. Forgiveness affords us the ability to soar to the mountaintop and look to our future with hope.

Pastor Hagee and I are privileged to know many wonderful people who survived the horrors of the Holocaust. One such individual was a man named Shoney Alex Braun who was taken from his home in Transylvania by the Nazis as a young boy of thirteen. His family was deported by train to Auschwitz Concentration Camp in Poland with thousands of others in his community.

Once they reached the camp, Shoney was immediately separated from his mother and sister. Shoney did not know that he would never see his mother and sister again.

As he, his brother, and their father were selected by Joseph Mengele, the infamous SS doctor known as the "Angel of Death," to enter the work camp, Shoney's mother and nine-year-old sister were led to an underground tunnel where they were immediately killed in the gas chamber.

While imprisoned, even though he was suffering the inhumanities and degrading horror of pure satanic hatred, Shoney chose to be thankful to God because he had not been separated from his beloved father and brother. After many months in various camps, one cold night, Shoney and his brother secretly met in the corner of their barrack to discuss what they could possibly give their father to celebrate his impending forty-second birthday. They had nothing to give; the Nazis had stripped them of everything. Suddenly, Shoney became excited; he realized he and his brother did own something of value— their daily bread rations.

Eagerly, the sons presented their love gift to their father on his birthday. Weeping at their generosity, the father refused to take the dry, hard, stale bread from his precious sons, for it was their only nourishment for the day. However, the boys convinced their father that nothing would make them happier than for him to accept their gifts. They wanted to honor the father they loved so dearly.

Finally, not wanting to hurt his sons' feelings, the father accepted their presents. Choking down his tears, Shoney's father prayed the prayer of blessing over the bread, and the grateful man ate his own ration as well as the bread of his two sons.

As he swallowed the last bite of the most valuable gift he had ever received, the three hugged one another, and then the sons blessed their father with a prayer and went to sleep.

During this horrid time in history, the Nazis were known for their infamous roll calls. Several times a day the villainous watchmen took count of the inmates to ensure there would be no escapees and to take away those who were too weak to stand. Those who were too frail to work would quickly meet their demise in the gas chambers or by deadly beatings.

The next morning at dawn, amidst the usual chaos, the prisoners dashed to their place in line for roll call. The guards repeated the count. An inmate was unaccounted for. Bright searchlights were positioned on the shivering prisoners. The guards went into the barracks in search of the missing man. Everyone waited. Suddenly, they returned with their prey—it was Shoney's father!

"This lazy dog was sleeping in the corner!" snarled the SS guard. "This dog has two sons in the camp!" The guard demanded that Shoney and his brother step forward. Once the boys stood by their father, the SS officer yelled to the prisoners, "It took ten minutes for us to find this dog. That is ten extra minutes Germany was kept from victory!"

After being deprived of any substantial nourishment for months, the boys' father was not used to so much bread, and consequently he fell fast asleep in the barracks and missed roll call. The boys were horrified as they saw their father taken from the barracks and paraded in front of the angry guards and frightened prisoners. There, on the day after he accepted his birthday gift, their much-loved father was kicked to death in front of his adored sons.[8]

The Jewish man who stood before Pastor Hagee and me went on to suffer the cruelty and inhumanities of one of the blackest times in history. Shoney's mother, father, brother, and sister were murdered by hatred, yet he was free of malice and bitterness.

As I heard him tell this story and others like it, which scarred most of his formative years, I asked him this question: "What kept you from becoming bitter?"

Triumphantly, he gently smiled and answered. "They took my home, they mangled my body, they took my family and all I treasured. But they could not take away my choice to forgive."

Shoney had chosen a better way—he chose the Torah way—the course mandated by Scripture:

> *And do not grieve the Holy Spirit of God, by whom you were sealed for the day of redemption. Let all bitterness, wrath, anger, clamor, and evil speaking be put away from you, with all malice. And be kind to one another, tenderhearted, forgiving one another, even as God in Christ forgave you.* (**Ephesians 4:30–32**)

When we forgive, as God forgave us, we become better.

Life Lesson Three:
Our God is the God of new beginnings

Naomi and Ruth did not know what was ahead of them. However, they did know they were home and trusted that God would somehow take care of them.

I have seen families in our church go through trials and tribulations, and I have seen most of them benefit from their new beginnings. My husband has a wonderful teaching that has changed my attitude about life and the challenges it often affords. He calls this teaching "The Promise, The Problem, and The Provision."

The concept Pastor Hagee teaches is that the Word of God is filled with His promises. Yet our life on earth guarantees a host of problems. How we act in these problems will determine how quickly God will send His provision. Wouldn't you know it, it depends on us!

The children of Israel received a promise: the land of milk and honey (EXOD. 3:8). They encountered the problem: Pharaoh and the wilderness (EXOD. 5:2; 16:3). And of the multitudes who left Egypt, only Joshua and Caleb inherited the promise (NUM. 14:30).

Millions died in the wilderness because of their refusal to accept by faith the promises God made to Abraham, Isaac, and Jacob concerning their inheritance of the land of milk and honey.

The distance between Egypt and the Promised Land did not take forty years to travel, but God had the children of Israel go around the mountain several times because of their ungodly behavior while in the problem.

Many of you who are going through this journey with me are in the midst of a problem. God has given you a promise regarding your problem in His Word. Are you sick in body? The Lord promises to heal all our diseases (PS. 103:3)! Is your marriage failing? The Word of God says He hates divorce, except for the scriptural reasons of adultery and abandonment (MAL. 2:16). Has your spouse told you he no longer loves you? The Lord says He holds the heart of man in the palm of His hand, and He can turn that heart as easily as He controls rivers of living waters (PROV. 21:1).

Have your children come under attack? The Lord says no weapon formed against you or your household will prosper (ISA. 54:17)! Are your finances lacking? The Lord promises to prosper you as you obey His statutes (1 CHRON. 22:13)!

We must learn to look to the Author of these promises, instead of dwelling on the enormous size of the problem. We must decide to trust the God we serve through our problem in order to receive His promised provision. We must praise Him for His wisdom and mercy, for He is always faithful:

I will bless the LORD at all times; His praise shall continually be in my mouth. (PSALM 34:1)

Picture the Lord's "promise field." I know many of you have found this field, and you peacefully abide there. We can say of God's promise field what we can't say of any other field: The soil is so rich and deep that we will never be able to glean all His "promise field" has to offer.

Taking hold of His promises enables the believer to see the problem through the eyes of the Promise Giver. In the eyes of a King's daughter these problems are simply beautiful stitches in the tapestry called life.

Corrie ten Boom, a Christian Dutch woman who also suffered Nazi imprisonment during the Second World War, often showed a piece of tapestry to her audiences. She would hold up the piece of cloth, first showing the exquisiteness of the embroidered side and all the intricate stitches of thread that formed a beautiful picture. This is the plan of God for our lives, she would say. Then she would flip the embroidery over to show the tangled, confused underside, illustrating how we view our lives from our human standpoint, especially while living through the problem.[9]

Joseph's life is an example of tangled adversity. Joseph grew up as his father Jacob's favorite son, yet because of his brothers' jealousy, his life became one of great trial and adversity.

Despite all his hardship, time and time again Joseph trusted in the God he served while he was in the problem, and time and time again God showed him favor and gave him a new beginning. When Joseph revealed himself to his brothers, he also revealed God's plan, which Joseph was able to see, despite the suffering:

But now, do not therefore be grieved or angry with yourselves because you sold me here; for God sent me before you to preserve life . . . And God sent me before you to preserve posterity for you in the

***earth, and to save your lives by a great deliverance. So now it was
not you who sent me here, but God.*** (GENESIS 45:5, 7–8)

Joseph saw the problem through the eyes of the Lord and trusted Him. He kept
his eye on God's promise, and God's provision finally came. Joseph remained
faithful to God and enjoyed the beauty of God's promise in the tapestry called
life.

Like Joseph, I want you to look at both sides of the embroidery. Accept
God's promise, remain faithful to Him in the problem, and expect His provision in your life.

Chapter Six

THE DIVINE APPOINTMENT

Naomi was trying to sweep the dusty floor of her once-immaculate home. There were no servants now, only the two of them. Naomi was also fretful, for Ruth had begged to go into the gleaning fields for several days now—and had made yet another plea a moment ago.

"I am so concerned for your travel into the fields," Naomi said. "My people do not understand your love for me, and they certainly do not understand your love for our God. I do not know how you will be received, for you are a foreigner in their eyes. I must protect you, my daughter." Naomi became more and more anxious for Ruth's safety.

"Yes, I know, Ruth . . . We must trust in Jehovah God . . . Yes . . . I agree, my daughter, we cannot depend on others, we must work to eat . . . I only wish I could go out into the field in your stead." Naomi's heart was heavy. She did not want Ruth to suffer her pain, her embarrassment. Ruth had not been disobedient; Naomi had been the one to sin against God.

Very early the next morning Ruth resumed her appeal to Naomi. Knowing she could not convince Ruth to stay, Naomi finally released her. "You may go, my child. But first grant me the privilege of saying a prayer of blessing for you as you glean the corners of the fields for our welfare."

Naomi walked over to the beautiful young woman who followed her to Bethlehem, the woman who had converted to Judaism and the woman who pledged to stay with her no matter what the cost. Oh, how she loved her precious daughter-in-law who was now kneeling obediently before her. Tears streamed down Naomi's face as she placed her hands on Ruth's head.

"The Lord bless you and keep you. The Lord make His face to shine upon you, and be gracious unto you. The Lord lift up His countenance upon you, and give you peace . . . May He direct your path and provide the bread we need for this day. May He protect you as you gather His provision and return to me. Amen."

Naomi watched as Ruth walked out of their barren home and down the desolate road, lit ever so softly by the dawn's first glimmer of light. Naomi's heart pounded within her, her mind spinning with questions as well as petitions to Jehovah: *Will Ruth return to me safely? Have You heard my prayer, Jehovah God? Have You forgiven my sin? . . . Oh, Lord, please do not punish my precious Ruth for my failure . . . I have no desire for riches; I have no desire for prestige. I only desire to feel Your presence and to know You have forgiven me. Lord, keep Ruth safe and bring her back to me.*

When Naomi could see Ruth no longer, she closed the door, wiped the tears from her face, and returned to her chores. She busied herself, washing their few tattered garments and sweeping the cobwebs from the corners of the little-used rooms, as if trying to remove the past from her mind. As the day came to a close, Ruth had yet to return.

Naomi could not fight off the waves of worry. *Has Ruth lost her way? Have the reapers of the field harmed her for being a Moabite? . . . I should never have allowed her to go. I'm responsible for her now. She is so kind, so loving, so trusting.* As Naomi waited she reminisced about the first time she met Ruth.

The time in Moab had been a difficult one for Naomi. She did not have many friends in the far country. She often visited with the women in the surrounding area about their families and would greet them warmly in the marketplace, but she and the women of Moab had little in common. Naomi kept the Jewish feasts and lived by the Law of Moses, and the women of Moab worshiped a multitude of gods. They just couldn't understand her faith in only one God. She hungered for the friendships she left behind in Bethlehem.

After the death of Elimelech, Naomi hoped she and her sons would return to the land of Judah, but she was disappointed when Chilion and Mahlon decided to stay in Moab. It seemed her sons were accustomed to living in the far country.

She also remembered grieving over Mahlon and Chilion's decisions to take Moabite women as wives—what would become of them? What would Jehovah think of their disobedience? She was certain God would never forgive them for their great transgression.

When the day came to meet Ruth, Naomi was not prepared for what she felt. As Ruth walked into Naomi's presence, a prevailing sense of joy came over Naomi.

Ruth's eyes were filled with love as she humbly glanced at Naomi. Ruth's gentle smile mirrored an inward kindness that surrounded her like an aura. She was the daughter of the king of Moab, yet she dressed modestly. Nevertheless, even in modesty, her clothing complemented her as if embracing the splendor of a fine statue. Ruth was the portrait of both inward radiance and outward beauty. She only lacked a belief in the God of Abraham, Isaac, and Jacob. And for this Naomi was saddened.

Naomi smiled as she relived Ruth's conversion on their journey to Bethlehem. Now Ruth was complete—she was a Jew. Yet she had no husband, for Mahlon was dead. Naomi became sad again, for she thought of Ruth who had no one but an old woman to share her future, an old woman who was frantically worried about the safety of her precious daughter-in-law.

THE BIBLE STUDY

There was a relative of Naomi's husband, a man of great wealth, of the family of Elimelech. His name was Boaz.

> *So Ruth the Moabitess said to Naomi, "Please let me go to the field, and glean heads of grain after him in whose sight I may find favor." And she said to her, "Go, my daughter."*
>
> *Then she left, and went and gleaned in the field after the reapers. And she happened to come to the part of the field belonging to Boaz, who was of the family of Elimelech.* (RUTH 2:1–3)

A relative of Naomi's husband. Relative is translated as the word *moda* in Hebrew, which means a "familiar relative" or "kinsman." Boaz was the son of Elimelech's brother.[1] Even though Naomi knew she had at least two close relatives, she had not dared to ask for their assistance, since she was ashamed for deserting her people during their time of need.

Once again we have a glimpse into the character and strength of these two women: Naomi, not willing to thrust herself upon a rich relative in her time of lack, and Ruth, the daughter of the king of Moab, yet not too proud to work the fields and shoulder the burden of support for herself and her mother-in-law.

A man of great wealth. This phrase is also translated as a "mighty man of valor." From the Hebrew, the full meaning of the description of Boaz is "a man of substance, who need not flatter or show partiality—a man endowed with the highest human qualities, encompassing all virtues, among them, generosity and the hatred of unjust gain."[2]

His name was Boaz. In the case of wicked men, their names were given before the word name: Goliath was his name. Nabal was his name. But the names of the righteous were preceded by the word *name:* His name was Kish. His name was Saul. His name was Jesse. His name was Mordecai. His name was Boaz. These righteous men of valor were acknowledged in this manner because they resembled their Creator, of whom it was written in Exodus 3, "I Am who I Am," which is translated in the Hebrew as "I Am the Name."[3]

The Holy Scriptures emphasize that Boaz was a man of God. He was a Torah scholar and one of the judges appointed over Bethlehem.[4] He was also the only Old Testament example of a Hebrew *goel*,[5] which is translated as "kinsman" and "redeemer." The phrase *kinsman-redeemer* can best be understood by defining two aspects of its root words.

The first definition is to buy back, to purchase by paying a price for that which was lost. This definition relates to the purchase of a relative's debt. If through misfortunate circumstances a man was forced to mortgage his property and was unable to recover its cost by the date of the maturity of the note, the property was passed on to the mortgager until the Year of Jubilee. However, at any time during this period the kinsman-redeemer, the next of kin, could pay the mortgage and restore its possession to the rightful owner:

> *If one of your brethren becomes poor, and has sold some of his possession, and if his redeeming relative comes to redeem it, then he may redeem what his brother sold.* (LEVITICUS 25:25)

This same policy applied to the person as well. If the debtor owned no property and sold himself into slavery to pay his debt, the kinsman-redeemer could, at any time, restore his next of kin to freedom by paying the price required to meet his debt:

> *Now if a sojourner or stranger close to you becomes rich, and one of your brethren who dwells by him becomes poor, and sells himself to the stranger or sojourner close to you, or to a member of the stranger's family, after he is sold he may be redeemed again . . . or anyone who is near of kin to him in his family may redeem him.* (LEVITICUS 25:47–49)

This definition of a kinsman-redeemer applies not only to redeeming the property or the debt of the departed relative, but also to redeeming the widow of his relative, according to the penal code of Deuteronomy 25:5–10.

The second definition of the kinsman-redeemer is to avenge the next of kin by blood. This definition refers to the cities of refuge, which were designated as places a man could flee if he had killed someone accidentally. Here, the man who killed was protected from the *goel* of the man he killed. However, if the accused murdered with premeditation, he was not permitted to enter the city of refuge, and the *goel* of the victim was allowed to avenge his relative's death:

> **The avenger of blood himself shall put the murderer to death; when he meets him, he shall put him to death.** (NUMBERS 35:19)

Boaz met the qualifications of a "kinsman-redeemer." He was related to Naomi, and therefore related to Ruth. He was a man of great wealth, so he was *able* to redeem her, and he was more than willing to redeem what was lost, as we will soon discover.

"Please let me go into the field and glean." Ruth is not purely asking for permission to glean the field to ease their hunger. She is much more sensitive than that. This request stresses the noble character of a "princess" who was willing to go into the fields as a common pauper to spare her mother-in-law the indignity of going out to provide for their needs where she would be subjected to the humiliating stares of those who knew her former affluence.

Gleanings were not the property of the owner of the field; they belonged to the poor. To glean meant to walk after the reapers and gather whatever remained. This was God's gift to the poor, according to Leviticus 19:9–10. *Jehovah Jireh*, the Lord who provides, had remembered His people and given them bread. The law of gleaning was a Jewish law that Ruth learned from Naomi:

When you reap the harvest of your land, you shall not wholly reap the corners of your field, nor shall you gather the gleanings of your harvest. And you shall not glean your vineyard, nor shall you gather every grape of your vineyard; you shall leave them for the poor and the stranger. (LEVITICUS 19:9–10)

"In whose sight I may find favor." Ruth wanted to find favor with the owner of the field. She would not glean the field unless she had the owner's permission, and then she would "glean the heads of grain after him," a continued gesture of modesty. Ruth qualified to glean the fields on two counts: she was a stranger and was also a widow.

And she happened. This is one of my favorite verses in the entire book of Ruth. This verse speaks of the majesty of the God we serve. First, imagine the thoughts that were going through Ruth's mind: *Where do I go? How will I be received? Will I be allowed to glean? Will I find my way back home to Naomi?*

The Hebrew text reads that she "went and came," signifying that she made her way with fear and trembling—and with much prayer. She went out a certain distance and walked back, and then went out again, marking her path so she would not lose her way home. Ruth did not know the land; she did not know the people or their customs. What courage it must have taken to embark on this enormous walk of faith!

Naomi had not given Ruth instructions where to go or how to get there. Ruth simply went out with the faith that *Jehovah Rohi*—the Lord, her Shepherd—would guide her path. At first glance the reader might be led to believe that the word *happened* suggests it was mere coincidence that Ruth came to the field of Boaz. This was simply not so; her steps were ordered by the Divine Creator.

Unfortunately, we do not completely comprehend that the Heavenly Architect, the Prime Cause of all, designs all the apparently random events in advance and plans our course to the last detail.[6] How unimportant it must have seemed for the steps of a young Moabitess to be directed by the Sovereign One. It might seem that God was merely providing food for the poor; to the contrary, He was orchestrating the creation of the greatest genealogical line known to mankind!

This verse refers to those moments of our lives that we do not direct, but which direct us. These moments may be unexpected events, but they are the most intentional messages sent by the One who directs and brings about all things.[7] The steps of Ruth did not just "happen"; they were divinely ordered by the God who would soon become even more real to her.

Who was of the family of Elimelech. This is designated as a prophetic statement in Hebrew commentaries. "The family of Elimelech" automatically qualifies Boaz as a kinsman-redeemer who could marry Ruth, the Moabitess, and ultimately father the Davidic dynasty.[8]

LIFE LESSONS

LIFE LESSON ONE:
JESUS CHRIST IS YOUR KINSMEN-REDEEMER

The entire premise of scriptural redemption is based on the person of the redeemer. Boaz was the "kinsman-redeemer" and "was the plain figure of Christ."[9] Just as Boaz was a blood relative of Naomi, so Christ is the blood relative of those He redeemed from sin when He shed His blood for His own at His cross:

> ***In Him we have redemption through His blood, the forgiveness of sins, according to the riches of His grace which He made to abound toward us in all wisdom and prudence.*** (EPHESIANS 1:7–8)

Christ is also beautifully fulfilled in the second qualification of a "kinsman-redeemer": to avenge the next of kin by blood. Jesus is the avenger of our souls. Sin and Satan are present to kill, steal, and destroy us and are therefore murderers of your soul and mine.

> **The thief does not come except to steal, and to kill, and to destroy. (JOHN 10:10)**

Satan is called a murderer in Scripture, and we are his victims. Jesus told the Pharisees:

> **You are of your father the devil, and the desires of your father you want to do. He was a murderer from the beginning, and does not stand in the truth, because there is no truth in him. When he speaks a lie, he speaks from his own resources, for he is a liar and the father of it. (JOHN 8:44)**

Satan introduced sin in the Garden of Eden and brought death to the human family. Sin is therefore a partner in the crime, for "the wages of sin is death."[10] The apostle Paul told the Romans of his own struggle with sin:

> **For sin, taking occasion by the commandment, deceived me, and by it killed me. (ROMANS 7:11)**

Yet, we have been restored by the blood of the Lamb, just as Paul was:

> **And you, being dead in your trespasses and the uncircumcision of your flesh, He has made alive together with Him, having forgiven you all trespasses, having wiped out the handwriting of requirements that was against us, which was contrary to us. And He has taken it out of**

the way, having nailed it to the cross. Having disarmed principalities and powers, He made a public spectacle of them, triumphing over them in it. (COLOSSIANS 2:13–15)

J. Vernon McGee states: "In the fullness of time, the avenger of blood came that 'through death He might destroy him who had the power of death, that is, the devil' (HEB. 2:14). He came to redeem us from sin and the law. He hates sin and Satan because they have been the cause of man's undoing. Christ did not pay the ransom to the Devil, but He did ransom us from the power of the Devil. Christ, in dealing with Satan and sin, is the avenger of blood kinsman. Our Redeemer loved us when were dead in sin, but He hated sin and Satan."[11]

Listen to the good news! We have been redeemed! Not by good works. Not by a ransom paid by man, but by the blood of the precious Son of God.

We were nothing. Now we are royalty, grafted into the root of Abraham, Isaac, and Jacob.

We had nothing. Now all that is the Lord's is our inheritance, because He has adopted us and made us His own.

We were dead, killed by our sin. Now we have forgiven and have everlasting life!

Rejoice with me! We are the King's daughters. Our value is immeasurable! Jesus paid our debt at the cross. He bought us with a great price and made the great exchange at the cross.

Imagine for a moment the price our Redeemer had to pay for our salvation. One of the ways I strive to lead the life He has ordained for me is to set my mind on that costly price.

Every Sunday morning at Cornerstone Church a dedicated team of volunteers translates our praise and worship and Pastor Hagee's sermons for the hearing impaired. I am amazed at the splendor of language when spoken without sound. The graceful movement of the interpreters' hands echoes the beauty of the words of an inspiring hymn or firmly emphasizes the power of a life-changing sermon.

My favorite interpretation occurs at the altar call when the sinner comes forward to receive forgiveness and accepts everlasting life. I know that the deaf can hear the suffering melody of the cross as they stand before the altar, tears streaming, their hands signing the name of Jesus: the little finger of the right hand draws a letter *J* in the center palm of the left hand, and the index finger of the left hand points to the center of the right palm, signifying His nail imprint. Even in silence, Jesus' name tells us of His suffering for the redemption of our souls.

LIFE LESSON TWO:
EVERYTHING IN YOUR LIFE WILL WORK WHEN YOU DO

Naomi could have gone to her relatives and requested aid, but she did not want to burden them with her needs. Additionally, Ruth was willing to put the royal status she enjoyed in Moab behind her and perform hard labor in the fields to help provide for the needs of her mother-in-law and herself. Had she not been willing to work in the fields, she would have missed her appointment with her divine destiny.

My husband tells our church that God provides worms for birds but He doesn't force them down their throats; birds must harvest the worms for themselves. So it is with His people. God provides us with good health, a bright mind, and the opportunity to work.

Our Father is not asking us to do anything He has not done Himself.

Genesis 1:1 describes God's work:

In the beginning God created the heavens and the earth.

And Genesis 2:3 announces the completion of His work:

> ***Then God blessed the seventh day and sanctified it, because in it He rested from all His work which God had created and made.***

God communicates four attributes of work to His people in Genesis. First, we must begin somewhere. God began at the beginning. This seems simple enough; however, some individuals refuse to begin at all, if they can't begin at the top.

My husband began picking cotton at eight years of age and worked in a grocery store sacking groceries when he was twelve. My father began selling produce out of the back of a truck with his father when he was a boy, picked peaches in the field with his mother as a young man, and later hauled produce throughout the country as a trucker when he married my mother. As we learn to be faithful in the small assignments, God can trust us with larger ones.

Second, God loved His work:

> ***And God saw that it was good.*** (GENESIS 1:12)

It is important to be happy with the work God has given us. A job is a tool the Master Potter uses to mold us into the individuals He has destined us to become. Therefore, we must do all that is set before us with excellence and a right attitude. God saw that His work was good when He examined it. We must do the same.

We must learn to love what we do to provide for our family, for he who loves his work never truly labors. If we can't look on our work and feel good about it, we must examine our heart and our attitude concerning our job. Whatever our assignment, God records our efforts in His heart and will reward us in His appointed time. We may not see the outcome in an instant, but we will be rewarded if we are faithful and perform our jobs to the best of our ability.

Third, God completed His assignment:

Thus the heavens and the earth, and all the host of them, were finished. And on the seventh day God ended His work which He had done. (GENESIS 2:1–2)

Many people have no problem beginning a job, but the challenge comes in completing it. When you look at today's résumés, it is rare to have someone stay at a job more than twenty-four months. Why?

Some of the answers I receive are: "I was bored." Or "I didn't want to deal with the politics." Or "I had no future in the company." We are often met with trials on our journey with our Redeemer. These trials are meant to strengthen us when we put our trust in the God of our salvation, for James tells us to:

Count it all joy when you fall into various trials, knowing that the testing of your faith produces patience. (JAMES 1:2–3)

Finally, God rested:

And He rested on the seventh day from all His work which He had done. (GENESIS 2:2)

If God rested, so must we. Rest is a gift from God. Rest is a time to reflect on His goodness. When we rest, we think more clearly and we become more productive. The enemy will try to deceive us into thinking that rest is a waste of time and nothing good will come of it. To the contrary, rest is a mandate from God. Not to rest is to be disobedient to His law and suffer the consequences of our rebellion. The Lord asks us to:

Rest in the LORD, and wait patiently for Him. (PSALM 37:7)

God is our example. Both He and His works are faithful:

The works of the LORD *are great, studied by all who have pleasure in them. His work is honorable and glorious, and His righteousness endures forever.* (PSALM 111:2–3)

When we work according to God's example, everything in our lives will work as well.

LIFE LESSON THREE:
OUR GOD IS A GOD OF DIVINE APPOINTMENTS

In the fall of 2003 my husband and I were returning from our twentieth trip to Israel. We host a very "hands on" trip for our friends and partners. Pastor Hagee leads the tour, teaches the Word of God, and meets with several dignitaries. And I, well, I am the ever-present, hovering mother hen who wants everything perfect for our guests. As always, we were greatly satisfied with our pilgrimage and equally exhausted by the end of the trip.

We immediately fell asleep after we boarded our El Al jet home and awakened six hours later, a bit more refreshed.

Suddenly, a visitor came to our seats. In our exhaustion, we were unaware of the other people seated in our section, but to the right of us, on the other side of the plane, sat two Orthodox rabbis. One was now standing in front of my husband and me.

The rabbi was a distinguished man of tall and slender stature. He had on a traditional black, vested suit with the cords of his "talit katan" hanging from his waist. Of course, he wore a yarmulke atop his head, and his face was bordered on either side by long, gray side curls that matched his gray beard. His dark, compassionate eyes were fixed on John as he asked him the question, "Do you know who I am?"

"No, I'm afraid I don't," replied my husband.

"They call me the Disco Rabbi!"

Due to the roaring noise of the jets, my husband thought he had misunderstood the rabbi. John turned to me and loudly asked, "Did he say 'Disco Rabbi'?"

Remaining seated due to the lack of space in the narrow aisle of the plane, I nodded yes. And my husband turned to the Rabbi and introduced himself.

Then the rabbi made this most unusual statement: "The Lord has told me to come to you and tell you my story."

We were now very eager to hear what he had to say. The rabbi sensed my husband and I had difficulty understanding his heavy Israeli accent, so he showed us a short video on his computer. The story we were about to witness changed our lives forever.

The Disco Rabbi's given name is Rabbi Yitzchak Dovid Grossman. In 1968 he moved into the city of Migdal Ha'Emek in the lower Galilee to be part of the humanitarian care that was desperately needed in the area. The city was designed to accommodate the high influx of Jewish immigrants from North African countries. However, the unexpected growth in immigrants led to job shortages and a lack of sufficient school facilities. As a further consequence, the city soon became known for its high crime rate.

After arriving in the area, Rabbi Grossman became aware of the young Jewish children who roamed the city streets, either orphans or children who had no proper parental supervision. These children would gather in the discotheques of Migdal Ha'Emek, instead of the local synagogues. They were wasting away their lives, instead of studying the Torah. The rabbi knew something had to be done to redeem these precious young souls, so he went where they were.

He held Torah studies in the discos and pubs and on the street corners. Wherever the young people gathered, he was there. Slowly, but surely, the tough exteriors of this new generation began to peel away. The gentle side of these young people, who were searching for their true identity, emerged.[12]

Rabbi Grossman's reputation as the Disco Rabbi preceded him. He was able to visit prisoners in Israeli jails, giving them words of encouragement and providing them with young rabbis to teach them the beauty of the Torah way of life.

After a while, the criminal activity of the town began a considerable downturn. Entrepreneurs started to establish factories, and the unemployed regained their pride as jobs became available.

In 1972, Rabbi Grossman founded Migdal Ohr (Hebrew for "Tower of Light") to provide education and social guidance to children from underprivileged and problem homes. This facility now reaches over 6,000 pupils, eighteen hundred of which are Jewish orphans from the former Soviet Union. These orphans managed to find refuge in Israel through Exodus Two, a program that brings the Jews of the world to Israel, fulfilling the blessing given in Ezekiel:

> *Thus says the Lord GOD: "When I have gathered the house of Israel from the peoples among whom they are scattered, and am hallowed in them in the sight of the Gentiles, then they will dwell in their own land which I gave to My servant Jacob. And they will dwell safely there, build houses, and plant vineyards; yes, they will dwell securely, when I execute judgments on all those around them who despise them. Then they shall know that I am the LORD their God."*
> **(EZEKIEL 28:25–26)**

As I heard more of the rabbi's testimony, I knew something beautiful was happening. To understand the significance of this moment, you need to know two facts about our personal lives.

First, on the night of our departure from Israel, my husband and I traditionally stand on the balcony of our hotel overlooking the breathtaking old city of Jerusalem and say a prayer. We give thanks unto the Lord for bringing us to Israel one more time. We thank Him for a safe trip where the lives of our friends and partners are changed forever. We pray for the peace of Jerusalem and the Jewish people. We pray for our children and grandchildren. On this particular trip, we added a special prayer for an event that would take place at Cornerstone Church two weeks after our return to the States.

Since 1981 we have hosted "A Night to Honor Israel," giving Christians of our community, and the nations of the world, an opportunity to honor Israel and the Jewish people. As we obey His command, we have seen countless blessings come our way, just as He promised in Genesis 12:3.

> *I will bless those who bless you, and I will curse him who curses you; and in you all the families of the earth shall be blessed.*

That year we were privileged to raise over two million dollars from Cornerstone Church and our partners around the globe whose desire it is to bless Israel. We knew that putting the funds in the right hands was a great responsibility, so we asked God to give us wisdom to make the proper decisions in dispersing the resources.

As my husband and the rabbi were talking I began to pray, sitting quietly in my seat by the window of the plane. *Lord, is this a divine appointment orchestrated by You? Is this the man we are to help as he helps Your seed? Show us, Father, that this encounter is of You!*

Rabbi Grossman had become so excited about his work that he unknowingly pressed the lever that caused John's seat to flip back into the sleeping position, and John's body with it, his arms flailing in the air. After the initial shock, John and the rabbi both began laughing.

"Rabbi! Rabbi! Help me get the chair back into position!" my husband cried between the bursts of laughter.

Red with embarrassment the Rabbi began to search for the proper button that would take my husband back to a sitting position.

When Rabbi Grossman finally managed to bring my husband's seat to its upright position, he took my husband's face in his hands and kissed him on the forehead!

This loving gesture had immense significance for John and me. Ever since we were married, we have used a saying to describe God's supernatural blessing and favor in our lives. Whenever something wonderful happens to us, which is not initiated by either of us, my husband says, "The Lord has just kissed us on the forehead." John and I treasure this phrase, a private saying between us that attempts to describe God's bountiful blessings on our lives.

At the moment the Disco Rabbi kissed John on the forehead, the Lord answered my prayer. Our meeting with this man was not a coincidence. This moment was God's divine appointment for our lives.

Since our meeting we have been used of God to present Rabbi Grossman with over $1.25 million dollars for the Jewish orphans he cares for. Praise be to God!

Coincidence or divine appointment? Do you recognize God's hand in such incidents? I hope so. Always remember: If you heed God's voice and obey His commandments, every step you take is one step closer to the destiny God has ordained for you.

The steps of a good man are ordered by the Lord, and He delights in his way. (PSALM 37:23)

Chapter Seven

THE KINSMAN

This was the beginning of an extraordinary day for Boaz. He awoke with a sense of anticipation, for his reapers would begin to harvest his fields today. As always during Morning Prayers, Boaz gave thanks to Jehovah for His bountiful provision.

Boaz remembered the number of times he had thanked God in prayer for abundance while his fields were still barren. He thanked God for allowing him to provide for those less fortunate than he during their time of lack. He thanked the God of Hope that the people of Bethlehem never lost heart during their time of trial. The famine had been long, and it had been hard, but somehow the Mighty One had sustained them.

Boaz knew *Hashem* was drawing attention to His people and to their rebellion with a season of famine, and he always believed in his heart the day would come when their time of testing would be over. Today was that day. Today was a day of harvest. Today was a day of restoration. Today was a day of new beginnings.

This day also marked the end of mourning for the wife of his youth. Boaz was saddened that she would not share this bright and glorious moment with him, but he knew she was in a much better place. She was a virtuous woman, full of goodness and kindness, and he sorely missed her.

Boaz did not want to spend this day indoors; he wanted to share in the joy of the harvest with the people. After Morning Prayers he did something he had not done in years. He mounted his horse and rode into his fields.

The air had a unique sweetness; the sun, an astounding glow. Even the birds' chirping sounded a melody of rejoicing. Boaz sensed an expectancy he had never known before. *What could it be? Could it be the harvest? Could our God be blessing us with a new day?* he wondered.

Whatever the reason, Boaz was determined to take all this beautiful moment had to offer and accept it as a gift from the One who gave all blessings.

As he rounded the stony path, Boaz began to witness the magnificent colors of the harvest. What beauty God had created with His pallet of gold and amber! The heavy stalks waving in the air, pregnant with their fruit, were ready for the gleaning as if to announce divine restoration for the people of Bethlehem. Today would be a good day; Boaz could feel it.

Suddenly, his eyes set their gaze on the most beautiful woman he had ever seen.

THE BIBLE STUDY

Now behold, Boaz came from Bethlehem, and said to the reapers, "The LORD be with you!" And they answered him, "The LORD bless you!"

Then Boaz said to his servant who was in charge of the reapers, "Whose young woman is this?"

So the servant who was in charge of the reapers answered and said, "It is the young Moabite woman who came back with Naomi from the country of Moab. And she said, 'Please let me glean and gather after the reapers among the sheaves.' So she came and has continued from morning until now, though she rested a little in the house." (RUTH 2:4–7)

Behold. In Hebrew the word *behold* suggests something unusual and uncommon. Boaz did not usually come into the field. He was a wealthy man who had overseers to supervise his harvest. These men would report the day's events to him, so it was not necessary for him to be in the gleaning fields. Why was he there?

Jewish scholars believe that the guiding hand of divine providence led him to the field on that particular day in order to meet Ruth.[1] God will lead His children into the path He has chosen for us; all we must do is listen for His direction and choose to follow His course. David spoke of this guidance in the Twenty-third Psalm:

He restores my soul; He leads me in the paths of righteousness for His name's sake. (PSALM 23:3)

"The Lord be with you!" The sages credit Boaz for originating the custom of greeting one's neighbor in the name of *Hashem,* in the name of the Lord. He did this to instill in the hearts of this lawless generation that the all-pervading presence of God was the sole source of mankind's blessing and favor.[2] We must learn from Boaz's example and constantly give praise to the Lord who is the source of all that is good in our lives.

"The Lord bless you!" The Hebrew translation is "May *Hashem* bless. May He bless you with an abundant harvest." This greeting not only referred to the bounty of Boaz's field but also to the fullness of his personal life. According to biblical genealogy, he had been recently widowed, and his visit to the fields came at the completion of his time of mourning.

Jewish sages believe that a man who dwells without a wife lives without blessing. Therefore, the reapers greeted Boaz with this prayer over his life: "May *Hashem* bless you with a worthy wife."[3]

I try to greet people with the phrase "God bless you" or the phrase "I bless you in the name of the Lord." I am always pleased to hear the responses I receive. Sometimes people say, "God bless you too" or, "Thank you," or they simply reply with a kind smile or a look of pleasant surprise. Whatever their response, I know I have left people with a blessing that will help them through their day, and I know the blessing will not return void. In blessing others I also have acknowledged my God, who is ever-present in my life and the source of every good blessing that comes to me.

A side note about Jewish genealogy: Unlike most cultures, which may or may not take time to record births, marriages, and deaths, the Jewish culture has always done so, because of God's mandate (NEH. 7:5).

I have met individuals within the Jewish community who can trace their genealogy to one of the original twelve tribes. The Bible is not comprised of a series of fables about mythical characters designed to present some moral code to whoever reads them. The Holy Scriptures are the inherent Word of our Creator, giving the believer insight into the interactions between the Great I Am and His chosen people. We are to believe its truths, learn from its pages, be guided by its precepts, and be inspired by its promises.

"Whose young woman is this?" Boaz was a judge in Bethlehem. He heard about all the happenings of the town at the city gates when he gathered with the other leaders to discuss the matters concerning the people. He knew that his relative Naomi had returned to Judah with a young Moabite. So why ask this question? Most Jewish scholars agree that Boaz was really distinguishing Ruth for her modesty among the other women in the fields.

The gleaning fields were filled with reapers. They were also filled with women who were widowed and were therefore also "gleaning" after the reapers. Some women were flirtatious with the hope of attracting a new husband. Often the men would see them bending immodestly to draw attention to themselves.

Rather than bending, Ruth sat as she gleaned the fallen ears of barleycorn. While the other women hiked up their skirts, she kept hers down. The other women conversed with the reapers, while Ruth remained silent.[4] She set herself apart from other women.

Christian scholars believe the encounter between Boaz and Ruth was love at first sight. The fact that Boaz had fallen desperately in love with Ruth is not concealed within the story, for the true love of a man and a woman is an arrangement of God and is never wrong, except when perverted by sin.[5]

"It is the young Moabite woman." Boaz asked the overseer of the field about Ruth. He informed Boaz that Ruth was qualified to glean the field because she had come to Bethlehem with Naomi as a convert, as a Jew.[6]

The phrase *young Moabite woman* implied two truths about Ruth. First, *young* implied that she was of child-bearing age. Jewish sources record Ruth's age as forty, still considered young and fruitful. Boaz was said to be eighty, still strong and ready to begin a new family by the standard of the day. Lest you think their ages were not very romantic, translate their ages to twenty for Ruth and forty for Boaz, and your modern mindset can paint the portrait of romance much easier.

Second, *a Moabite woman* implied Ruth was not under the ban of the Moabites, for she was a woman, and this ban only applied to men by authority of the Oral Law.[7]

"Please let me glean and gather." The overseer mentioned Ruth's request to emphasize her modesty and good manners. Even though it was not necessary to ask permission to glean the harvest fields since it was the law, this young woman came to the overseer and humbly asked for permission to glean.

Boaz had heard enough. What he felt in his heart for Ruth was confirmed by what the overseer said about her. He knew that the time had come for him to take the next step: to publicly proclaim his status as Naomi and Ruth's kinsman-redeemer.

LIFE LESSONS

LIFE LESSON ONE:
PROCLAIM THE BLESSING

The power of the spoken word is without measure. When you speak badly to your children or your spouse, you proclaim curses over their lives. Phrases such as "You will never amount to anything!" or "What's wrong with you, can't you understand?" or "You are just like your father; you're both unbearable!" are curses that curtail the potential your children and loved ones have for their lives. A curse is defined as "a calling to send evil or injury down on a person, to afflict or blaspheme."[8] Is that what you want to offer those you love?

I have encountered many individuals who have been so negatively impacted by spoken curses that their lives have forever lost meaning and purpose. They have no hope for the future. When they marry, they perpetuate the negative cycle of the spoken curse over their lives and the lives of their children. They are emotionally and spiritually handicapped.

This is the origin of the biblical phrase *generational curses*. From generation to generation, we fail to break the negative words that have been spoken over our lives. Seven simple steps and a prayer of deliverance can break these curses from our families and their future.

In his book, *Blessing or Cursing: You Can Choose*, Derek Prince lists seven vital steps that will release us from generational curses:

1. Confess your faith in Christ and in His sacrifice on your behalf.

2. Repent of all of your rebellion and your sin.

3. Claim forgiveness of all sins.

4. Forgive other people who have ever harmed you or wronged you.

5. Renounce all contact with anything occult or satanic.

6. Pray the prayer of release from any curse.

7. Believe that you have received your release and go on with your life in God's blessing!

After you have taken these steps, a prayer of deliverance will remove these generational curses from your life. Please recite this prayer:

PRAYER OF DELIVERANCE
FROM GENERATIONAL CURSES

Lord Jesus Christ, I believe that You are the Son of God and the only way to God, the Father; and that You died on the cross for my sins and rose again from the dead.

I give up all my rebellion and all my sin, and I submit myself to You as my Lord.

I confess all my sins before You and ask for Your forgiveness—especially for any sins that exposed me to a curse. Release me also from the consequences of my ancestors' sins.

By a decision of my will, I forgive all who have harmed me or wronged me—just as I want God to forgive me. In particular I forgive _____.

I renounce all contact with anything occult or satanic—if I have any "contact objects," I commit myself to destroy them. I cancel all Satan's claims against me.

Lord Jesus, I believe that on the cross You took on Yourself every curse that could ever come upon me. So I ask You now to release me from every curse over my life—in Your name, Lord Jesus Christ!

By faith I now receive my release, and I thank You for it! Amen.[9]

You have now been released from your family's generational curses. Begin to accept God's blessings for your life. He is so ready to give them to you.

Our God not only expects us to receive His blessings, He also instructs us to pronounce blessings over each other in His powerful name:

The blessing of the LORD be upon you; We bless you in the name of the LORD. (PSALM 129:8)

The blessing is so powerful that the Word of the Lord instructs us to even bless our enemies:

> **Bless those who persecute you; bless and do not curse.**
> (ROMANS 12:14)

Blessing is defined as "the invoking of divine favor," as "the gift of divine favor," as "a desire to impart prosperity and success," and as "approval and anything that gives happiness and prevents misfortune."[10] In spiritual terms, the blessing is the impartation of the spoken Word of God by God's delegated authority. Now I ask you, which would you rather proclaim from your mouth: a curse or a blessing?

What about receiving the blessing? It is amazing to me how little use we make of the spiritual blessings God gives us. In fact, we often make little use of God Himself! Even though He is our God, we seldom give ourselves to Him, and we ask so little of Him. Yet He is able to do all things, all we must do is ask!

The Lord gives us every opportunity to rely on Him for comfort and help. He desires us to seek Him. He wants us to depend on Him. Jesus said:

> **Come to Me, all you who labor and are heavy laden, and I will give you rest.** (MATTHEW 11:28)

The more we ask the Lord, the more He will give us, and the more we will depend on Him. The more we depend on Him, the less we will do without His presence and guidance in our lives.

We should never want when we have a God who will supply all of our needs. We should never fear when we have a God who will comfort us, for the Word of God says:

> **The LORD is my light and my salvation; Whom shall I fear?**
> (PSALM 27:1)

He can supply us with everything. Better still He desires to *be* everything to His children!

We must learn to go to Him often in prayer, to go to Him for blessings, to go to Him in faith at all times. If we lose everything and keep our faith in God, we will lose nothing. But if we gain the world and lose our faith in God, we have nothing. We are the King's daughters! Our heavenly Father who owns the wealth of the world and holds the earth in the palm of His hand is waiting for us to draw closer to Him.

Some of our church members, like so many others in America, had a problem with leaving church before the end of Sunday morning services. When the altar call was given, my husband could see some people begin to leave their seats so they could exit the parking lot a few minutes early. This would grieve him, because their early departure caused others who were considering a commitment to Christ to be abruptly interrupted, distracting them from their eternal decision. Consequently, they would choose not to participate in what the Holy Spirit had prepared for them through the service—their eternal life!

Then, during a preaching series entitled "The Power of the Blessing," my husband ended every sermon in the series with a blessing over the congregation. As he dismissed the people, he asked them to raise their hands for the impartation of the blessing. As God's delegated authority, my husband would impart blessings over the lives of our church members and all they put their hands to throughout the coming week.

Soon we noticed something remarkable: No one left early. They waited for the blessing. They needed the blessing. They wanted the blessing. Testimonies began to flow, giving glory to the Lord for the good things He had done in that week through the faithfulness of His Word and the power of His blessing. Since that time, my husband imparts the blessing of God at the end of every service, and our son Matthew is doing the same as he carries on the mantle placed on Him by the God of all blessings.

No one leaves until the blessing is imparted.

LIFE LESSON TWO:
SET YOURSELF APART FROM THE WORLD

The Word of God tells us not to be

> *conformed to this world, but be transformed by the renewing of your mind, that you may prove what is that good and acceptable and perfect will of God.* (ROMANS 12:2)

Ruth set herself apart from all the other women in the fields, and that drew attention to her.

I often observe the young men and women of our church as they try to overcome the temptation of the world. They are afraid to be set apart; they want to be accepted. They want to be like the masses. Yet God asks us not to emulate the world, and in that obedience we will be rewarded.

We are a unique people, set apart to God. According to the Bible, the more we obey God, the more we are blessed. Yet the more we obey Him, the more the world looks at us as strange because God's Word doesn't conform to the world. The world can't understand the people of God.

We feel incredible love for One we have never met. We talk to a God we cannot see. We empty ourselves in order to be full. We admit we are wrong so we may be reconciled. We are strongest when we are weakest. We give up in order to keep. We see the invisible, hear the inaudible, and accomplish the impossible—all with the help of the One who gave His life for us. In fact, our foundations are based on the virtues of His very life.[11]

We are, by the very nature of the God we serve, set apart.

Chapter Eight

THE FAVOR

urprised that his master was in the harvest fields, the overseer came running to Boaz soon after he dismounted his horse. After Boaz greeted his workers in the name of the Lord, a custom he had begun during the famine, the men returned his greeting with a blessing.

Boaz acknowledged the workers' blessing, yet ignored the day's report, for he could hardly take his eyes from Ruth. The woman he gazed upon was a vision of beauty as she gracefully moved through the stalks of barley. She looked radiant under the sun's rays. Boaz awoke from his daze and inquired about Ruth. Excitedly, the overseer answered Boaz, giving him only a glowing report of Ruth's behavior in the field. As the overseer gave his account, Boaz felt a tug at his heart. *Who is going to care for this fair maiden? If she has been so bold as to accept our God as hers, then who will Hashem send to redeem her and Naomi?*

As a relative of Elimelech, Boaz knew there was another kinsman-redeemer closer to Naomi than he; therefore he had not thought of redeeming Naomi—until now.

As Ruth gathered the barley that would sustain her and her mother-in-law, she could feel the cool breeze brushing against her face. The soft, gentle wind felt like fine linen. She remembered the elegant feel of linen, for she wore it often as a princess in Moab.

Even though her thoughts of beautiful garments provided a pleasant memory, Ruth was grateful for the thicker clothing she had on today, for it protected her from the noonday sun. Ruth had worked diligently since early morning, and she anticipated with great joy Naomi's surprise when she saw all Ruth had gleaned.

As she offered thanks to the one true God for leading her to a bountiful field, her silent prayer was interrupted by the sound of a man's voice. Startled, she looked up and at once met Boaz's eyes.

THE BIBLE STUDY

Then Boaz said to Ruth, "You will listen, my daughter, will you not? Do not go to glean in another field, nor go from here, but stay close by my young women.

"Let your eyes be on the field which they reap, and go after them. Have I not commanded the young men not to touch you? And when you are thirsty, go to the vessels and drink from what the young men have drawn."

So she fell on her face, bowed down to the ground, and said to him, "Why have I found favor in your eyes, that you should take notice of me, since I am a foreigner?"

And Boaz answered and said to her, "It has been fully reported to me, all that you have done for your mother-in-law since the death of your husband, and how you have left your father and your mother and the land of your birth, and have come to a people whom you did not know before.

"The LORD repay your work, and a full reward be given you by the LORD God of Israel, under whose wings you have come for refuge."

Then she said, "Let me find favor in your sight, my lord; for you have comforted me, and have spoken kindly to your maidservant, though I am not like one of your maidservants." (RUTH 2:8–13)

"You will listen, my daughter." First of all, Boaz was giving Ruth assurance that she was welcome in his field. Jewish scholars believe this statement had a much deeper allegorical connotation. Boaz was informing the young Moabitess that there was no reason for her to glean in another "spiritual field," for the Law of Moses stated[1]:

You shall have no other gods before Me. (EXODUS 20:3)

"Let your eyes be on the field." It was believed that a generous person would bring blessing. Boaz knew that Ruth had a generous heart, for she spent the day in hard labor on behalf of her mother-in-law. This belief was later recorded in the Proverbs[2]:

He who has a generous eye will be blessed, for he gives of his bread to the poor. (PROVERBS 22:9)

"Not to touch you." Boaz lived by the Torah; therefore, he thought and communicated by its precepts. Deuteronomy 10:19 instructed the believer to "love the stranger," for the Jew was once a stranger in the land of Egypt. Boaz was informing Ruth that the reapers of the field would not discourage her, not only as she gleaned but also in her newfound faith in Jehovah God.[3]

"Go to the vessels and drink." The wells that contained pure water were far from the fields, and only the strong men could fetch and carry the jugs of water a long distance. Therefore the women and the poor would have to drink the inferior water that was drawn from nearby wells. Boaz was continuing to favor Ruth by inviting her to drink from the fresh water drawn from the pure wells.[4]

So she fell on her face, bowed down to the ground. Always possessing a mindset of gratitude, Ruth expressed her gratefulness in the most dramatic way possible. Remember, Ruth was the daughter of the king of Moab; she was used to people bowing down before her. Ruth displayed her sincere and humble spirit as she bowed before Boaz in a gesture of appreciation for Boaz's goodness and favor on her behalf.

"Why have I found favor . . . since I am a foreigner?" Boaz's favor was probably the first time Ruth had been shown any kindness in Bethlehem, other than the kindness of Naomi. She fully expected to be treated like a foreigner, like a daughter of Moab who was not fit to enter into the assembly of *Hashem*.[5] Ruth was asking Boaz why she had found favor in his eyes.

"It has been fully reported to me." In Hebrew the word *reported* is *told* and is doubled in this verse for emphasis. Boaz was explaining to Ruth that his favor upon her came because her kind deeds had been discussed by the people at the city gates and in the fields.[6]

One of the unique characteristics of this beautiful book in Scripture is the presence of dialogue. You don't have to imagine what the protagonists of the story are thinking; you know through their conversations. Over half of the eighty-five verses in the book of Ruth are dialogue; therefore we are right in the midst of what transpired in this remarkable love story.[7]

"The Lord repay your work and a full reward be given you." This statement by Boaz is interpreted at two levels. The Word of God is like the layers of an artichoke: On the surface the Word gives one message, and the more we study it, new layers are revealed until we finally get to the center of its meaning. Unless you take the time to study the Word, you will never get to the core of its message.

The first meaning of the verse is simply a blessing for Ruth; Boaz is imparting a prayer for divine blessings, or the promise of them, over Ruth's life.

The second meaning is much more profound. The phrase *full reward* refers to a more valuable blessing; some Jewish scholars credit Ruth's merits as much greater than those of Abraham. After all, Abraham left his father's house only in response to God's call, in which He clearly said, "Get out of your country, from your family and from your father's house" (GEN. 12:1). However, Ruth left on her own initiative—without divine call and despite Naomi's attempt to dissuade her—in order to come under the wings of *Hashem.*[8]

"Under whose wings you have come for refuge." In order to fully understand the power of taking refuge under God's wings, Jewish scholars reflect on the various kinds of wings found in Scripture.

> **(ISA. 24:16)** *The earth has wings—"From the [wings] of the earth we have heard songs."*
>
> **(PS. 139:9)** *The morning has wings—"If I take the wings of the morning . . ."*
>
> **(EZEK. 10:5)** *The cherubim have wings—"And the sound of the wings of the cherubim . . ."*
>
> **(ISA. 6:2)** *The seraphim have wings—"Each one [seraph] had six wings."*

The Hebrew interpretation of this verse relates to the degree of shelter and divine protection found in the wings of the Almighty. Ruth acted kindly toward Naomi, and for this she would be rewarded. Great is the power of those who act benevolently, for they find shelter, neither in the shadow of the wings of the earth, nor in the shadows of the morning, nor in the shadow of the wings of the cherubim, nor in the shadow of the wings of the seraphim, but only in the shadow of Him at whose Word the world was created.[9]

Under His wings, the God of all order was orchestrating the events in the life of this young foreigner so she could soon occupy a very deliberate position and be an integral link in "The Scarlet Thread"—the divine bloodline running through Scripture. Our God offers that same kind of protection and care for all who believe:

> *How precious is Your lovingkindness, O God! Therefore the children of men put their trust under the shadow of Your wings.*
> (PSALM 36:7)

LIFE LESSONS

LIFE LESSON ONE:
REMAIN IN THE FIELDS OF THE LORD

There is a direct correlation between Christ and Boaz, and Ruth and the Church. The field belonged to Boaz, a wealthy man who owned many fields. Ruth had no reason to go into any other field to gather food. Boaz provided all she needed.

As believers, we have no reason to go to anyone else but Christ, for He told His church:

> *Do not love the world or the things in the world.* (1 JOHN 2:15)

There is enough for the Christian in Christ; therefore it is not necessary for the believer to go into the fields of the world to find comfort or reward. One kernel from an ear of corn in the field of the Lord is worth more than all the fields the world has to offer.

Ask Him for the desires of your heart, and He will fill whatever emptiness you have.

For those of you who have left old friendships and acquaintances, who have left mother and father or brother and sister, to come into the world of the believer, allow me to encourage you: Our Savior will reward you with His favor and His protection. He will reward you with His companionship. You have left Moab and followed the Lord into an alien land. Soon you will find comfort under the covering of His wings; everything you need will be found there, and you will not remain a stranger for long. Boaz showed kindness to Ruth, just as Christ shows love to the believer who has forsaken all to follow Him. As King David, we must learn to depend on the Lord for our covering and protection.

> *Keep me as the apple of Your eye; hide me under the shadow of Your wings.* (PSALM 17:8)

For those of you who accepted Christ years ago and have forgotten what it is to feel like a stranger in the land of the faithful, I ask that you extend kindness to the new convert.

Jesus personally spoke of the importance of loving one another (JOHN 13:34–35). The love He has for us cannot be measured or duplicated. His love cannot be bought or sold. His love cannot be earned or traded. Our Savior's love can only be freely given and freely accepted. You will search the world over and never find this kind of love. Stay in the field of the Lord and glean what He has for you. Soon you will feel right at home.

LIFE LESSON TWO:
DIVINE FAVOR FOLLOWS OBEDIENCE

On a cold Sunday night the week of Christmas several years ago, my husband was visiting with our congregation after teaching on specific prayer. Pastor Hagee challenged our flock to pray and ask God in such specific terms that when His provision came there would be nothing left to chance; it would be obvious: God had provided. "If you want a bicycle, then ask for a red bicycle with chrome handlebars and shiny spoke wheels! Give God the opportunity to show off!"

The line formed quickly as the people saw Pastor Hagee giving hugs. He is a loving man, and to this day his sheep are energized by his strong, encouraging arms when he compassionately wraps them around their problems.

One of the people in line was a young boy around twelve years of age who had come to church with a friend. He waited quietly and patiently for his turn to speak to my husband. I was moved as I witnessed my husband kneel to look into the young man's eyes. He listened to the child intently, and then he enveloped him with his large, loving arms and began to weep. Pastor Hagee then stood and wiped the tears from both of their faces. The young man walked out of the church, and my husband continued to visit with those left in line.

On our way home John told me all that had occurred. "The young boy you saw speaking to me came to church tonight with one of his friends. He broke my heart as he told me that God had made him the man of the house, since his father had left him, his four brothers and sisters, and his mother. He asked me to agree with him that he would find a job to care for the needs of his family.

"He asked me to pray that God would bring him a red bicycle with chrome handlebars and shiny spoke wheels so he could secure a paper route and help his mother support his family. He told me he wanted to be specific."

Tears streamed down my husband's face as he continued his heart-wrenching story. "I asked him to stay and wait for me so I could get more information from him, but he left immediately. But you will never guess what happened next!"

By this time I was crying as well and could not wait for the rest of the story. "What happened?" I cried out.

"A doctor was in the visiting line just four people behind this precious little boy. The man extended his greetings and wished our family a blessed Christmas. Then he told me something that made my jaw drop."

"What!" was my more than curious response.

"The doctor told me he had a bicycle he wanted to donate to our church for some young person to enjoy since he had no time to use it himself. He said, 'The bike is brand-new!'"

Excited almost beyond words, I yelled, "Oh my, John! The Lord has provided!"

"Yes, I know, but when I looked around for the young man, he was gone. I know his name—it's Robert—but I know nothing more about him. I don't know how to find him."

That statement led me to stand on one of my favorite verses: "being confident of this very thing, that He who has begun a good work in you will complete it until the day of Jesus Christ" (PHIL. 1:6). "God will help us find him!" I confidently pronounced. We held hands and prayed that the Lord would lead us to this young man.

The following Wednesday was the day before Christmas, and I, along with other volunteers in our church, was filling food baskets and wrapping gifts that were to be delivered to the families of our congregation and the community who would otherwise not have Christmas. It was near the end of the day, and the last batches of baskets and gifts were ready for delivery.

Suddenly, a young woman from our church came running from the parking lot. "Diana, is it too late to receive a Christmas basket?" she shouted as she tried to catch her breath.

"No, it's never too late. We have prepared several extras," I answered as I handed her one of the food baskets. My friend gladly received the gift and began to tell me her story.

"Several weeks ago I met this woman who was left stranded by her husband. She is a wonderful woman and works very hard; however, her husband left her with so much debt she can hardly put food on the table, and she has been especially depressed during the holiday season."

My skin tingled with excitement. *Can this be?* I thought to myself. *Lord, have You brought this young boy to us?* "Does she have a son about twelve years of age?" I asked.

"Yes, she does. His name is Robert. He is a fine young man, and he is trying to establish a paper route to help his mother with the expenses of the house and the needs of his brothers and sisters. This is truly a good family."

I knew it! God was showing off!

I gave the young woman an account of the previous Sunday evening and asked her if she could make an extra stop at the doctor's house on the way to her divine appointment. We both cried and gave praise to the Lord for His uncommon favor. Then she left to get the bicycle and deliver food and Christmas gifts to the family on the night before our Savior's sacred birth.

Later that evening my friend called me to recount the events of this very special day. "Diana, you will never believe all that God has done!"

"Try me!" I answered excitedly.

My friend began to tell me the miracle story. "I went to the family's home, and Robert came to the door. His mother was unaware of my visit to her home, because their phone has been disconnected. Robert told me that she could not come to the door, because she was in bed with a migraine. I told him I had a very big surprise for her and the family.

"Robert hesitated a moment and then let me into their home. He went to his mother's bedroom, and after a few minutes, he returned with his mother, his hand clenched in hers. Oh Diana, she looked so tired and dejected!

"Robert's mom told me that the day had been a difficult one. She had gone from agency to agency, looking for resources to help provide for a modest Christmas for her family. Everywhere she went the story was the same: She was too late to qualify for aid. All the agencies advised her to go to a local church for assistance. Since the family had no church, she knew there was little chance for help. She didn't know how she was going to tell her children there would be no Christmas this year.

"Robert held his mother's hand tightly and informed her he would tell his brothers and sisters. He gently told her he didn't want her to worry any longer.

"Diana, then I told them what you asked me to tell them: 'Jesus has heard your cry. Today will be a day of His provision. Today our Father will show you His divine favor.' I could sense that neither Robert nor his mother could understand what I was saying, so I asked my husband to bring in the gifts.

"He went to the car and began to unload food baskets until their cupboards were full to overflowing. Then he unpacked the Christmas tree we had purchased before we arrived to their home as well as all the gifts the church had sent. Finally, we asked Robert to come to the door for the final surprise. We showed him the 'answered prayer' that was strapped to the roof of my husband's car."

My heart was leaping within me, and I interrupted my friend's story. "What did he say?"

"His eyes opened wide, and he smiled and said 'I knew God would answer my prayer, I just knew it!' With that he ran to the car and helped my husband take the bike off the roof. By now the whole family was jumping up and down and clapping their hands. We went into the living room and sat down, and my husband said, 'We need to offer a prayer of thanksgiving to the Lord.'

"He took their hands, and before he began thanking the Lord for His provision, my husband led the entire family in a prayer of salvation! Diana, they all accepted Christ on Christmas Eve! Thank you so much for letting my husband and me be a part of this miracle!"

I told my friend we had all been chosen to participate in a series of divine appointments orchestrated by the Master Conductor of our lives. We had answered God's call to take part, and because we were obedient, we were blessed beyond words. I wanted to ask my friend one last question before I said goodbye: "What color was the bicycle?"

Her answer was one last confirmation of our God's infinite mercy and favor. "It was a beautiful bicycle. It had all the bells and whistles anyone could desire. It was red with chrome handlebars and shiny spoke wheels."

Our Lord is continually orchestrating a great symphony in our lives. He is ready to provide for our every need. He is ready to shower His divine favor over us. He wants to show off for you! Ruth was eager to obey the law of gleaning. The Lord God of Israel brought favor to her through Boaz. Robert was ready to help supply for his family. Both found favor with God. Divine favor follows obedience:

If you walk in My statutes and keep My commandments, and perform them, then I will give you rain in its season, the land shall yield its produce, and the trees of the field shall yield their fruit. For I will look on you favorably and make you fruitful, multiply you and confirm My covenant with you. (LEVITICUS 26:3–4, 9)

LIFE LESSON THREE:
LEARN TO LIVE UNDER HIS SHELTERING WINGS

When my family and I went on a cruise to Alaska, I was amazed with the majesty of God's creation. The beauty of the coastline was simply breathtaking. One of the most beautiful sights I witnessed was that of the regal bald eagle sailing effortlessly through the air. Sitting on the balcony of our stateroom, I used my binoculars to get a closer look at this magnificent bird.

I finally located an eagle that was hovering over her chicks in her nest. Her wings were enormous as they arched high above her chirping offspring. Inside the massively strong wings were soft white feathers, obviously present to give comfort to the young cradled beneath her.

Oh, how like the wings of this majestic bird are those of our Creator! He promises to cover us with His protective wings and deliver us from the enemy. God never underestimates the enemy, and in the midst of the battle He will comfort us with His sheltering wings.

When my mother-in-law was diagnosed with cancer, her prognosis was grim. The doctors informed her she had colon cancer, and the treatment they proposed was comprised of eight weeks of radiation followed by a radical colostomy. Even then, her expected survival was less than one year. Our family gathered around what the doctors predicted would be her deathbed, and under the leadership of my father-in-law, we covered her with a prayer of healing.

Vada Hagee is my Naomi. I have learned to love God by watching her. I have learned to trust God by her precious example. When my mother-in-law fell in love with Jesus, it was for life. When she reads His Word, it is like reading a love letter from her Redeemer; she can hardly keep from crying, for she cherishes every promise He gives.

When my mother-in-law heard her prognosis, she confidently proclaimed, "Well, this is what the doctors believe. I respect them for their knowledge, but I will trust in the Word of the Lord."

With that statement the battle for her life was on. She chose her weapon: the Word of the living God—the Word of *Jehovah Rophe,* the Lord our Healer.

When her treatment began, she called me and informed me that the radiation therapist had warned her of the devastating side effects the radiation would have on her soft, fragile, pale skin. She also told me that she went to the Holy Scriptures and felt the Lord direct her to Psalm 91.

"I have committed it to memory, and I will stand on it during the radiation. I fully believe I will be spared from all the side effects of the treatments."

My mother-in-law did as she said, and after eight weeks of radiation her skin did not have the slightest sign of irritation. One might conclude that the treatment was ineffective; however, the following week she went into the colostomy surgery, which was supposed to take six hours but took less than two. What was intended to be a colostomy was transformed into a simple surgery to remove a small tumor whose deadly cancer was fully contained. What was to be her last year of life has turned into twenty-three more beautiful years of walking in love with her Savior.

Vada Hagee is ninety-two years of age and loves the Lord more than when she first met Him. Their love for each other is beautiful. The only desire He has yet to grant her is to meet Him face to face. I feel He will grant her loving request soon. Her life can be expressed by the psalm that gave her such comfort and healing during her struggle with cancer:

He who dwells in the secret place of the Most High shall abide under the shadow of the Almighty. I will say of the LORD, "He is my refuge and my fortress; my God, in Him I will trust. Surely He shall deliver you from the snare of the fowler and from the perilous pestilence. He shall cover you with His feathers, and under His wings you shall take refuge; His truth shall be your shield and buckler. You shall not be afraid of the terror by night, nor of the arrow that flies by day, nor of the pestilence that walks in darkness, nor of the destruction that lays waste at noonday. A thousand may fall at your side, and ten thousand at your right hand; but it shall not come near you. Only with your eyes shall you look, and see the reward of the wicked. Because you have made the LORD, who is my refuge, even the Most High, your dwelling place, no evil shall befall you, nor shall any plague come near your dwelling; for He shall give His angels charge over you, to keep you in all your ways. In their hands they shall bear you up, lest you dash your foot against a stone. You shall tread upon the lion and the cobra, the young lion and the serpent you shall trample underfoot. "Because he has set his love upon Me, therefore I will deliver him; I will set him on high, because he has known My name. He shall call upon Me, and I will answer him; I will be with him in trouble; I will deliver him and honor him. With long life I will satisfy him, and show him My salvation." (PSALM 91)

Just as my mother-in-law did, we need to call upon the Lord so He can deliver us from our sicknesses and honor us with His promises. We need to live under His sheltering wings every day of our lives:

But to you who fear [reverence] My name the Sun of Righteousness shall arise with healing in His wings. (MALACHI 4:2)

Chapter Nine

HANDS FULL ON PURPOSE

Ruth was attracted to Boaz from the moment she saw him, yet she could not understand why. He was much older than she was. Nevertheless, she was drawn by the wisdom that seemed to emanate from his eyes. Ruth was also overwhelmed by the lovingkindness he showed toward her, the magnitude of which she had never felt before.

Boaz was a Jew, and she was a foreigner, but she received an acceptance from him that she had received from no other. When he gave his invitation to join him at his table, she bowed her head and walked slowly toward him. Boaz motioned for Ruth to sit beside his reapers. She discreetly covered her face with her scarf to hide the blush of her cheeks as she asked herself the question, *Do I belong here?*

Just a few short hours ago Ruth felt completely lost as she tried to find her way to the barley fields. Once there, she felt so inadequate and insecure. Her past life as a king's daughter had not prepared her for the hard work of the harvest. Earlier in the day, her body became weary as she tried to gather as many stalks as possible to assure enough food for Naomi and herself. Now she was resting at the master's table, partaking of his generous bounty. She could hardly absorb what was happening—*Hashem* had truly been good to her!

Boaz felt as if he was being led by a force outside of himself. He intuitively sensed that Ruth was a kind, humble, and gracious woman. Now he knew it to be true. He could not take his eyes from what seemed to be the most beautiful woman he had ever seen. He wanted to keep her near, and something within him desperately desired to provide for her. He did not know what lay ahead, but he was certain that *Hashem* might be part of all that was occurring.

Boaz gave the blessing over the meal and invited Ruth to take the bread and dip it into the wine. She reached for the bread, took a small portion, and dipped it in the wine and put it to her lips. She could not remember when she had eaten anything so good.

In an added generous gesture, Boaz passed more bread to her. Ruth was very hungry, for she had not eaten a proper meal in months; but even in her hunger, she did not overlook the loving benevolence her host extended to her. She thanked him for his generosity and gratefully ate of his offering until she was satisfied. Then she placed some bread into her apron so she could take a portion of this delicious meal to Naomi. Oh, if only Naomi could share this beautiful moment with her!

As the meal was ending, Ruth arose to return to her work in the fields. Before she left the table, she could feel the stares of the others sitting around her. Some of the reapers were looking at her as if to ask, *What have you done to merit such favor? You, a woman, and a Moabite at that!*

Ruth knew that not everyone at the table felt as they did. Some of the reapers were obviously happy for her; she could see it in their eyes. They had witnessed her strong work ethic since daylight, and they realized that she was not looking for favoritism, only an opportunity to glean the field. Their affection for Boaz was evident, and many of the reapers were happy to see his interest in this beautiful Gentile convert.

Ruth kept her eyes on Boaz, for she saw security in his strong features; his confident smile gave her comfort. She bowed her head and offered a silent prayer of thanks to the God who had brought her to this refuge of provision.

Then Ruth modestly thanked her benevolent host and returned to work. Boaz watched Ruth as she walked back into his fields, and when he was certain she could not hear him, he motioned his overseer aside for private instruction: "Let her glean even among the sheaves, and do not reproach her. Also let grain from the bundles fall purposely for her; leave it that she may glean, and do not rebuke her."

THE BIBLE STUDY

Now Boaz said to her at mealtime, "Come here, and eat of the bread, and dip your piece of bread in the vinegar." So she sat beside the reapers, and he passed parched grain to her; and she ate and was satisfied, and kept some back.

And when she rose up to glean, Boaz commanded his young men, saying, "Let her glean even among the sheaves, and do not reproach her. Also let grain from the bundles fall purposely for her; leave it that she may glean, and do not rebuke her."

So she gleaned in the field until evening, and beat out what she had gleaned, and it was about an ephah of barley. (RUTH 2:14–17)

"Eat of the bread." Ruth was not only invited to the master's table, Boaz asked her to partake of the meal as well. He wanted Ruth to eat and be fully nourished. He wanted to draw her closer to him.

Our Redeemer wants us to eat of His Word until our souls have life-sustaining nourishment, and He wants us to drink of His fountain of living water until we are filled to overflowing. Scripture assures us of our Lord's desire to feed our souls:

I am the living bread which came down from heaven. If anyone eats of this bread, he will live forever; and the bread that I shall give is My flesh, which I shall give for the life of the world. (JOHN 6:51)

If anyone thirsts, let him come to Me and drink. He who believes in Me, as the Scripture has said, out of his heart will flow rivers of living water. (JOHN 7:37–38)

"Dip your piece of bread in the vinegar." The average reader will naturally think of vinegar as a bitter-tasting substance that would bring no comfort whatsoever. To the contrary, this dipping sauce was a compound of nectars expressed from sweet fruits such as grapes mingled with water to produce a weak wine-like substance.

This kind of drink is still commonly used in the harvest fields of Italy, for it is not exceedingly strong, is cooling, and gives flavor to bread when the reapers refresh themselves at midday.[1] In essence, Boaz invited Ruth to come to his table and partake in a meal of bread and wine.

What a sweet foreshadowing of God's goodness. Before Boaz became Ruth's kinsman-redeemer, he invited her to have a meal of bread and wine. Moreover, before Christ became our Redeemer at the cross, He invited His own to take communion with Him—a meal of bread and wine:

> ***And as they were eating, Jesus took bread, blessed and broke it, and gave it to the disciples and said, "Take, eat; this is My body." Then He took the cup, and gave thanks, and gave it to them, saying, "Drink from it, all of you. For this is My blood of the new covenant, which is shed for many for the remission of sins.*** (MATTHEW 26:26–28)

Think of it! We are invited to eat at the Master's table and partake of all He has prepared for us. As we take our place at His table, our Redeemer cannot take His eyes from us for He knows of the beautiful plans He has made for us, and He wants us to fulfill our destiny! What a gift! What favor!

She sat beside the reapers. Boaz did all he could to keep Ruth from feeling like an intruder in his field. She sat beside the reapers, not behind them as a servant. Boaz gave her comparable status with those who had been in his household for years. He wanted Ruth to feel as if she belonged in his field. She was a foreigner, yet he was bringing her into his inner circle.

Our Redeemer gives us all equal status when we come to His cross. He is not a respecter of persons. It does not matter if we come into His kingdom as a child or as an elderly person, if we come into His kingdom ignorant of His Word or a scholar of it. In His eyes, we have the same value and inheritance. There is no foreigner, no man, woman, or child who cannot walk through the redeeming blood of our Savior in atonement for his or her sins and receive everlasting life:

> *Also the sons of the foreigner who join themselves to the LORD, to serve Him, and to love the name of the Lord, to be His servants— everyone who keeps from defiling the Sabbath, and holds fast My covenant—even them I will bring to My holy mountain, and make them joyful in My house of prayer.* (ISAIAH 56:6–7)

Our Redeemer is, in fact, the author of every good and perfect gift:

> *Every good gift and every perfect gift is from above, and comes down from the Father of lights, with whom there is no variation or shadow of turning.* (JAMES 1:17)

In our Redeemer's presence, the redeemed find peace, security, and joy. His presence is a sanctuary where no harm can enter in:

> *I will say of the LORD, "He is my refuge and my fortress; my God, in Him I will trust."* (PSALM 91:2)

He passed parched grain to her. Picture this remarkable scene. Boaz is sitting at the head of the table, his reapers beside him, and Ruth, the beautiful Moabitess, sitting beside the reapers, equal in the master's sight. She was the least of them, yet he treated her as the greatest of them by purposely handing her more grain. He did this because he knew she needed more than the others at his table.

Now put yourself in this picture. You are sitting at the Master's table, by His invitation. You sit beside those who have sat at His table for years, yet He hands you more from His endless bounty than He does the others. He knows your every need.

You are His, and He wants you to feel at home when you come to His table. He wants you to be full with all He has to offer:

> *On this mountain the* Lord *Almighty will prepare a feast of rich food for all peoples, a banquet of aged wine—the best of meats and the finest of wines.* (Isaiah 25:6 niv)

She ate and was satisfied, and kept some back. Ruth ate at the table of the master until she was satisfied, but she also kept some back for Naomi. She decided not to enjoy her feast alone. Ruth remembered her beloved mother-in-law, who was not as fortunate to partake at such a bountiful table.

"And do not reproach her." The poor were not allowed to glean between the sheaves, but Boaz commanded his reapers: "Even if Ruth gleans improperly because of her lack of knowledge of the law, you are not to embarrass her by confronting her."[2]

When new converts come to the Lord, they are often ignorant of the conditions that our Lord calls us to abide by. We, who have been in the Lord longer and are aware of the requirements Christ puts on our lives, should be mindful of those who have recently received Christ as Savior. We should guide them gently as we were guided by His loving kindness, grace, and mercy.

I try to make as many deposits in the bank of kindness, mercy, and grace as I can, for one day I know I will need to make a withdrawal from that same bank and the amount I have available to me will be equal to what I have deposited, for Scripture says:

> *Blessed are the merciful, for they shall obtain mercy.* (Matthew 5:7)

"The bundles fall purposely for her." Boaz was so determined to provide for Ruth that he ordered his reapers to make certain to drop sheaves at her feet so she would be sure to have more than enough.

Boaz was also showing phenomenal sensitivity toward Ruth by not embarrassing her in front of the reapers. He wanted his reapers to purposely forget the sheaves and make it appear to Ruth that they were accidentally left behind. In doing so he was fulfilling the Jewish commandment that required sustaining the needs of the poor without causing them humiliation or shame. In executing this act, Boaz was emulating God. God will always provide for his own. David saw this truth in his own experience:[3]

I have been young, and now am old; yet I have not seen the righteous forsaken, nor his descendants begging bread. (PSALM 37:25)

Beat out what she had gleaned . . . an ephah of barley. When Ruth had finished gleaning, she did not go home immediately to rest from her hard day's labor. First, she beat the grain out from the sheaves. Ruth did this not only to spare her mother-in-law the work, but also to spare herself the added weight on her journey home.[4]

The fruit of Boaz's generosity and the diligence of Ruth's labor was equivalent to approximately four gallons of barley.[5]

LIFE LESSONS

LIFE LESSON ONE:
YOU WILL BE SATISFIED AT THE MASTER'S TABLE

You may attempt to find fulfillment elsewhere, but you will not be satisfied until you become a child of the living God. If you try to find contentment for your life without the presence of the Lord, you will be greatly disappointed. You will work and not find prosperity; you will look for love and find only heartache. You will seek out joy, only to be filled with sadness. You will strive for good health, yet your soul will become frail and weak.

Oh, but I have good news for you! When you believe in Him and trust in His death on the cross for your salvation, then you shall be completely satisfied. Your mind will be satisfied with the knowledge that Christ is the author of hope. Your heart will be satisfied with contentment, for He is all the love and affection you will need to be full and complete. Your conscience will be satisfied with perfect peace as you set your mind on His teachings and His promises. Your purpose will be satisfied, for to know Christ is to be found in Him.

One of the kindest men I have had the privilege of knowing was Derek Prince, a true friend to my husband and me. Derek devoted his life to the teaching of the gospel of Jesus Christ, and what a great teacher he was. He had an anointed authority of Scripture and his faith in the Word of the living God rivaled no other; he lived the Word, and he was satisfied with its fullness.

In July of 1941, while serving in the British army, Derek had a supernatural encounter with the Lord. He said of that experience:

Out of that encounter, I formed two conclusions which I have never had reason to change: first, that Jesus Christ is alive; second, that the Bible is a true, relevant, up-to-date book.

These two conclusions radically and permanently altered the whole course of my life. Immediately, the Bible became clear and intelligible to me; prayer and communion with God became as natural as breathing; my main desires, motives and purposes in life were transformed overnight.

I had found what I was searching for! The meaning and purpose of life is a Person!"[6]

While on his deathbed, prior to meeting His beloved Savior in glory, Derek asked one last question of the Lord he so faithfully served. With tears in his eyes, he looked at a disciple of his who stood by his bedside and in sincerest humility asked, "Have I done everything I am supposed to do?"

Here was a man who took the Word of God to the nations of the earth. He spoke in the villages of the poor who never had the opportunity to know of the saving knowledge of Jesus Christ. He laid hands on the sick and prayed for them in the name of the *Jehovah Rophe,* and they were healed. He delivered the oppressed captives to freedom by the power of the Lord.

Derek did all of these works and more in obedience to the Word of the One he loved so dearly.

For fifty-eight of his eighty-eight years of life, Derek gave all praise to the God of Abraham, Isaac, and Jacob for his achievements in ministry; he knew the source of his success was the Lord. Derek truly loved his Savior. Those who knew him were blessed to sit under his teachings and hear of his complete devotion to his Redeemer. Yet, he asked the question, "Have I done everything?"

Derek ate at the table of the Master until he was satisfied, but he did not stop there. He "kept some back" and gave to all those who would receive the good news.

Yes, Derek Prince did all he was supposed to do and more. I can hear the Lord telling him:

***Well done, good and faithful servant; you were faithful over a few things, I will make you ruler over many things. Enter into the joy of your lord.* (MATT. 25:21)**

You will not be satisfied until you share of the bountiful provision He has given you. Ask the Master, and He will show you what He wants of you, and as you obey Him, your soul will be filled to overflowing.

LIFE LESSON TWO:
GOD HAS PREPARED BANQUETS FOR HIS REAPERS

God prepares a great banquet for His children every time His Word is taught and preached. Yet I am often saddened by some of the sheep who are members of our church, and other churches around the world who do not participate in the feasts the Lord has set before them.

Every Sunday morning and evening we gather in the name of the Lord and feast at His table. Throughout the year, we have camp meetings where some of the finest and most anointed speakers in the nation join my husband to present the Word of God.

As the shepherd's wife, I purposely take time to give special invitations to all the members of our church to partake at the Master's table, especially during these wonderful times of revival. I inform them that the Lord of Hosts has heard our cry for more and has prepared a meal for our hungry souls. He promises in His Word that we will not hunger or thirst if we eat and drink from His table. All are invited, and the meal is free.

Invariably, on Monday mornings or on the day following one of the Lord's feasts, I will receive phone calls from some of our sheep, in which they complain of bad marriages, sick bodies, or wayward children. When I ask if they partook of the feast offered by the Spirit of the living God the previous day, they answer with no. "No, I was too tired." "No, I was too busy." "No, I had company, I had a business appointment, or I needed family time."

These church members are suffering from spiritual malnutrition, yet they have neither time nor desire to feast with Him who can satisfy any hunger they may have. How sad the Lord must feel. He has prepared His feast for us and set it on His banqueting table from the beginning of time. He knew what we would need to be full and satisfied, yet we refuse to come to the banquet. How disappointed He must be when He comes to His table and His guests of honor are not there.

As the Lord manifests the provisions of His Word, all will be filled with the Bread of Life. We can always extract sweet divine nourishment from the meditation of His teachings. When we hear of His doctrines of grace and mercy, we fuel ourselves with enthusiasm. When Jesus Christ and His cross are lifted up, there is food enough and to spare. When the glorious work of the Holy Spirit is remembered and partaken from, there is sustenance for our every need.

Accept the Lord's invitation to His banquet table, and you will never hunger or thirst again.

LIFE LESSON THREE:
TRUE FAITH PRODUCES FAITHFULNESS

Ruth was a woman of faith, and she was found faithful in every task.[7] Even though Boaz extended extraordinary privileges and provision to her, Ruth was faithful to return to the gleaning field. In order for Ruth to take her harvest home, she had to work diligently while in the field.

The Lord promises that while the earth remains there will always be a time for planting and a time for reaping (GEN. 8:22). The Great Master of the harvest needs faithful reapers to work in His fields until the fruit of our labor has been gathered unto Him:

> **Then He said to His disciples, "The harvest truly is plentiful, but the laborers are few. Therefore pray the Lord of the harvest to send out laborers into His harvest." (MATTHEW 9:37–38)**

The Lord asked His disciples to pray that laborers might be sent forth to the harvest. Additionally in the next chapter of Matthew, He sent out His disciples so they could lead others by their example:

And as you go, preach, saying, "The kingdom of heaven is at hand."
Heal the sick, cleanse the lepers, raise the dead, cast out demons.
Freely you have received, freely give. (MATTHEW 10:7–8)

After His crucifixion and resurrection, He enlarged His commission to include the world:

And He said to them, "Go into all the world and preach the gospel
to every creature." (MARK 16:15)

Every believer ought to be in the field of the One who is greater than Boaz. As His disciples, we must have faith that His Word will transform all who hear of its truths. A living faith is a going faith; a vital faith is an evangelizing faith.

When the Christian goes into the fields of the Lord, he will find that "hands full on purpose" have been left by our Great Redeemer, which will enable the believer to do more than glean; he or she will one day reap a bountiful harvest in white fields.[8] We must simply be willing to go.

Many of us who are intimidated by God's Word resist sharing the love that Jesus has shown us with others for fear of being rejected and fear of what He will require of us. We basically lack trust in the God we serve. I was certain that I would fail and embarrass Him if I dared try to share His Word with others, and consequently for years I did nothing.

A young woman was speaking to a guest evangelist on the subject of consecration, of giving herself wholly to God. She said, "I dare not give myself wholly to God, for fear He will send me out to China as a missionary."

The evangelist said, "If some cold, snowy morning a little bird should come, half frozen, pecking at your window, and it would let you take it in and feed it, thereby putting itself entirely in your power, what would you do? Would you grip it in your hand and crush it? Or would you give it shelter, warmth, food, and care?"

A new light came into the young woman's eyes. She said, "Oh, now I see, I see. I can trust God!"

Two years later, the evangelist came to the same church to minister, and the young woman excitedly approached him and recalled their previous conversation. She told him how she had finally abandoned herself to God—and then her face lit up with a smile and said, "And do you know where God is going to allow me to serve Him?" With a twinkle in her eye that radiated a supernatural contentment she answered her own question—"In China!"[9]

Trust God.

Chapter Ten

THE HOPE

Naomi felt an intense trepidation for Ruth. It was almost nightfall and no sign of her precious daughter-in-law. *Where could she be? Has someone harmed her? Could some vicious animal have mauled her and left her by the side of the road suffering, only to die in a strange country? What has become of my darling Ruth?*

Naomi fell to her knees and began to call upon the Name. *Hashem, I ask You to bring Ruth safely back to me! Do not judge her for my sin! You have brought me home to my people, but I cannot bear life without Ruth! Spare her, Father! Bring her safely to me!*

Naomi rose to her feet and wiped the tears from her face. How weary she was of washing her face with tears of sorrow. She went to the door and walked outside in some hope of seeing Ruth, but she saw nothing.

Then suddenly, as if from nowhere, a small figure appeared on the horizon. *Can it be? Can it be my Ruth! Yes! Yes! It is Ruth! Hashem has answered my prayer! . . . Praise be to the living God! He has heard my cry and brought Ruth home to me! I will sing of His mercies forever, for He is faithful!* Naomi could not contain herself. She ran from the house and met Ruth on her path home.

As the two women walked the distance back to Naomi's house, both were filled with joy—Naomi, for Ruth's safe return, and Ruth for the provisions she held in her arms for Naomi. Happiness made Ruth's heavy load seem lighter as she carried her harvest back to Naomi, and now she could show her mother-in-law all she had gathered.

When they reached the house, and before Naomi could open her mouth to speak, Ruth began to show Naomi her bounty of grain. Naomi could not believe her eyes! Not only had *Hashem* kept her beloved daughter-in-law safe, He had also rewarded them with food enough and to spare.

Enthusiastically, Naomi began to ask Ruth question after question—she wanted to hear all the details of Ruth's day. "Where have you gleaned today? Where did you work? Who took notice of you so you could gather so much grain?"

When Ruth told Naomi of her encounter with the master of the field, the older woman could not believe what she heard! Boaz! Our kinsman! It was Boaz who gave! She leaped to her feet and danced in a circle, waving her arms above her in praise to the One and Only!

"Blessed be he of the Lord, who has not forsaken His kindness for the living and the dead!" Naomi shouted praises unto the Lord and clapped her hands in front of Ruth in pure exhilaration! "Ruth, my darling Ruth, this man is a relation of ours! Boaz is one of our close relatives!"

Ruth sat before Naomi and watched her in amazement. Never had she seen Naomi so joyful. For the first time since she had known this wonderful woman, Ruth saw hope in Naomi's eyes.

"What did you say, my sweet? I didn't hear you . . . Boaz asked you to stay in his field? Oh, yes. Yes! This is good advice. It is good that you go out with his young women, so that people do not meet you in any other field." Naomi paced back and forth in excitement trying to sort her many thoughts.

"Look at me, Ruth, where are my manners? I have been so overjoyed over your astonishing news that I have offered you nothing to comfort you from your hard day's labor." Naomi turned to walk to the cupboard, and paused and thought for a moment as she remembered that her shelves were empty. "Amusing I should say this, Ruth, for I have nothing to offer you but my arms of welcome."

Ruth smiled and eagerly turned the pockets of her apron inside out to produce what she had lovingly hidden away from Boaz's table for her precious mother-in-law. The hungry Naomi saw generosity's portrait unveiled before her as she witnessed Ruth tenderly laying out the bread from Boaz's table.

Tears flowed from Naomi's eyes, but this time they were tears of joy as she held the bread of promise in her hands. Naomi took Ruth's hand and offered a prayer of thanksgiving to *Jehovah Jireh*. "Blessed are You Adonai, our God, and Ruler of the Universe, who brings forth bread from the earth. It is good and delightful to give thanks to You, O Lord. We will sing praises to Your Name, O Most High, for You show forth Your loving-kindness in the morning and Your faithfulness by night. Make us glad according to the days You have afflicted us and the years we have seen evil. Let Your glory appear to Your servants and Your majesty to their children. Let the favor of the Lord our God be upon us and confirm for us the work of our hands as we partake of this bread that You have so mercifully provided. Amen."

Naomi ate of the bread, and even though she had not had a proper meal in months, she became quickly satisfied. She shared the evening meal with Ruth, and there was still bread enough and to spare. Then Naomi cleaned off the table and put the remainder of the meal away. She felt her heart joyfully beating within her as her head spun with thoughts for the future. For the first time in years, Naomi felt hope.

The hand of *Hashem* was indeed guiding Naomi and Ruth to their divine destiny!

THE BIBLE STUDY

Then she took it up and went into the city, and her mother-in-law saw what she had gleaned. So she brought out and gave to her what she had kept back after she had been satisfied.

And her mother-in-law said to her, "Where have you gleaned today? And where did you work? Blessed be the one who took notice of you." So she told her mother-in-law with whom she had worked, and said, "The man's name with whom I worked today is Boaz."

Then Naomi said to her daughter-in-law, "Blessed be he of the LORD, who has not forsaken His kindness to the living and the dead!" And Naomi said to her, "This man is a relation of ours, one of our close relatives."

Ruth the Moabitess said, "He also said to me, 'You shall stay close by my young men until they have finished all my harvest.'" And Naomi said to Ruth her daughter-in-law, "It is good, my daughter, that you go out with his young women, and that people do not meet you in any other field."

So she stayed close by the young women of Boaz, to glean until the end of barley harvest and wheat harvest; and she dwelt with her mother-in-law. (RUTH 2:18–23)

What she had kept back after she had been satisfied. Realizing that Naomi felt apologetic about having nothing to serve her daughter-in-law, Ruth immediately shared the bread she kept back and assured Naomi that she had eaten well while in the field of Boaz.

Naomi was astonished at the quantity of grain Ruth had gleaned, and her amazement was compounded when Ruth gave her the leftovers of the noon meal, for it confirmed that Ruth had truly been blessed while she was in the field of Boaz.[1]

When the Master provides, there is always enough to satisfy and more:

For thus says the LORD God of Israel: "The bin of flour shall not be used up, nor shall the jar of oil run dry, until the day the LORD sends rain on the earth." So she went away and did according to the word of Elijah; and she and he and her household ate for many days. The bin of flour was not used up, nor did the jar of oil run dry, according to the word of the LORD which He spoke by Elijah. (**1 KINGS 17:14–16**)

Then He commanded the multitudes to sit down on the grass. And He took the five loaves and the two fish, and looking up to heaven, He blessed and broke and gave the loaves to the disciples; and the disciples gave to the multitudes. So they all ate and were filled, and they took up twelve baskets full of the fragments that remained. (**MATTHEW 14:19–20**)

Whether for a household or a multitude, our God is the God of more than enough. He is faithful to provide for His own. His provision is a demonstration of His amazing grace that has no boundary and no limit. Even the prodigal son realized that the God of his father provided more than enough to his servants. Yet the far country provided nothing for him:

How many of my father's hired servants have bread enough and to spare, and I perish with hunger. (**LUKE 15:17**)

"Where have you gleaned today?" It was obvious to Naomi that Ruth had worked the fields with intensity due to the amount of grain she had carried home. And because of her experience as a landowner, Naomi knew that Ruth must have received additional help, for an *ephah* was more than one woman could have gathered in a day.

Naomi also knew that it was usually forbidden for the gleaner to beat the stalks while still in the field. Therefore, noticing Ruth had come home with beaten grain, Naomi was also asking Ruth the question, "Who was so kind to you while you were in the field?"[2]

"Blessed be the one." The verse in the Hebrew reads, "with whom I worked." The Midrash teaches that the poor do more for the landowner than the landowner does for the poor. This law is demonstrated in its fullness because it is believed that the land-owner profits more spiritually than materially from the generosity he dispenses, while the poor only gain temporarily from the charity they receive from the landowner.[3]

Boaz was a giver. It is said that you make a living by what you get and make a life by what you give.

> *I have shown you in every way, by laboring like this, that you must support the weak. And remember the words of the Lord Jesus, that He said, "It is more blessed to give than to receive."* (ACTS 20:35)

Ruth could not outgive Boaz, and God's children cannot outgive Him. When we give to God's people, we receive a spiritual reward that is worth its weight in gold. Naomi wanted to know the name of the landowner who had been so good to Ruth for it was customary to offer a prayer of blessing on his behalf:

> *Blessed is he who considers the poor; The LORD will deliver him in time of trouble. The LORD will preserve him and keep him alive, and he will be blessed on the earth.* (PSALM 41:1–2)

"The man's name . . . is Boaz." The name of the landowner is an answer to Naomi's prayer, for the name is that of her kinsman-redeemer. Naomi received this as a sign from the Lord that He would bring deliverance to her and to her daughter-in-law.

Boaz's character resembled the traits of the God he served. His name was Boaz, the man of valor. Boaz, the master of the field. Boaz, the provider. Boaz, the kinsman-redeemer. Boaz truly resembled the nature of the Name above any other name.

"Blessed be he of the LORD." When Naomi heard the name of the field owner, she knew he was already blessed of God, for he was a righteous man, a *tzedakah*. Before knowing his name, she blessed him with her own blessing. After his name was revealed to her, she blessed him in the name of the Lord.

"His kindness to the living and the dead!" This was a happy day for Naomi— a day of atonement, a day of hope for the survival of her family. By supporting the "living"—Naomi and Ruth—God, through Boaz, was supporting the "dead"—Elimelech and Mahlon—by sparing their widows from starvation or the shame of gathering in the fields of strangers. In addition, it was not demeaning for Ruth to glean in the field of Boaz, for he was a relative and a redeemer— her dignity was spared.

The *living* in Hebrew refers to the plural form of the word. Somehow, Naomi instinctively knew that both she and Ruth would fulfill their divine purpose now that there was the hope of a redeemer. The older woman realized that *Hashem* had forgiven her. He had forgotten her sin, and He had given her a blessed hope for the future.

"One of our close relatives." Boaz was a *goel,* and as such, it was his duty to marry the widow of his kinsman, provided he was the next of kin (DEUT. 25:5–6).

However, there was one very large obstacle: Ruth was a Moabite. Though the Torah prohibited a Jew from marrying a Moabite—even a convert—the Oral Law offered an exception. Jewish sages believe there were two laws: the written law that God gave to Moses on Mount Sinai and a second set of laws, the Oral Law, also given to Moses at Sinai and transmitted by word of mouth from generation to generation.[4]

The Oral Law dictated that the prohibition only affected Moabite men and did not apply to Moabite women. This oral tradition was not well known at the time these events were occurring, because the number of Moabite converts seeking to marry Jews was minimal—only one in fact, and her name was Ruth![5]

According to the Levirate Law, Ruth should take the initiative and present her case to her kinsman because she was a widow. If this were the first marriage, the woman would never initiate the proposal; that privilege was reserved for the groom. Yet Levirate tradition allowed for the widow to let her kinsman know of her desire to be redeemed. If the kinsman refused her proposal, she could take him into court and disgrace him.[6]

However, Ruth was not fully aware of her rights at this point, and Naomi felt certain that Boaz would take the initiative and redeem Ruth before she had to execute her right of redemption. The obvious interest Boaz showed for Ruth gave Naomi confidence for their future relationship.

Levirate marriage is a classic example of the Mosaic Law expressing the rights of a woman over a man. However, this law also held another purpose for its existence. It is believed in Judaism that after a woman is married to a man, she becomes as one of his limbs, an extension of her husband. Nature ordained this through the experience of the first father, Adam, whose ribs were taken by God and fashioned into a woman: his wife, Eve.

The Jews believed it was an act of divine mercy to allow a man who was married and died childless to reproduce children through his brother, who was like a part of himself. This act would serve as a memorial to the childless man and give the offspring from the Levirate marriage the right to take the deceased's place in serving the Creator—since he had no other heir in this physical world except for his surviving wife.[7]

"Until they have finished all my harvest." Ruth descended from a self-centered, miserly people—the Moabites, who refused to give God's chosen people food when they traveled through the wilderness. Ruth first experienced unique loving-kindness under the care of Naomi, and now she marveled at the generosity she was receiving from Boaz.

Boaz invited Ruth to stay as long as the harvest remained. This statement confirmed to Naomi and Ruth that the attention Boaz imparted to Ruth was not in passing.

"That you should go out with his young women, and that people do not meet you in any other field." Naomi accomplished two things with this statement. First, she countered Boaz's suggestion—"You shall stay close to my young men"—by telling Ruth to stay near the women of Boaz's field, thereby avoiding any appearance of wrong intentions.

Second, Naomi emphasized the magnitude of granting Boaz's request to stay in his field. Naomi advised Ruth to refuse any offer to go into another gleaning field if she were entreated to do so. Naomi did not want Ruth to seem ungracious toward Boaz's benevolent hospitality.[8]

Until the end of the barley harvest. The barley and wheat harvest lasted for three months. During this time Ruth went into Boaz's field and gleaned all day, returning to Naomi every evening as she had promised—"wherever you lodge, I will lodge." Coincidentally, or not so coincidentally, three months was also the mandatory waiting period that would have to elapse before a convert was permitted to marry a Jew.[9] Only God knew what would soon happen.

In Jewish tradition, Ruth is loved. She ranks among the matriarchs. She is known as the "Mother of Royalty." Sarah, Rebekah, Rachel, and Leah gave the Jews the twelve tribes, but Ruth gave them a king.

King David is a descendant of Ruth. Without Ruth, Israel might not have had a king, at least not David of whom it is said by the Jews, *"Khai vekayam"*— He lives and shall go on living until the end of time.

King David provided a sense of immortality and—because of his link to the Messiah—a hope for redemption. The Jews believe that because of Ruth they have their King David—and their hope.[10]

Everything was now in place. The God of the universe was setting His grand plan in motion. Redemption was His plan, and soon His will would be done.

LIFE LESSONS

LIFE LESSON ONE:
HOPE SEES THE INVISIBLE

Once upon a time there was a man named Abraham who was chosen by God. The almighty God loved Abraham a great deal and therefore made a covenant with him. God promised Abraham that he would be the father of many nations, and this same covenant would also be with his son Isaac and his descendants after him.

Now at the time, Abraham and his wife, Sarah, were old and had no children. But God's promise came to be and Sarah bore a son named Isaac, and he was known as "The Son of Promise." Abraham and Sarah loved their son very much, and they loved God for His faithfulness.

One day God decided to test and prove Abraham's love and loyalty to Him, so He called on Abraham and asked him to offer his beloved son as a burnt offering on Mt. Moriah. In obedience to the God he loved, Abraham rose early in the morning and led Isaac to Mount Moriah.

Isaac said to Abraham, "My father! See, here are the fire and the wood, but where is the lamb for the burnt sacrifice?"

Abraham replied, "My son, God Himself will provide a lamb for the burnt offering."

When they came to the place God had ordained, Abraham built an altar; then he laid the wood and bound Isaac and laid him on the altar. Abraham stretched forth his hand and took hold of the knife. Then suddenly, Abraham heard the Lord calling to him. The voice of the Lord said, "Do not lay your hand on your son or do anything to him, for now I know that you fear and revere God, since you have not held back from Me, even giving Me your only son."

Then Abraham glanced around, and behold, behind him was a ram caught in a thicket by his horns. Abraham took the ram and offered it as an ascending sacrifice instead of his beloved son.

Abraham called the name of that place "The Lord Will Provide."

With every step Abraham took up the mountain, Isaac, the sacrifice, was one step closer to the altar. Abraham had faith that God would provide, even though neither he nor Isaac could see the provision.

Abraham believed God when He promised that Isaac's destiny was to inherit the promises made in Genesis 12. When Abraham said, "God will provide for Himself the lamb for a burnt offering" (GEN. 22:8), he was foreshadowing the sacrifice of the spotless Lamb, God's son, who would climb this same mountain four thousand years later to take away the sin of the world.[11] Abraham spoke in faith, acted in obedience to God's instruction, and, without knowing, uttered a prophetic word concerning the redemption of humanity.

Abraham hoped for what he could not see, and God provided, just as He does for us today:

For we were saved in this hope, but hope that is seen is not hope; for why does one still hope for what he sees? But if we hope for what we do not see, we eagerly wait for it with perseverance. (ROMANS 8:24–25)

Hope sees the invisible.

LIFE LESSON TWO:
HOPE TOUCHES THE INTANGIBLE

There was a gifted professor of music named Herman who taught piano at the college level. One night at a university concert, a distinguished piano virtuoso suddenly became ill while performing a very difficult piece.

No sooner had the artist retired from the stage than Herman rose from his seat in the audience, walked on stage, sat down at the piano, and with great mastery completed the performance. At a reception later that evening, one of the students asked Herman how he was able to perform such a demanding piece so beautifully without notice and with no rehearsal.

Herman replied, "In 1939, when I was a budding young concert pianist, I was arrested and placed in a Nazi concentration camp. Putting it mildly, the future looked bleak. But I knew that in order to keep the flicker of hope alive that I might someday play again, I needed to practice every day.

"I began fingering a piece from my repertoire on my bare board bed late one night. The next night I added a second piece and soon I was running through my entire repertoire on the dry rotting boards. I did this every night for five years. It so happens that the piece I played tonight at the concert hall was part of that repertoire. That constant practice is what kept my hope alive. Every day I renewed my hope that I would one day be able to play my music again on a real piano, and in freedom."[12]

Herman could not touch the piano, but he could feel his music. Many of you reading this study cannot touch God and therefore have little hope for tomorrow. But I can assure you, based upon the Word of God, one day soon you will feel His presence, for the Master Architect is never far from us, even in our despair. You must have faith that He is present even in your wilderness.

The book of Acts records this encouraging message, which is intended to be embraced by every believer:

So that they should seek God, in the hope that they might feel after Him and find Him, although He is not far from each one of us. For in Him we live and move and have our being; as even some of your [own] poets have said, For we are also His offspring. (ACTS 17:27–28 AMP)

Hope touches the intangible.

LIFE LESSON THREE:
HOPE ACCOMPLISHES THE IMPOSSIBLE

A number of years ago, in a mental institution outside Boston, a young girl known as "Little Annie" was locked in the dungeon, diagnosed as hopelessly insane. Annie was confined to a living death in a small cell with little light and cold, barren walls.

About that time an elderly nurse was nearing retirement. She felt there was hope for all of God's children, so she started taking her lunch into the dungeon and eating outside Little Annie's cell. She felt perhaps she should communicate love and hope to the little girl.

In many ways, Little Annie was like an animal. On occasions, she would violently attack the person who came into her space. At other times, she would completely ignore them. When the elderly nurse started visiting her, Little Annie gave no indication that she was even aware of her presence. One day the elderly nurse brought some brownies to the dungeon and left them outside the bars of Annie's cell. Little Annie gave no hint she knew they were there, but when the nurse returned the next day, the brownies were gone.

From that time on, the nurse would bring brownies when she made her Thursday visit. Soon after, the doctors in the institution noticed a change was taking place. After a period of time, they decided to move Little Annie upstairs.

Finally, the day came when the "hopeless case" was told she could return home. But Little Annie did not wish to leave. She chose to stay, to help others. Annie was the woman who eventually cared for, taught, and nurtured Helen Keller, for Little Annie's name was Anne Sullivan.[13]

Anne Sullivan was shown the love of God by the old nurse, and that love produced hope for the impossible:

> *Now may the God of hope fill you with all joy and peace in believing, that you may abound in hope by the power of the Holy Spirit.* (ROMANS 15:13)

Because of such hope, Anne was able to show a child who was sightless, speechless, and without hearing about the love of God and teach her that with Him nothing was impossible. Helen had no sight, but became full of vision because Anne taught her to hope in the God of the impossible.

We have no hope besides Him. We cannot hope in ourselves, for we will fail. We cannot hope in the world, for it is corrupt. We cannot hope in others, for they will disappoint us. We can only hope in Christ: our Bridegroom, our Savior, our Redeemer, our King.

As His children, we should rejoice, for we can do all things through Him who strengthens us. He is the source of our strength and because of His supernatural power we can abound in all hope, for He is our blessed hope:

> *. . . looking for the blessed hope and glorious appearing of our great God and Savior Jesus Christ, who gave Himself for us, that He might redeem us from every lawless deed.* (TITUS 2:13–14)

Hope accomplishes the impossible.

Chapter Eleven

THE THRESHING FLOOR

Ruth remained loyal to her pledge to Naomi—every morning Ruth would leave to gather in Boaz's field, and every evening she would return home to Naomi. Each day for three months, Naomi sat and waited for Ruth's return after gleaning in the field of the man Naomi felt certain would redeem them.

Naomi waited with anticipation for Ruth to bring news concerning her long-desired dream—that Boaz would finally extend the full measure of kindness—the rebuilding of Naomi's deceased family by marrying Ruth. But Boaz made no attempt to fulfill this good deed.

Questions and speculations pounded Naomi's head through the day as she awaited Ruth's return. *Can it be that Boaz has no interest in Ruth? I think not, for he continues to treat her with kindness.*

Can it be that Boaz is prepared to give Ruth bread and nothing more? Or is he still mourning the memory of his dead wife, blessed be her soul, for his wife died the very same day we came to Bethlehem? I think not, for why would Boaz show interest in Ruth in the first place, and besides, the time of his official mourning period has been over for months.

Can it be that Boaz thinks he is too old for such a beautiful and young woman as Ruth? Perhaps, but only Hashem knows the answer.

One day Naomi made a critical decision. She had had enough! She had waited for Boaz to act for a sufficient amount of time, to no avail. She would now become involved, very involved!

After the evening meal, Naomi sat Ruth down and began to broach the subject of marriage, a subject she and Ruth had successfully avoided for three months. Every sentence was cautiously weighed and measured. For weeks now, Naomi had worded this conversation in her mind, because she did not want to offend Ruth.

"My little bird, we must discuss something of great importance . . . your future."

Ruth looked into Naomi's eyes and could instantly discern that her mother-in-law had given serious thought to the discussion they were about to have, so she listened intently.

As Naomi began her well-rehearsed monologue, she spoke without taking a breath. "My precious daughter, shall I not seek rest and a home for you that you may prosper? Is Boaz not our relative? Look, I know he is winnowing barley tonight on the threshing floor. I want you to wash and anoint yourself. I want you to put on your best garments and go to his threshing floor. However, I do not want you to make yourself known to the man until he has finished eating and drinking."

Ruth could not believe her ears. Naomi was asking her to be very aggressive in her approach to Boaz, something both women had shunned in the past. Ruth did not know exactly what to think of Naomi's directives, but she was confident that Naomi's love for her was pure. She believed that her mother-in-law would only give her good counsel; therefore, Ruth knew it was time to prepare for the next step.

Naomi was so intent in her statements to Ruth that she did not notice Ruth's inquisitive stare. Oblivious, Naomi continued to share her plans. "When he lies down, notice the place where he lies, and when you go to him in the dark of night, uncover his feet and lie down next to him. He will tell you what to do."

When Naomi was finally done with her detailed instructions, even though she was overwhelmed, Ruth looked at her mother-in-law and simply said, "All that you say to me, I will do."

THE BIBLE STUDY

Then Naomi her mother-in-law said to her, "My daughter, shall I not seek security for you, that it may be well with you? Now Boaz, whose young women you were with, is he not our relative? In fact, he is winnowing barley tonight at the threshing floor.

"Therefore wash yourself and anoint yourself, put on your best garment and go down to the threshing floor; but do not make yourself known to the man until he has finished eating and drinking. Then it shall be, when he lies down, that you shall notice the place where he lies; and you shall go in, uncover his feet, and lie down; and he will tell you what you should do."

And she said to her, "All that you say to me I will do." So she went down to the threshing floor and did according to all that her mother-in-law instructed her. (RUTH 3:1–6)

"My daughter." Naomi was not coming to Ruth as a meddling mother-in-law, but as one who cared for her as if she were her own daughter. She had nothing but good intentions for Ruth's future.

"Seek security for you." It was obvious to both women that Ruth had found favor in the eyes of Boaz. It was also clear that for whatever reason, Boaz did not pursue his interest. It was as if after finding Ruth, he lost her and was resigned to his loss.[1]

Naomi set aside thoughts of her personal future; instead, she was determined to find rest and spiritual satisfaction for her dear, dear Ruth.[2]

We can deduce that by the end of the barley harvest, Boaz, the rich kinsman, and Ruth, the stranger from Moab, were very much in love. Boaz was concerned about asking for her hand in marriage because of the difference in their ages and her extraordinary beauty. He felt certain Ruth would be attracted to a much younger, stronger man. Ruth, on the other hand, did not make her feelings known because of her modest character, even though she was moved by his gracious and generous spirit.

Boaz gave Ruth no hint of his intentions while they worked together during the harvest; now Naomi suggested to Ruth that it was up to her to make the next move so Boaz could know of her willingness to entertain further "negotiations" towards marriage. Naomi also knew that Ruth and Boaz would make a suitable union; therefore, Naomi took the part of the matchmaker in this rare, yet beautiful, story.

The incidents that brought Ruth and Boaz to this point had not occurred because of Naomi's doings; they occurred because the supernatural hand of God was moving everyone into place to accomplish His purpose.

Naomi did not invite Ruth to follow her to Bethlehem; she discouraged her in accordance to the laws concerning proselytes. Even Ruth's going out into the field, which led to the new chain of events, was her own idea and not Naomi's. The Holy Spirit of God carried out His mission when He brought Boaz and Ruth together.[3]

The Hebrew word *manoach,* meaning security and rest, also implies several benefits that would come from the match of Boaz and Ruth. First of all, Ruth would be redeemed. Second, the house of Elimelech would be resurrected through the marriage of Mahlon's widow to Boaz. The third benefit was prophetic and of most importance and was known only to God Himself: What began to take shape in Boaz's field would provide the foundation and support for the coming of the Messiah, the Redeemer of the Jewish people and the world, for the word *manoach* also means "comforter."[4]

But the Comforter, which is the Holy Ghost, whom the Father will send in my name, he shall teach you all things, and bring all things to your remembrance. (JOHN 14:26 KJV)

"Winnowing barley tonight." Barley needed to be threshed before it was winnowed. In the threshing process the stalks of barley would be beaten on the ground or tread upon by animals in order to separate the grain from the chaff or surrounding husk. The grain was then winnowed—scooped up on flat, tray-like baskets, then tossed into the air where a constant breeze would catch the lightweight husk and blow it away, leaving the heavier grain to fall back on the tray. Finally, the grain was poured into containers for storing.

The best wind for threshing came at night. Naomi knew that Boaz would come to the threshing floor in the evening because her husband, Elimelech, who was a land-owner before he left for Moab, did the same. Naomi was certain Boaz would help stand guard to protect his harvest from theft, which was rampant at this time in history. In addition, Naomi knew Boaz, a Torah scholar, was not permitted to be alone at night to avoid the appearance of evil.[5]

This moment in the harvest was a time to celebrate and to make vocal man's thanks to *Jehovah Jireh* for His abundant provision. It may be much easier for me to picture this scene than it is for many of you because I come from Mexican heritage, and we have mastered the art of celebration!

We celebrate the birth of a baby and celebrate his or her christening. We celebrate days of independence: both Mexico's and America's! We celebrate birthdays, and we celebrate when our children graduate from kindergarten, elementary and junior and senior high school, college, and graduate school. If our children become doctors or lawyers—wow, do we ever celebrate!

We celebrate when our children get engaged and get married, and, of course, we celebrate our anniversaries. We celebrate the birth of Christ and His resurrection! For these celebrations, the *comadres* spend all day making delicious foods like *tamales, enchiladas,* and *bunuelos.* We invite our mothers, fathers, grandparents, children and grandchildren, our in-laws, nieces, and nephews; and, of course, there are the cousins—oh yes, we all have a multitude of cousins! There is festive Mariachi music, piñatas, and dancing! We are a joyful, passionate people, and we enjoy the journey of life! Pastor Hagee and I have many Jewish friends, and by experience, we know that festive celebrating is something Mexicans and Jews have in common.

The time on the threshing floor was truly a time of rejoicing. A multitude of workers were there, some even with their children. All the reapers and the gleaners were on the threshing floor, offering thanks to the God who gave them their rich harvest. It would not have been unusual to see Ruth present to celebrate the end of a successful harvest. After the winnowing, which lasted late into the night, the people participated in an evening meal and retired for the evening on the threshing floor to guard the winnowed grain.[6]

At this moment in time no one could fathom that the threshing floor of Boaz was about to host an episode in the life drama of Ruth that would forever change the course of biblical history!

"Wash yourself and anoint yourself." Naomi fully knew that every move Ruth made needed heavenly assistance to prevent her actions from being misinterpreted by Boaz. Moreover, Naomi wanted Ruth's actions to be seen as pure in the eyes of God and therefore crowned with His approval. It was not enough that Ruth had come to take shelter under the wings of the Divine Presence; she required more purification.[7]

When Naomi told Ruth to "wash yourself and anoint yourself," Naomi was not instructing Ruth to bathe, for Ruth was a believer, and cleanliness was mandatory. Naomi was asking Ruth to purge herself from the impurity of the idolatry of Moab; she wanted Ruth to take a ritual bath known as a *mikveh*.[8]

The ritual bath or *mikveh* is one of the oldest institutions in the Jewish community. The water for this bath must be from an underground source (such as a spring or rainwater), melted snow, or ice. No matter what the source, the water cannot be collected by a human agency; the water must fall into a built-in or hewn-out pool or bath. The pipes through which the water passes must be free of cavities in which water can collect or stagnate. None of the materials that construct the pipes can be made of anything that can attract sources of impurity in the biblical sense.

The ritual bath must also be under the care of a rabbinical supervisor. When an individual enters the *mikveh,* it is imperative that the person wash and be completely immersed. Immersion in the *mikveh* is only valid if not a speck of dirt comes between the person and the water. It is not a bath; it is a spiritual cleansing.

Many Jews undergo immersion in this ritual bath just before the Sabbath and on the eve of Yom Kippur, the Day of Atonement. Another purpose for the *mikveh* is to immerse the proselytes as the symbolic separation from an unclean past, which is part of their completed journey into Judaism.[9]

In biblical times, many Jewish homes had *mikvehs.* Elimelech was a wealthy land-owner before he left for Moab; he was also a judge, and therefore we can assume that his home contained a *mikveh.*

Symbolically, the ritual bath was the final break Ruth would make with her unhappy past in Moab. Her past was filled with want, sadness, grief, and generational curses, but her future would be filled with satisfaction, expectation, and rejoicing! Ruth's redeemer gave her a hope that she would become new again, just as our Redeemer promises us:

> *Therefore, if anyone is in Christ, he is a new creation; old things have passed away; behold, all things have become new.*
> (2 CORINTHIANS 5:17)

The Hebrew root of the word *Mikveh* is hope. The National Anthem of Israel shares this same root within its title "Hatikveh." The scriptural connection between the waters of purification and hope is God's redemptive power, which is the foundation of our faith and the hope of His people Israel.

Therefore You are great, O Lord GOD. For there is none like You, nor is there any God besides You, according to all that we have heard with our ears.

And who is like Your people, like Israel, the one nation on the earth whom God went to redeem for Himself as a people, to make for Himself a name—and to do for Yourself great and awesome deeds for Your land—before Your people whom You redeemed for Yourself from Egypt, the nations, and their gods?

For you have made Your people Israel Your very own people forever; and You, LORD, have become their God. (2 SAMUEL 7:22–24)

Naomi also asked Ruth to anoint herself with perfumes, which was a custom of Jewish nobility.[10] Ruth had cleansed herself from the idol worship of the past, and now she was noble, bathed in purifying water, and baptized into the people of God. Naomi wanted Ruth to have the scent of a king's daughter—an aroma of myrrh and perfumed oils—when she came into the presence of her redeemer.

"Your best garment." In some Jewish traditions it is said that a man should have two sets of garments: one for weekdays and one for the Sabbath. The best clothes either woman possessed was her Sabbath dress. Naomi wanted Ruth to prepare her finest clothing to wear before her redeemer.

In the Hebrew, the text says that Naomi wanted Ruth to carry her dress with her so as not to be noticed wearing her Sabbath dress on another day.[11] Naomi had planned this night for over three months. She had considered every detail, and she wanted everything to be perfect.

"Finished eating and drinking." Naomi is acting like a true mother-in-law. She is advising Ruth not to even approach Boaz until he is content with a full meal. I tell the women of our Bible studies: When it comes to attaining successful relationships with our spouses, timing is everything!

"Uncover his feet." Jewish sages believe that "God has been engaged in creating the light of the Messiah since the beginning of the world." Therefore, Naomi sensed that Boaz, the mighty man of valor, was the one God had chosen to be Ruth's redeemer, even though there was one kinsman who was closer to Naomi than Boaz. The name of this nearer kinsman was Tov. Elimelech had two brothers, Tov and Salmon. Salmon was Boaz's father and was deceased. Tov was Boaz's uncle who was very much alive and, therefore, the closest relative to Naomi.[12]

Naomi was suggesting that Ruth uncover Boaz's feet to remind him, who was a kinsman, of his moral obligation to marry her if Tov would not. If a "brother" of the deceased refuses to enter into Levirate marriage, he undergoes a process called *chatlitzah,* involving the removal of his shoe, which is symbolic of removing his possessive right over the widow. I will discuss this custom at length in a later chapter, but for now Naomi was instructing Ruth to uncover Boaz's feet as a gesture reminiscent of *chatlitzah,* in the hope that it would make Boaz aware of his moral obligation to her.[13]

"He will tell you what you should do." Naomi knew that Boaz had three choices. He could reject Ruth completely and chastise her for her forward conduct. Second, he could advise Ruth to approach the closer kinsman, Tov, his uncle; or third, he could accept Ruth's proposal and redeem her in marriage. Naomi was not certain of the outcome, but she was sure of one fact: God knew the outcome, and He would protect Ruth in her quest to seek rest and security.[14]

"I will do." These words exemplify Ruth's submissive spirit to authority. The young Moabite convert was not looking for marriage; she was content to be with Naomi and worship the God of the Jews for the remainder of her life. Ruth trusted Naomi and the God she prayed to and knew that whatever Naomi suggested was divinely inspired and was intended for the purposes of heaven.[15] Even though the assignment Naomi gave seemed contrary to the modesty and dignity

Ruth possessed, she was willing to carry out Naomi's wishes without any motive of personal gain. Scripture instructs us to submit to authority:

> *Likewise you younger people, submit yourselves to your elders. Yes, all of you be submissive to one another, and be clothed with humility, for "God resists the proud, but gives grace to the humble." Therefore humble yourselves under the mighty hand of God, that He may exalt you in due time, casting all your care upon Him, for He cares for you.* (1 PETER 5:5–7)

LIFE LESSONS

LIFE LESSON ONE: PREPARE YOURSELF

As believers, we must prepare ourselves when we come before our Redeemer. I remember how impressed I was when I first read the Book of Esther and became aware of the amount of preparation Esther went through before being presented to an earthly king:

> *Each young woman's turn came to go in to King Ahasuerus after she had completed twelve months' preparation, according to the regulations for the women, for thus were the days of their preparation apportioned: six months with oil of myrrh, and six months with perfumes and preparations for beautifying women.* (ESTHER 2:12)

As I read this Scripture I asked myself the question, *How do we prepare ourselves to come before our heavenly King?*

One of the best ways I can answer this question is to encourage you to be prepared to do God's will. To do this, we must obey His commandments and do so with a humble and gracious spirit. Scripture makes this instruction very clear:

> *If you return to the LORD with all your hearts, then put away the foreign gods . . . from among you, and prepare your hearts for the LORD, and serve Him only; and He will deliver you.*
> **(1 SAMUEL 7:3)**

Scripture tells us that our God can use *any* vessel that is pure and ready to hear His voice and obey His commandments to accomplish His purpose:

> *But in a great house there are not only vessels of gold and silver, but also of wood and clay, some for honor and some for dishonor. Therefore if anyone cleanses himself from the latter, he will be a vessel for honor, sanctified and useful for the Master, prepared for every good work.* **(2 TIMOTHY 2:20–21)**

When God wants an important work accomplished in this world, or a wrong righted, He goes about it in a very remarkable way. He does not release His thunderbolts of judgement. He simply has a tiny, helpless baby born, perhaps in an obscure home, of very humble parents. His Son then knocks on the door of the parents' hearts, and they invite Jesus in. They in turn train that baby with His love, His principles, and His direction, which is inspired by the truth of His Word, and then—God waits.[16]

God waits for us to prepare ourselves, He waits for the desire to serve Him to awaken within us, and He waits on us to reach our divine destiny.

LIFE LESSON TWO: PURIFY YOURSELF

The threshing floor was a place of separation—where the dry, worthless husk was separated from the valuable and nutritious grain.

God's Word is the place of separation for the believer. The inspired Word of God produces seven practical effects within each one of us. These seven transforming effects are faith, the new birth, complete spiritual nourishment, healing and health for our physical bodies, mental illumination and understanding, victory over Satan and sin, and cleansing and sanctification.[17]

We are going to discuss the seventh effect: cleansing and sanctification. The word *sanctify* comes from the word *saint. Sanctify* also means to be made "holy." So the word *sanctification* is to "make holy" or to "make saintly." At first I had difficulty understanding the concept of holiness, because my religious background linked holiness to sainthood. I could not imagine myself as sanctified, since I have never seen myself as a canonized saint. However, the New Testament mentions five distinct agents in connection with sanctification and the believer:

1. **The Spirit of God—**"*God from the beginning chose you for salvation through sanctification by the Spirit and belief in the truth.*" (2 THESSALONIANS 2:13)

2. **The Word of God—**"*Sanctify them by Your truth. Your word is truth.*" (JOHN 17:17)

3. **The Altar—**"*For which is greater, the gift or the altar that sanctifies the gift?*" (MATTHEW 23:19)

4. **The Blood of Christ—**"*Of how much worse punishment, do you suppose, will he be thought worthy who has trampled the Son of God underfoot, counted the blood of the covenant by which he was sanctified a common thing, and insulted the Spirit of grace?*" (HEBREWS 10:29)

5. **Our Faith**—*"To open their eyes, in order to turn them from darkness to light, and from the power of Satan to God, that they may receive forgiveness of sins and an inheritance among those who are sanctified by faith in Me."* (ACTS 26:18)

In summary, the Holy Spirit initiates the work of sanctification in the heart and mind of each one whom God has chosen for His eternal purposes. Through the truth of God's Word (as it is revealed in the heart and mind), the Holy Spirit speaks, reveals the altar of sacrifice (different in each one of our lives), separates the believer from all that holds him back from God, and draws him to a place of surrender and consecration upon the altar.

This altar is the place of separation from the world: It is the Christian's threshing floor.

However, the exact extent to which each of these four sanctifying agents—the Spirit, the Word, the altar, and the blood—accomplish their sanctifying work in each believer is decided by the fifth factor in the process—the individual faith each one of us possesses. God never violates His law of faith:

As you have believed, so let it be done for you. (MATTHEW 8:13)

The key text for the work of sanctification is found in Ephesians:

Christ also loved the church and gave Himself for her, that He might sanctify and cleanse her with the washing of water by the word, that He might present her to Himself a glorious church, not having spot or wrinkle or any such thing, but that she should be holy and without blemish. (EPHESIANS 5:25–27)

Several key points in the above Scripture deserve attention. First, the processes of cleansing and sanctification are closely joined together, and although they are similar, they are not identical. The distinction between them is this: that which is truly sanctified must, of necessity, be absolutely pure and clean; but that which is pure and clean need not necessarily be sanctified in the fullest sense. In other words, it is possible to have purity, or cleanness, without sanctification, but it is not possible to have sanctification without purity and cleanness.

Second, Ephesians 5 reflects one main, definite purpose for which Christ redeemed His church: that He might "sanctify and cleanse her" (v. 26). Therefore, the purpose of Christ's atoning death for His bride as a whole, and for each individual Christian in particular, is not fulfilled until those who are redeemed by His death have gone through a subsequent process of cleansing and sanctifying (v. 27).

The third point to notice in the passage in Ephesians is that Christ uses "the washing of water by the word" (v. 26) as the means to cleanse and sanctify the church.[18] If God's Word is the means of sanctifying and cleansing; then in this respect the operation of God's Word is compared to the washing of pure water. Therefore, His Word is the Christian's *mikveh*.

When believers are drawn to the cross of Christ and immerse themselves in the Word of God, they set themselves apart by sacrificing their sin on God's altar. Then they are cleansed and made pure by Christ's blood and by the faith they have in Him. As water is the source of life for the physical body, so the Word of God is the source of life for the spirit.

Sanctification is a process. You are to prepare yourself, you are to purify yourself, and you are to present yourself.

Life Lesson Three: Present Yourself

Ruth was ready to present herself in her finest raiment to her redeemer. What do we, as children of God, have to offer our Redeemer?

We know that all righteousness is as filthy rags (Isa. 64:6), so what could we possibly present to Him who is holy? Holiness is a part of God's eternal, unchanging nature. God was holy before sin ever entered the universe, and God will still be holy when sin has once again been banished forever.[19] Paul shows us in part that which we can present our Savior—ourselves:

> ***I beseech you therefore, brethren, by the mercies of God, that you present your bodies a living sacrifice, holy, acceptable to God, which is your reasonable service. And do not be conformed to this world, but be transformed by the renewing of your mind, that you may prove what is that good and acceptable and perfect will of God. (ROMANS 12:1–2)***

Paul is describing four successive stages in the process of our presentation before the Lord:

1. Presenting our bodies as living sacrifices upon God's altar. The altar sanctifies that which is presented upon it.

2. Not being conformed to the world. Instead being separated from its vanity and sin.

3. Being transformed by the renewing of our minds: learning to think in entirely new terms and values.

4. Knowing God's will for our lives; this revelation is granted only to the renewed mind in Christ. The old, carnal mind can never know or understand God's perfect will.

Notice how important God's Word is to this process. Derek Prince said it best:

> Once Jacob dreamed of a ladder reaching from earth to heaven, for the Christian, the counterpart to that ladder is found in God's Word. Its foot is set on earth, but its head reaches heaven—the plane of God's being.

Each rung in that ladder is a promise. As we lay hold by the hands and feet of faith upon the promises of God's Word, we lift ourselves up by them out of the earthly realm and closer to the heavenly realm. Each promise of God's Word, as we claim it, lifts us higher above earth's corruption and imparts to us a further measure of God's nature.[20]

Scripture simply describes this ascending process as having "the mind of Christ" (1 COR. 2:16).

Sanctification is by faith. True faith allows us to present ourselves to our Father as a living and acceptable sacrifice; therefore we, as believers in the Promise Keeper of all promise keepers, should strive to mature in our divine journey with Him:

> *And you, who once were alienated and enemies in your mind by wicked works, yet now He has reconciled in the body of His flesh through death, to present you holy, and blameless, and above reproach in His sight—if indeed you continue in the faith, grounded and steadfast, and are not moved away from the hope of the gospel which you heard, which was preached to every creature under heaven, of which I, Paul, became a minister . . . Him we preach, warning every man and teaching every man in all wisdom, that we may present every man perfect in Christ Jesus.* (COLOSSIANS 1:21–23, 28)

We are called to prepare ourselves, to purify ourselves, and to present ourselves to our heavenly Father. This process begins on the threshing floor, God's altar, and is accomplished through the *mikveh,* the pure water, of God's Word until we are truly daughters of the King.

Chapter Twelve

THE BLESSING

E ven though Boaz was a wealthy man, he was also a righteous man. In order to share in the suffering of the townspeople during the long famine, he gave most of his food away to those less fortunate and did without during the time of lack in Bethlehem. However, today was different. Today, Boaz would eat until he was satisfied. Today, Boaz and the people of Bethlehem had enough and some to spare!

Boaz laughed with his reapers and greeted their families. It was a festive time, and in accordance to Torah law Boaz joyfully led his people in a prayer of thanksgiving for the blessing *Hashem* had given them.

"Blessed are You, Adonai, our God, Ruler of the Universe, who creates many forms of nourishment. Blessed are You, Adonai, our God, Ruler of the Universe, who creates the fruit of the vine. We come into Your courts with humble hearts as we praise You and give You thanks for Your bountiful provision. We bless You, Lord God of Israel, for Your righteousness endures forever. You are true to Your covenant and faithful to remember Your people. We thank You for the good land You have given us. You have redeemed us from destruction and crowned us with Your loving-kindness and tender mercies. You have satisfied our mouths with good things. We bless You, Lord, and all of Your great works, for You are clothed in honor and majesty. Amen."

Tired from the long day's work, Boaz bid his guests goodnight and went alone to the far end of the threshing floor near a stack of bundles, and there he made his bed. He laid his head on the straw and quickly fell asleep. God was good, for Boaz's modesty and humility had caused him to go far from his servants, which allowed Ruth to approach him without being noticed.

In the deep of darkness Ruth came quietly, her shawl wrapped around her face to avoid being recognized. She stepped softly as she made her way by Boaz's feet, and it was there that she lay.

Around midnight Boaz awakened, for he was used to rising in the middle of the night for worship and Torah study, which was the tradition of his fathers. Suddenly, he was startled to encounter someone lying at his feet. He put out his hand and felt the head of a woman!

"Who are you?" he asked.

"I am Ruth, your handmaiden. Please spread the corner of your garment over your handmaiden, for you are a close relative." Ruth spoke with a quiver in her voice, not sure of Boaz's response, yet her trust remained in the Lord. "God's wings are the righteous, whose merit protects the world. Grant me refuge beneath your wing."

Ruth's face, illuminated by the soft glow of the moon, was as radiant as the face of a woman in love. Boaz was taken by her beauty and innocence. As Naomi had hoped, Ruth's vulnerability aroused Boaz's compassion. Ruth lay at Boaz's feet as a baby bird without a nest or a mother's wing to shelter it.

Boaz was overwhelmed with Ruth's kindness to Naomi, her desire for his God, and now, her love for him. Several younger, stronger men would have gladly taken this woman as their wife, but she chose him! He rose to his knees, took her face in his hands, and with tears in his eyes spoke softly to her.

"Blessed are you of the Lord, my daughter! May the Lord deal kindly with you as you have dealt with the deceased; may your reward be complete from the Lord beneath whose wings you have come to take refuge, and in caring for the destitute Naomi. Your kindness now is greater than this kindness. You have not gone after young men, whether poor or rich."

Then Boaz draped his fringed, four-sided garment over Ruth's shoulders. The beautiful young woman smiled with contentment as she felt secure under his covering. This was the only night she had spent away from Naomi, but she knew God would not be ashamed of her coming to Boaz in the middle of the night, for her intent was pure, and *Hashem* knew her intent.

Ruth wanted God's will for her life. Never had she thought of anything but God's will. *Hashem* was forever present in her deeds and in her thoughts, and today she would be rewarded.

THE BIBLE STUDY

And after Boaz had eaten and drunk, and his heart was cheerful, he went to lie down at the end of the heap of grain; and she came softly, uncovered his feet, and lay down.

Now it happened at midnight that the man was startled, and turned himself; and there, a woman was lying at his feet.

And he said, "Who are you?" So she answered, "I am Ruth, your maidservant. Take your maidservant under your wing, for you are a close relative."

Then he said, "Blessed are you of the Lord, my daughter! For you have shown more kindness at the end than at the beginning, in that you did not go after young men, whether poor or rich."
(RUTH 3:7–10)

After Boaz had eaten. Having winnowed his grain, and beheld its abundance, Boaz ate his fill for the first time in years. He blessed his meal before eating and offered a prayer of thanksgiving after his meal in fulfillment of the Torah command:

When you have eaten and are full, then you shall bless the Lord your God for the good land which He has given you. **(DEUTERONOMY 8:10)**

I have been at the home of Orthodox rabbis and been humbled by the thanks they offer before and after they partake of their meal. Jewish prayer is an encompassing part of the daily life of an observant Jew, one who keeps the Law. Before a Jew goes to sleep, he asks God to protect his slumber. When a Jew rises in the morning, he thanks God for preserving him through the night. A Jew says a blessing before eating and grace afterward.

I remember the humility I felt when I first witnessed my Jewish friends wash their hands before the meal. From the moment they cleansed their hands they did not speak to anyone other than to God in prayer. Later they explained to me that they do not speak from the time they pray over the ritual of cleansing their hands until they pray the blessing over the bread. In this way they refrain from defiling their lips with vain words prior to blessing the meal and partaking of the bread. However, the ritual of cleansing and praying over the meal exceeds that of thanksgiving; Ezekiel compared the altar of the Lord to a table:

> **The altar was of wood, three cubits high, and its length two cubits. Its corners, its length, and its sides were of wood; and he said to me, "This is the table that is before the Lord."** (EZEKIEL 41:22)

The altar is where the high priest serves the Lord. The Jews believe the table where we partake of our meals is symbolic of that altar. The act of cleansing one's hands and praying over the food is a symbol, which demonstrates the preparation and ability to serve God on a continual basis. The acts of cleansing and partaking at our table are joined, as are the acts of preparation and serving at the altar of the Lord. These beautiful deeds of cleansing, preparation, and thanksgiving before the Lord makes it possible for everyone, not just the rabbi, to become a priest over his or her miniature temple, which is the home.

The ritual of cleansing ultimately connects the meal (the sacrifice), the person (the priest), and the table (the altar).

His heart was cheerful. Jewish sages say that Boaz's heart, as a result of studying God's Word, was filled with the spirit of the Lord, and therefore was not tempted to do evil when he found a beautiful woman lying at his feet as he awoke for midnight prayers. His mind was rich with pure thoughts so Boaz was able to hear the voice of God and do what was right for Ruth.[1]

At midnight. As I mentioned previously, Boaz was a righteous man who was very observant to Jewish law and tradition. Every night he rose at midnight to study the Torah.

> ***At midnight I will rise to give thanks to You, because of Your righteous judgments. I am a companion of all who fear You, and of those who keep Your precepts.*** (PSALM 119:62–63)

Boaz's ancestors passed this tradition on to him, and it is recorded that Boaz passed the tradition to his heir.[2]

However, there is something more to verse eight than detailing time; this verse also marks the middle of the Book of Ruth, which ties to the symbolic fact that these epic events took place in the middle of the night.

The expressions "it came to pass at midnight" and "at midnight" are found three times in the Old Testament:

> ***And it came to pass at midnight that the LORD struck all the firstborn in the land of Egypt.*** (EXODUS 12:29)

> ***And Samson lay low till midnight; then he arose at midnight, took hold of the doors of the gate of the city and the two gateposts, pulled them up, bar and all, put them on his shoulders, and carried them to the top of the hill that faces Hebron.*** (JUDGES 16:3)

Now it happened at midnight that the man was startled, and turned himself; and there, a woman was lying at his feet. (RUTH 3:8)

The onset of redemption, or the gaining of freedom, is common to all three of these instances, for the Jews believe that midnight is the time prayers are answered. The second common thread that is woven into the three incidences is that they all occurred on the night of Passover.

The Talmud, which is a compilation of biblical commentary and legal rulings, says that our future redemption will occur on Passover, "at midnight," which has the numerical value of *190* as does the word *end,* the term designating the end of the world as we know it and the beginning of the messianic era.[3]

Under your wing. The word *wing* is understood to mean the corner of a garment. Ruth was essentially asking Boaz, "Please place the corner of your garment over me as a token of marriage." The word *wing* is also seen as a metaphor borrowed from birds who shield with their wings during mating. In this sense, these words are used as a symbol of marriage.[4]

The sheltering aspect of marriage is symbolized by a four-sided fringed garment, which reflects a nuptial canopy or *chupah.* Three of our five children have been married under a marriage canopy, which incorporated my husband's treasured prayer shawl.

As Ruth sought the covering of her redeemer, we, the bride of Christ, seek our Redeemer's covering as well.

How precious is Your lovingkindness, O God! Therefore the children of men put their trust under the shadow of Your wings. They are abundantly satisfied with the fullness of Your house, and You give them drink from the river of Your pleasures. For with You is the fountain of life; in Your light we see light. (PSALM 36:7–9)

"Blessed are you." God said to Abraham, "In you all the families of the earth shall be blessed" (GEN. 12:3). Torah scholars believe this blessing refers to all the righteous converts who will be "grafted" into the tree of Israel. Thus, when Boaz referred to Ruth as "his daughter," he was telling her she was more than one of his handmaidens; she was a righteous convert.

When Boaz blessed Ruth, he was also praising her for her habit of showing kindness. First, Ruth helped to bury her husband in a proper Jewish tradition (RUTH 1:8). Second, Ruth showed kindness in caring for Naomi (RUTH 2:11). Third, Ruth showed kindness to her soul as she embraced Judaism (RUTH 2:12).

Conversion is considered a good deed. There are three types of converts in Judaism. One converts to eat:

> *You may give it (meat) to the alien who is within your gates, that he may eat it.* (DEUTERONOMY 14:21)

Others convert in order to receive charity:

> *And you shall not glean your vineyard, nor shall you gather every grape of your vineyard; you shall leave them for the poor and the stranger.* (LEVITICUS 19:10)

Still others convert for the sake of heaven:

> *One ordinance shall be for you of the assembly and for the stranger who dwells with you, an ordinance forever throughout your generations; as you are, so shall the stranger be before the Lord.* (NUMBERS 15:15)

The next act of kindness Ruth expressed involved Boaz. She sought to marry Boaz because she loved him and was taken with his goodness. The general decadence and immorality of the generation of this time would have led Ruth to search after a rich man, but she chose to marry a righteous man who loved the Lord God of Israel. For this good deed Boaz took special notice.

By not going after the young, rich men, Ruth proved that she had converted purely for the sake of heaven, and therefore was blessed of God, who cherishes sincere converts.[5]

> *Gather the people together, men and women and little ones, and the stranger who is within your gates [the convert], that they may hear and that they may learn to fear the Lord your God and carefully observe all the words of this law.* (DEUTERONOMY 31:12)

All three of these types of converts have walked into Cornerstone Church at one time or another. The first kind of convert comes into our flock with the pretense of sincere motives, and within months they are introducing get-rich-quick programs, luring trusting sheep into their designs with the promises of instant prosperity. My husband has a keen sense of smell, and he tells me he can distinguish the scent of goats from sheep with great accuracy. Under most circumstances, he will ask these types of individuals to make a choice: Either attend our church for the sake of worship and fellowship or choose to take your business schemes elsewhere.

Other converts walk in the door in dire need. They are eagerly welcomed and are provided food, clothing, and essentials for their daily upkeep. In time, we notice that they don't want to attend classes or support groups that we have put in place to help them break from their past of "lack and want." They want to stay in their place of need. We seek job interviews for them, but they are too busy to make the appointments. We attempt to put them in trade programs but they feel they are not suited for "that kind of work." They simply want charity without discipleship and accountability.

Still others are true converts who grace the altar of our church every Sunday.

I never tire of watching these precious individuals come to the altar of forgiveness and cry out to their Redeemer. They long for His mantle to fall upon their past and give them a new hope for tomorrow. They seek nothing but a relationship with the God of Abraham, Isaac, and Jacob. They too are like baby birds without nests, seeking refuge under the wings of the Almighty. They are what makes our ministry rewarding. They will be blessed of God, for He cherishes sincere converts.

> *Therefore remember that you, once Gentiles in the flesh . . . that at that time you were without Christ, being aliens from the commonwealth of Israel and strangers from the covenants of promise, having no hope and without God in the world. But now in Christ Jesus you who once were far off have been brought near by the blood of Christ.* (EPHESIANS 2:11–13)

LIFE LESSONS

LIFE LESSON ONE:
OUR REDEEMER COVERS US WITH HIS ROBE OF RIGHTEOUSNESS

Boaz, the redeemer and bridegroom, draped his garment over Ruth, the Gentile and bride. This adoring gesture symbolized his love for her and his desire to protect her. Ruth's plea for protection portrayed the ultimate act of yielding:

> *I will greatly rejoice in the LORD, my soul shall be joyful in my God; for He has clothed me with the garments of salvation. He has covered me with the robe of righteousness, as a bridegroom decks himself with ornaments, and as a bride adorns herself with her jewels.* (ISAIAH 61:10)

Christ, the Redeemer and Bridegroom, drapes His robe of righteousness around the church, the Gentile and His bride.

For Boaz and Ruth this act of love and devotion occurred on the threshing floor, the place of separation of the grain from the chaff. For Christ and the sinner, this act occurs at the cross, our place of separation from the world.

> *But God forbid that I should boast except in the cross of our Lord Jesus Christ, by whom the world has been crucified to me, and I to the world.* (GALATIANS 6:14)

When we, the sinner, come to the cross of Christ and yield to His love, our Redeemer drapes His pure white robe of righteousness over our lives and covers our sin with His purity. It is that simple. The act of redemption, the act of deliverance from sin and its penalties, is set in motion:

> *Fear not, for I have redeemed you; I have called you by your name; you are Mine.* (ISAIAH 43:1)

We now become a work in progress. The more we are convicted of our offenses, the more we seek repentance and cleansing. As we mature in Christ, we realize we have an inheritance for we are the King's daughters. He promises to give us the desire of our hearts, for we have been purchased with a great price:

> *For he who is called in the Lord while a slave is the Lord's freedman. Likewise he who is called while free is Christ's slave. You were bought at a price; do not become slaves of men. Brethren, let each one remain with God in that state in which he was called.* (1 CORINTHIANS 7:22–24)

Christ gave His life so we may have ours! He has given us an invaluable inheritance. The white robe of righteousness of the Son of God is draped around our sinful lives, giving us access to the Father's throne where He sees us through His Son and not through our sin! We are the King's daughters! We must begin to think like the King's daughters—we must begin to act like the King's daughters—we must begin to live like the King's daughters!

Wear the Robe of righteousness proudly, however, always remember this truth: You did not earn it—Jesus did.

LIFE LESSON TWO:
THERE IS POWER IN IMPARTING THE BLESSING

God's purpose for the blessing is a redemptive one and is an example of "divine substitution." This plan is clearly demonstrated in Jacob's blessing of his grandsons Ephraim and Manasseh in Genesis 48. Jacob's son, Joseph, brought his sons to his father:

> *And Joseph took them both, Ephraim with his right hand toward Israel's left hand, and Manasseh with his left hand toward Israel's right hand, and brought them near him.*
>
> *Then Israel stretched out his right hand and laid it on Ephraim's head, who was the younger, and his left hand on Manasseh's head, guiding his hands knowingly, for Manasseh was the firstborn.*
>
> *And he blessed Joseph, and said . . . "Bless the lads; let my name be named upon them, and the name of my fathers Abraham and Isaac; and let them grow into a multitude in the midst of the earth."*
> (**GENESIS 48:13–16**)

Many of you have heard the term "the laying on of hands," but don't fully understand its meaning. Neither did I until I was taught by my husband, our dear friend Pastor Bill Ligon, and Derek Prince. "The laying on of hands" is an act in which one person in spiritual authority places his hands upon another with some definite spiritual purpose, which can have one of three intentions or a combination of all three:

1. To transmit spiritual blessing or authority

2. To publicly acknowledge a person's particular spiritual blessing or authority God has given him

3. To publicly commit a person to God for some special task or ministry[6]

I am going to discuss the first purpose of imparting the blessing with "the laying on of hands." When Joseph brought his sons Ephraim and Manasseh to his father, Jacob, the patriarch blessed his grandchildren by laying hands on their heads. It was the tradition to put the right hand on the oldest son and the left hand on the younger. Jacob bestowed his personal blessing to his grandchildren but with crossed hands.

Witnessing his father's crossed hands, Joseph felt the aged patriarch made a mistake. Joseph attempted to reverse the order by putting his father's right hand, the greater blessing, on the first son, Manasseh, and his father's left hand, the lesser blessing, on the second son, Ephraim, but Jacob refused.

> *But his father refused and said, "I know, my son, I know. He [Manasseh] also shall become a people, and he also shall be great; but truly his younger brother [Ephraim] shall be greater than he, and his descendants shall become a multitude of nations."*
> (GENESIS 48:19)

This entire experience is a "type and shadow" of Christ and the sinner coming to the cross of Calvary. When a sinner comes to the cross, he cries out for a blessing from God. God hears the sinner's cry for mercy and, out of His pure love, blesses the sinner by imparting the blessing of his firstborn, Jesus Christ, to the sinner.

The great effect of the blessing of salvation is that God, the Father, substitutes the life of His Son, Jesus, for the death of the sinner. The sinner (you and me) who deserves to die, instead lives, and the Savior, who is pure and deserves to live, dies instead.

God shows Divine preference when He gives eternal life to the sinner, for we receive the resurrection life of the firstborn as the ultimate blessing.[7] This beautiful exchange is described in Galatians:

> ***Christ has redeemed us from the curse of the law, having become a curse for us (for it is written, "Cursed is everyone who hangs on a tree") [DEUT. 21:23], that the blessing of Abraham might come upon the Gentiles in Christ Jesus, that we might receive the promise of the Spirit through faith.* (GALATIANS 3:13–14)**

The act of Jesus willingly giving up His birthright is reflected in His own words:

> ***. . . just as the Son of Man did not come to be served, but to serve, and to give His life a ransom for many.* (MATTHEW 20:28)**

This great exchange was made at His cross:

Jesus was *punished* that we might be *forgiven.*
Jesus was *wounded* that we might be *healed.*
Jesus was made *sin* with our *sinfulness* that we might be made
    righteous with His *righteousness.*
Jesus died our *death* that we might receive His *life.*

Jesus was made a *curse* that we might share His *abundance*.

Jesus bore our *shame* that we might share His *glory*.

Jesus endured our *rejection* that we might have His *acceptance*
 with the Father.

Jesus was *cut off* by death that we might be *joined* to God eternally.

Our *old man* was put to death in Him that the *new man* might
 come to life in us.[8]

Sin no longer has dominion over us, because Christ, in His atonement, His exchange at the cross, made it possible for the sinner to become dead to sin but alive to God and His righteousness.[9]

A man named Nikolai Berdyaev abandoned Marxism for Christianity. When asked what brought him to his Christian faith, he insisted it was neither history, nor theology, nor the church, but purely the actions of a woman, a Christian who was simply called Mother Maria.

Nikolai was present at a concentration camp when the Nazis were murdering Jews in the gas chambers. As the Nazi officer arbitrarily chose who would go to one line and live or to the other line and die, a frantic mother was sent to the "life-line," and her helpless baby was sent to the line leading to the death chamber. Crying out in agony the desperate mother refused to part with her baby, so she joined her baby in the "death-line."

Mother Maria, who had been chosen to live, noticed that the officer was only interested in meeting a numeric quota of dead Jews; therefore, she discreetly exchanged places with the mother and her baby.[10] She chose death so that others could live.

This self-sacrificing action revealed to Berdyaev what atonement really means, which is the heart of Christianity.

Chapter Thirteen

THE ROMANCE

The threshing floor remained quiet and still. In the far corner near the stacked containers of barley, Boaz and Ruth knelt before each other as he spoke to Ruth in the hushed tones of tender whispers. "Rest assured, Ruth, I will not turn you away. Fear not, for I am not ashamed to marry a Moabite convert. I know that you are a kind and virtuous woman, and the people of Bethlehem discern that you are righteous and worthy of marrying a judge of Israel."

Boaz wanted to do all he could to put Ruth's concerns to rest, so he continued to reassure Ruth that God motivated her actions. "Do not fear that you have blemished your reputation by coming here tonight. No one will condemn your action, for all know that you act solely for the sake of heaven."

Boaz began to explain to Ruth some of what he knew about her situation. "I know there is a kinsman who is closer related to Naomi than I."

Ruth looked inquisitively into Boaz's eyes, desperately trying to understand what he was saying to her.

Boaz could tell the news of another redeemer discouraged Ruth. The look of apprehension on her face made Boaz's heart ache. "Be assured, I will force this matter to a swift conclusion," he said. And in order to provide her with added security and confidence of his intentions, he made a vow to her, "As the Lord lives, I will perform the duty of marriage if the one closer than I refuses." Then Boaz asked Ruth to stay by his side until morning.

Ruth knew Boaz was a righteous man, and even though she could not fully understand the entire course of events that were coming together, she had to trust him. She lay at Boaz's feet with deep concern over the future. Ruth was thoroughly exhausted, for the day had proven to be much more demanding than she had anticipated. Finally she fell asleep.

Boaz lay awake for the remainder of the night, anguishing over the desecration he would bring to God's name if he and Ruth were even slightly suspected of immoral conduct. He loved God too much to let this happen and loved Ruth in such a pure way that he did not want her chaste reputation tainted, so he continued to pray until daybreak.

A translucent gray fog softly lingered over the earth as at last dawn considered its awakening. Boaz ceased from praying and awakened Ruth. She quickly rose from the threshing floor and began to prepare for her journey home while it was still too dark for even a close friend to recognize another.

Before Ruth left, Boaz gave her six barleycorns to take with her. As she fixed her eyes on the barley he put in her scarf, Boaz knew that Ruth recognized his offering as sufficient food for a little more than a day. He assured his beloved that she would only need food for one more day before entering the house of her husband.

As the morning star began to show on the horizon, Ruth walked the path back to Naomi's home with the six barleycorns Boaz had given her. She would be so happy to see Naomi, for she felt secure in her presence. Her journey home was filled with expectancy for the day's events. Over and over Ruth reflected on Boaz's oath to her: "As the Lord lives, I will perform the duty."

THE BIBLE STUDY

"And now, my daughter, do not fear. I will do for you all that you request, for all the people of my town know that you are a virtuous woman. Now it is true that I am a close relative; however, there is a relative closer than I. Stay this night, and in the morning it shall

be that if he will perform the duty of a close relative for you—good; let him do it. But if he does not want to perform the duty for you, then I will perform the duty for you, as the Lord lives! Lie down until morning."

So she lay at his feet until morning, and she arose before one could recognize another. Then he said, "Do not let it be known that the woman came to the threshing floor." Also he said, "Bring the shawl that is on you and hold it." And when she held it, he measured six ephahs of barley, and laid it on her. Then she went into the city. (RUTH 3:11–15)

"A relative closer than I." The kinsman-redeemer who was a closer relative to Naomi and Ruth was named Tov. Boaz's father, Salmon, Elimelech and Tov were brothers; thereby Tov was a closer relative than Boaz, who was a nephew.[1]

Tov's name is not mentioned in the text, even though genealogical records show that he existed. He is simply referred to as "Plony Almoni," which in Hebrew means "so and so." Jewish scholars believe his name was not worth mentioning, since he decided not to redeem the beautiful convert from Moab.[2]

"Perform the duty." Boaz did not have the power to grant Ruth's request immediately. Yet, his love for her was so pure that he not only assured Ruth he would do what she needed, he apologized for not being able to marry her as quickly as they both desired.

The closer relative, "the so and so," had to be given the option of redeeming Mahlon's field and his bride even though he had the opportunity to do so prior to this day, but failed to take previous action.[3]

"As the LORD lives." This expression indicates an oath. Boaz gave Ruth his word in order to give her peace of mind. Even though he tried to convince her he was in control of the situation and would care for her, Boaz could see that Ruth was worried for her future and the future security of her mother-in-law.[4]

Lay at his feet. Jewish scholars teach that Boaz prostrated himself before the Lord in prayer throughout the night while Ruth slept by his feet. If Ruth's visit became public knowledge and they were suspected of immoral conduct, it would be a desecration to the name of God, something Boaz did not want.[5] He remained in prayer so no impure thought could defile his mind.

Six ephahs of barley. The original Hebrew read "six measures or six barley-corns." One interpretation of this verse is that Ruth and Naomi would have only enough food for one more meal, indicating that Boaz intended to redeem the two women by the end of the day.[6]

Even though the initial meaning of the verse further illustrates Boaz's commitment to Ruth, there is a prophetic meaning of the verse as well, which proves to be much more insightful. We will discuss this prophecy in the next chapter.

LIFE LESSONS

Life Lesson:
To love is to redeem

Allow me to share a beautiful love story with you. Like the Book of Ruth, this story encompasses the love of a mother for her children, the love of a man for a woman, and the supernatural redemption of a family.

Her name was Leah. She was born in the early 1900s in the small village of Kregly. At the time, this territory belonged to Russia. Later, in 1914, the Polish army occupied the land and controlled it for twenty-five years.

When Leah was sixteen, she fell in love and married a young man whose name was Josef Hemerling. Together, Leah and Josef moved to the larger city of Baranovichy where they opened a surplus store, supplying clothes, soft goods, and food staples to the Polish army. Over the years they became very successful and were afforded the finest luxuries. Life could not have been better.

The Hemerlings were blessed with three daughters: Renia, Hannah, and Feigela; and a son, Shmulek. Life in this gracious and loving Jewish home was full of joy. Leah felt so fortunate to have so many blessings to share with others and thanked Jehovah often for His goodness as she invited Jewish soldiers every Friday night to their Sabbath table.

Life was abruptly interrupted when in 1941 the German army invaded Baranovichy. Instantly, the people became apprehensive and gravely troubled, for the Nazis brought with them a demonic presence that seemed to permeate the very air they breathed. Life was, at best, uncertain.

On the tenth day of German occupation, Hitler's elite SS soldiers captured over one hundred townspeople. The Germans brutally interrogated their captives and demanded to know the names of the richest families in town. Terrified of the consequences, the frightened citizens provided the SS with names. Leah and Josef were listed among them.

The heads of the selected households were told to bring ten kilograms of gold and fifty kilograms of silver to a specific location outside of the city, in return they and their families would be spared any Nazi penalties. Josef and the others brought the ransom quota to the Judenraad, Jewish middlemen appointed to deal with the Jews. Once the Germans confiscated the gold and silver, the unsuspecting men were ushered into the woods. There, before a large, freshly dug pit, the SS systematically shot them to death.

Leah waited for Josef's return. Midnight came, and still no word from her beloved husband. She anxiously stood by the window of her dark parlor, looking through her beautiful, lace Austrian curtains, a cherished anniversary gift from Josef. Suddenly, a family friend appeared from the shadows onto Leah's doorstep.

Leah received the news of her husband's murder. It was as if time stood still. Leah's lungs refused to take in air; she wanted to scream but no sound came from her mouth. Leah was numb, and Her Josef was gone. Leah's grief quickly turned to panic as she thought of her children. *I must save the children!*

Leah awoke and dressed her disoriented children in several layers of clothing and packed a small bundle for each of them to carry on their journey to the town of Kletzk, thirty kilometers away, where Leah's sister, Sara, lived with her husband and their four young daughters.

The day after Leah arrived, a Gentile friend of her sister informed them that a huge massacre of all Jews was to take place in Kletzk the next day. Leah immediately began her return journey home. Soon after Leah left, the men of Kletzk were massacred at the outskirts of the city, and Sara and her four children were deported to Siberia.

Upon Leah's return to Baranovichy, all the Jews were taken from their homes. Leah took her mother, Mary, her four children, and a small bag of belongings, and moved to the designated area of town the Nazis renamed the Jewish ghetto. In one day, thousands of people found themselves housed in just six square city blocks.

While in the ghetto, Leah eventually shared one room of a small house with sixteen other people. The healthy were allowed to leave the ghetto during the day to work, while the sick, elderly, and very young children remained within the walls of the filthy, disease-infested area.

Day by day, conditions in the ghetto worsened as food and water became scarce. Leah was fortunate to work at a bakery; she would hide bread discreetly on her body and bring it back to her mother and her four hungry children. While at the bakery, Leah was able to befriend a Russian man who became taken with her kind spirit and unique beauty.

Every morning under SS escort, Leah and Renia, her oldest daughter who was then twelve, were escorted out of the ghetto to work. The two were grateful to be able to get away from the plague-ridden ghetto through the day but were sad to leave Mary and the three children behind. Soon a fence was built around the ghetto, and every evening the workers were searched at its entrance, so Leah could no longer bring bread to her family.

While Leah and Renia were working outside the fence, Mary received terrifying news that the Nazis were on a killing spree, and she hurriedly gathered Hannah, Feigela, Shmulek, and the other young children under her care to hide in the cellar of the building they inhabited.

On the third day after Yom Kippur, the dreaded massacre took place. Soldiers came to the place where Mary and her beloved grandchildren and the others hid.

Unfortunately, an infant in their group began to cry. Frantically his mother tried to comfort him yet he continued to scream. The woman knew that the incessant crying would expose everyone in the basement, including her other children. With tears in her eyes, she held her hand over her baby's mouth until the crying finally stopped; she suffocated her precious baby to save the others.

But it was too late; the Nazis heard the baby's cry and discovered Mary and her precious grandchildren in their hiding place. The terrified family responded to the orders of the SS who shouted, "Raus! Raus!" "Out! Out!"

Later Leah learned that as Mary and her children were being led to the firing squad, Mary led her grandchildren in Sh'ma Israel (Hear O Israel).

The Sh'ma is the first prayer a Jewish child learns and the last prayer an observant Jew says before sleep each night; it is also the last prayer a Jew says before death. The Sh'ma is as close as you can get to a Jewish statement of faith. It is comprised of three paragraphs derived from Deuteronomy 6:4–9 and Numbers 15:37–41.[7] One of the most important components of this sacred prayer is its beginning: *"Sh'ma, Israel, Adonai Eloheinu, Adonai Echad.* Hear, O Israel, the Lord our God, the Lord is One." The tortuous vision of Mary and her three children huddling in prayer waiting for death played in Leah's mind for the rest of her life.

Soon conditions in the ghetto became intolerable. There was no food, no clean water. Disease permeated the air like a smothering blanket. Leah and Renia wept as they stepped over the lifeless corpses of men, women, and children to get to their jobs outside the ghetto.

One day, even in the midst of the agonizing suffering, God's supernatural protection covered Leah and Renia. On the way back to the ghetto, in the dark of night, Leah and Renia slipped away from the escorted group of workers. Miraculously, as if they became invisible, the two women went unnoticed. God's hand had indeed protected them!

Leah and Renia arrived at the home of their friends in the cold of night. Both the terrified women were agonizing in pain as pieces of flesh tore from their red, swollen, and bleeding feet due walking in the freezing snow. Yet even in severe misery, the fugitives were greatly relieved to find a place of refuge from the encroaching enemy.

Leah and her daughter had been hiding from the Nazis in the icy fields of Baranovichy for days in the hunt for food and cover. Finally, in desperation, Leah knew she had to ask their Christian friends, the Sleizen family, to hide them in their farmhouse, which she had visited many times before frantic survival dictated their lives. The Sleizens knew they could be deported to a concentration camp or instantly executed for hiding Jews, but they decided to do what was right in the sight of God—they brought their friends into their home.

In order to effectively hide the two women, the Sleizens dug a hole in their bedroom floor. The family placed a rug and sofa over the grave-like opening. The space was long enough to accommodate Leah's height and wide enough to cradle both mother and daughter as they lay side by side. This dark, cold, damp sepulcher became their refuge.

At three o'clock every morning Mrs. Sleizen would free Leah and Renia from their blackened tomb, allowing them to stretch their cramped bodies, eat a bit of food, and have sufficient time for them to carry out their basic necessities.

Day after day the mother and daughter lay there. When Renia cried in desperation, Leah would touch her and say, "Soon the war will be over. We are going to get out of here. We will go back home. Everything is going to be fine. Jehovah God will see to it my darling!"

Finally, after eight hundred and forty days—twenty-eight tortuous long months—mother and daughter were freed from their sepulcher and given passports and birth certificates with Christian names that the Sleizens managed to obtain.

The day Leah and her daughter were freed from their hiding place, the Germans began retreating from the territory due to the encroaching Russian army, and pandemonium was everywhere. The Nazi SS were randomly firing at those frantically running in the streets, trying to kill as many Jews as they could who had survived their devastating occupation.

As shots were wildly fired in the air, Leah held Renia tightly to her body. If one of them was shot, she would rather they both die by the same bullet so they would be spared the agony of losing each other.

Amidst the chaos Leah became reunited with the Russian man who had befriended her at the bakery outside the Jewish ghetto. She pleaded with him to help obtain the release of her sister Sara and her four daughters from Siberia. The Russian man inexplicably agreed, Sara and her daughters were released from the Siberian work camp and were reunited with Leah. Once again, the hand of God was on Leah and her family.

Jewish partisans who hid in the forest to escape the vicious SS also returned to the deserted town of Baranovichy, banding themselves in large groups to fight the remaining Germans. Those returning desperately searched for their loved ones, but found few. Later, Leah learned that out of a population of 45,000 people, Renia and a young boy were the only children to survive the demonic slaughter and deprivation of the Nazi hoards.

Among the brave who survived was Samuel Bratkovsky, who lost his wife and two young sons during the Nazi occupation. Grief became a constant companion as Samuel resisted the SS. Soon the partisans began gathering to share their heartrending stories with one another. Samuel's loneliness seemed all-consuming until he laid eyes on Leah, and he instantly became enchanted with the weary yet still beautiful woman.

What Boaz felt for Ruth, Samuel felt for Leah. He wanted to protect her and Renia. He became enamored with her concern for others and her innate kindness that radiated from her striking eyes. However, Leah was still deeply distraught over Josef's death and remained very much in love with her beloved husband.

Another partisan who became enamored with the Hemerling women was Pesach Burzak. Renia, now seventeen, was instantly drawn to his dark, handsome features, and he was impressed with the innocent beauty of the frail young woman. Their friendship, however, was short lived, and sad goodbyes were spoken as Pesach joined a group of partisans leaving Russia.

Rampant lawlessness prevailed, and Leah began to feel unsafe in the midst of the incredible chaos. She met with other Jewish survivors and partisans, and they collectively decided to leave Baranovichy.

The long, treacherous passage through the steep mountains began as the group traveled by night and rested through the day to avoid detection from the maverick SS troops who combed the hillsides.

At sunset as the group awoke from their rest to prepare for the night's travel, Sara noticed four-year-old Carmella missing. She somehow wandered away while the others were sleeping. Frantically, they searched the surrounding area, but to no avail. The group unanimously decided it was too risky to go back in search of the young child for it would put the whole group in jeopardy. Devastated, they left Carmella behind.

The next day Samuel was also missing, and Leah assumed that he decided to stay in a nearby town. He was a good man and she would miss his kindness, but her feelings for Samuel were smothered by the grief she felt for her little niece, Carmella.

For two days the group crossed the steep and jagged Alps between Austria and Italy. At sunrise on the third day they noticed someone walking toward them. As the solitary figure approached, Leah could see a man carrying a young child in his arms. It was Samuel, and he was holding Carmella! He had risked his life to save the helpless young girl from the wilderness and certain death!

Samuel loved Leah so much that he risked his own life to find Carmella, for he could not bear to watch Leah witness another loss in her family. In redeeming Carmella, Samuel kindled a love in Leah that would last a lifetime.

When the family arrived in Milan, they boarded a train to Rome. Leah had no money for passage; her only possession was a fragment of a torn and tattered Jewish prayer book.

As the conductor asked for tickets, Leah took a deep breath, gave a silent prayer, and handed him one of the torn pages from her cherished prayer book. Amazingly, he accepted the remnant of sacred Scripture as their fare. This was another sign from the Almighty that His hand was very much upon their lives.

Once in Rome, the group lived in the vestibule of an old, abandoned synagogue. There the group shared their hopes and dreams for tomorrow. It had been so long since they had hope, and to speak about their future together was a gift they all cherished. It was here in the synagogue, an earthly symbol of the eternal God, where the marriage of Leah Hemerling and Samuel Bratkovsky took place.

One cold Friday evening after reciting Sabbath prayers, Leah and Renia reclaimed their Jewish names. The new family made a vow to each other: "We will never be separated again. We will live freely as Jews and move to Israel, the homeland of our patriarchs—Abraham, Isaac, and Jacob."

Jews would come and go from the vestibule of the old synagogue where Leah, Samuel, Sara, Sara's daughters, and Renia lived. One such man was the handsome Pesach Berzak whom Renia had fallen in love with months before. The two were reunited and within weeks they too were married in the old Roman synagogue. Leah's family was being restored and they were about to embark on a journey to freedom in Israel.

Israel, known as Palestine at the time, was under British rule from 1917 to 1948. Immigration to Israel was virtually impossible because of the White

Paper Policy put in place by the British in 1939, which stated that no more than 5,000 Jews could immigrate into Palestine in one given year. Jews who arrived in Palestine without "proper British papers" were immediately arrested by the British and returned by ship to Europe and into the hands of the crazed Hitler and the deadly gas chamber. During the war, the Nazi dictator killed over 20,000 Jews a day in accordance with his "final solution," which eventually took over 6,000,000 Jewish lives—2,000,000 of them children.

Jews who had survived Hitler looked toward Palestine as their salvation. An illegal, underground immigration group agreed to transport Jews to Israel if they promised to live on a kibbutz, a place of communal living where survivors of the Holocaust could begin life anew and build a Jewish homeland. The forged immigration visas were like gold, yet God's favor allowed Leah to book passage to Israel.

Renia, now pregnant with her first child, received priority status to get on the ship to Israel. A week after the departure of her daughter and son-in-law, Leah and Samuel excitedly boarded an old cargo ship to the Promised Land.

Unfortunately, just as they saw the shimmering lights of their beloved destination appear on the horizon, the British navy intercepted the ship and its illegal cargo and diverted them to Cyprus. There, this man and woman who had lost so much—and given each other the precious little they had left—were housed in a makeshift detention camp.

Leah became seriously ill with typhoid. Samuel kept a twenty-four-hour vigil by her side, tending to the needs of this beautiful woman he loved with all of his being. With Samuel's love and care and God's healing touch, Leah miraculously recovered, and the two remained in the camp for nearly a year until, providentially, they were finally put onto another ship bound for Israel.

They arrived in Israel to be reunited with Renia and Pesach and to meet their new nine-month-old granddaughter, Henia. The sight of this adorable baby was a sign from God that He was not yet weary with mankind.

However, their short-lived peace was once again interrupted by war. Samuel and Pesach fought in the 1948 war for Israel's independence. They, along with thousands of other Jews and the hand of almighty God, were successful in bringing a rebirth to their Jewish homeland, *Eretz Israel*—the land of Israel.

The Lord God of Israel had promised the Jews they would dwell in Jerusalem forever, and He had promised that a nation would be born in a day:

For David said, "The Lord God of Israel has given rest to His people, that they may dwell in Jerusalem forever."
(1 CHRONICLES 23:25)

Who has heard such a thing? Who has seen such things?
Shall the earth be made to give birth in one day?
Or shall a nation be born at once? For as soon as Zion was in labor,
She gave birth to her children. **(ISAIAH 66:8)**

On May 14, 1948, these promises were fulfilled!

For fifty-two years Leah and Samuel remained devoted to each other, until Leah's death at age 89. Samuel lived until the age of 101. Henia, Leah's granddaughter by Renia, never knew that Samuel was not her natural grandfather until the day of her marriage in 1968.

After her shock, Henia realized this incredible man was much more than a relative. Samuel was a gift given to her beloved grandmother, Leah, by the God who had shown her great favor by sparing her and her daughter, Renia, during the ravages of Hitler's war against the Jews.

Renia said she always felt God was with them. "So much that happened was the pure favor of God—there is no other explanation. Some people's requests were turned down; others were not." Renia and her mother often wondered why such decisions were made. Nothing just "happened" in the lives of these chosen two; the sovereign hand of God directed their path and redeemed them from death.

Today, Henia is one of my dearest friends, and I had the great honor of meeting Samuel, a kind man who was devoted to Leah and her family. Samuel was a man who loved the Lord and treasured life to the fullest and remains a cherished member of the family. He is sorely missed, but the unselfish love he had for his precious wife Leah, is still spoken of to this day.

Henia has photographs of Leah, Samuel, Renia, and her father, Pesach, in his Polish partisan uniform. She also has photos of her grandmother, Leah, with her four children: Renia, Hannah, Feigela, and Shmulek. These precious memories were spared extinction, for Leah had hidden these valued photographs in her corset next to her most sacred possession—the tattered prayer book.

The Lord God of Israel continues to bless both Leah and Samuel through the legacy they left behind. Their cherished Henia married Richard Leibman, and together they had three children: Bryan, Lara, and Neville. Bryan married Eleonora, and together they had two children: Julia Leah and Daniel Isaac.

Hitler did not extinguish this noble Jewish line; he could not, for they were redeemed by the hand of God. God's intervention allowed Leah's great-great-granddaughter—Julia Leah—to be born.

Julia Leah freely lives as a Jew in a country that honors justice and religious freedom. The family will never be separated again. In Bryan Leibman's words, "Julia Leah will be proud to carry Leah's legacy forward.

Pesach (in partisan uniform), Renia, Leah, Samuel

top—Renia, left—Hannah, center—Shmulek, right—Feigela

Chapter Fourteen

THE PROPHECY

Sleep eluded Naomi the entire night. She lay on her bed, yet her mind was filled with tormenting questions as she impatiently waited for Ruth's return. *Did I do right in sending Ruth to the threshing floor? Did Boaz recognize and appreciate Ruth's purpose? Or did he, God forbid, humiliate her? Is there any hope still left for Ruth? Is there any hope left for me?*

Finally, she arose from her anguish, her body trembling with uncertainty. She began to pace back and forth in front of the window, glancing at the horizon for what seemed to be an infinite number of times.

Then, finally, she discerned the form of a human shadow approaching her home. As the first light of morning gradually grew brighter, Naomi could see that the form was that of a woman—it was Ruth!

As Ruth arrived home it was all Naomi could do to refrain from asking Ruth a myriad of questions, but she restrained herself and kept silent.

The beautiful young woman looked into Naomi's eyes, and Naomi returned the look with compassion. She asked one short question with utmost care and with true motherly concern. "Is this you, my daughter?"

At the time, it was not possible for Ruth to tell Naomi everything that was welled up within her heart concerning all that occurred on the threshing floor. She was trying to sort through all her memories of the evening, for she was very weary from the long night. With her soft and quiet answer to Naomi's question, Ruth immediately calmed her mother-in-law. "Yes . . . it's me, your daughter, and I have something for you."

As one interpreting a pleasant dream in which dormant hopes rise, Ruth handed over the evidence of Boaz's provision within her scarf and reported all that Boaz had said and done. She added, "Boaz sent you a message as well. He said, 'Do not go empty-handed to your mother-in-law.'"

Naomi looked at the six barleycorns and accepted them as a gift of consolation from Boaz, for it was she who had stood at the city gates and declared, "I went out full and the Lord has brought me back empty." However, Naomi, being a virtuous and learned woman in her own right, discerned there was something more than kindness to the gift Boaz had sent with Ruth.

She knew the *yes* of a righteous man was *yes* and his *no, no*—for Ruth reported that Boaz said he would not rest until he finished the deed this day. His promise was sufficient guarantee for Naomi to feel secure about the day's outcome. She assured Ruth that Boaz would act on their behalf, but as for the six barleycorns, Naomi knew the message within them far exceeded her imagination—within them was a prophetic word from *Hashem*.

THE BIBLE STUDY

> *When she came to her mother-in-law, she said, "Is that you, my daughter?" Then she told her all that the man had done for her. And she said, "These six ephahs of barley he gave me; for he said to me, 'Do not go empty-handed to your mother-in-law.'"*
>
> *Then she said, "Sit still, my daughter, until you know how the matter will turn out; for the man will not rest until he has concluded the matter this day."* (RUTH 3:16–18)

"Is that you?" Naomi was asking Ruth the question—"Are you still mine, or do you belong to Boaz?"[1]

Six ephahs. As stated in the previous chapter, the six *ephahs* were actually six barleycorns and were sufficient food for Naomi and Ruth to share for one day. This was a sign to both women that by the end of the day they would be under the care of a kinsman-redeemer who would meet their needs forevermore.

However, the six barleycorns also brought with them a prophetic message: Ruth's descendants would include six *tzaddikim,* or men of charity, each possessing six outstanding, righteous attributes. The names of these six men would be David, Chananiah, Mishael, Azariah, Daniel, and the Messiah.[2]

David's six traits are described in 1 Samuel:

> *Then one of the servants answered and said, "Look, I have seen a son of Jesse the Bethlehemite, who is skillful in playing, a mighty man of valor, a man of war, prudent in speech, and a handsome person; and the LORD is with him." (1 SAMUEL 16:18)*

These six virtues are believed to be represented in the six-pointed Shield of David, the *Magen* David, which is borne on the banner of Israel.[3]

The six virtuous character traits assigned to the Messiah are found in Isaiah when the prophet describes the reign of Jesse's offspring:[4]

> *There shall come forth a Rod from the stem of Jesse, and a Branch shall grow out of his roots. The Spirit of the Lord shall rest upon Him, the Spirit of wisdom and understanding, the Spirit of counsel and might, the Spirit of knowledge and of the fear of the LORD.*
>
> *His delight is in the fear of the LORD, and He shall not judge by the sight of His eyes, nor decide by the hearing of His ears; but with righteousness He shall judge the poor, and decide with equity for the meek of the earth; He shall strike the earth with the rod of His*

mouth, and with the breath of His lips He shall slay the wicked. Righteousness shall be the belt of His loins, and faithfulness the belt of His waist. (ISAIAH 11:1–5)

The prophetic message within the six barleycorns was set in motion—Ruth would one day become the Mother of Royalty.

"The man will not rest." The chapter opened with Naomi seeking rest for Ruth, and it closes with that rest attained. Boaz vowed he would not cease until he had found rest on Ruth's behalf.[5] Naomi did not send her daughter-in-law on yet another mission to find security; to the contrary, she advised her to remain at home and enjoy the assurance that another would provide. She told Ruth to remove all thoughts of restless anxiety from her mind, as Boaz had become restless on her behalf.

"He has concluded the matter." Naomi was advising Ruth as both a mother and a matchmaker. The word *matchmaker* most likely conjures up in your mind the image of *Yente* from the movie *Fiddler on the Roof,* but this is not the image the Torah considers a true matchmaker.

Matchmaking is a righteous deed, *a mitzvah,* and God Himself is concerned with it. Finding one's life partner is not a simple matter. The Bible describes Isaac, one of Scripture's most eligible bachelors, and the difficult search for his soul partner. He came from the greatest family in his generation. He was wealthy beyond words. He was handsome and brilliant, as well, but he could not find a wife. I am sure many women were vying for his hand, but his *basherte* could not be found.

His father Abraham commissioned the executor of his estate and his most trusted servant, Eliezer, to find a bride for his beloved son. Even though Eliezer was laden with riches and represented a worthy catch, he still asked for God's help to bring the perfect wife to Isaac:[6]

"O LORD God of my master Abraham, please give me success this day, and show kindness to my master Abraham. Behold, here I stand by the well of water, and the daughters of the men of the city are coming out to draw water. Now let it be that the young woman to whom I say, 'Please let down your pitcher that I may drink,' and she says, 'Drink, and I will also give your camels a drink'—let her be the one You have appointed for Your servant Isaac. And by this I will know that You have shown kindness to my master."
(**GENESIS 24:12–14**)

God was faithful and brought Eliezer His hand-chosen wife for Isaac. Eliezer encountered a *shidduch,* a match, for Isaac, and her name was Rebekah. Rebekah was Isaac's *basherte*—his destined one—and she was brought to Eliezer by God Himself. When God makes a match, you can be sure it is a good one!

And with God's help, Naomi put in play the plan to bring Ruth and Boaz together. However, the sovereign God of all creation already had a matchmaking plan of His own in place.

God gave Moses an order in Deuteronomy 2:9:

Then the LORD said to me, "Do not harass Moab, nor contend with them in battle."

Why would God say this about a country that had contended with Israel?

He did so because Ruth, the precious jewel, the Mother of Royalty, had not yet been fashioned, for Ruth only emerged in history during the period of the judges. She was born the daughter of the king of Moab. When her father, Eglon, died, another king was appointed over the region, and Ruth remained a charge in his house and in the field of Moab until Elimelech arrived there. Eventually, Elimelech's son, Mahlon, took Ruth for his wife, and Naomi, her mother-in-law, would lead her to Bethlehem.[7]

Bethlehem would eventually receive David, Ruth's grandson, and finally, the Messiah, for within the walls of Bethlehem a baby would be born who was God incarnate.

LIFE LESSONS

LIFE LESSON:
YOUR KINSMAN-REDEEMER WILL GIVE YOU REST

The *rest* our kinsman-Redeemer represents is the *rest* a sinner can only find in redemption. After God created the heavens and the earth, He rested. This is known as "creation rest." All was good, and nothing needed to be done to improve it.

Then man sinned and God broke His "creation rest." God began to put His redemption plan in motion to get man out of the pit of his transgressions. From that day in the garden until today, God has not rested; instead, He has walked with us through our difficulties, just as He assured Moses:

> *My Presence will go with you, and I will give you rest.*
> (**EXODUS 33:14**)

Jesus gave His disciples the same assurance:

> *My Father has been working until now, and I have been working.*
> (**JOHN 5:17**)

God will not rest until redemption is finished and sin is destroyed. Boaz is the only example in Scripture that fits the kinsman-redeemer aspect of redemption, which is essential for atonement.[8] God's people have longed for atonement:

Provide atonement, O LORD, for Your people Israel, whom You have redeemed. (**DEUTERONOMY 21:8**)

But not until One greater than Boaz came did God's people receive atonement:

In Him we have redemption through His blood, the forgiveness of sins, according to the riches of His grace. (**EPHESIANS 1:7**)

As our Boaz, Christ came down and redeemed us that we might have "redemption rest" from the penalty of our sins. He lives today within our hearts so that we may find rest in His power. Just as Boaz did, He has become restless for us until we cease from our own works and trust in Him.

There remains therefore a rest for the people of God. For he who has entered His rest has himself also ceased from his works as God did from His. (**HEBREWS 4:9–10**)

This type of rest comes when we no longer trust in our works for our redemption. This rest comes when we receive Christ's work of redemption on the cross as the penalty for our sins.[9] This rest comes when we trust in Him daily and commit our problems and difficulties to Him as He instructs us with His Word:

Blessed is the man whom You instruct, O LORD, and teach out of Your law, that You may give him rest from the days of adversity. (**PSALM 94:12–13**)

Why should you worry and fret about your problems when the Almighty God promises to walk beside you? Have you forgotten what Christ has done for you? Trust in Him and He will give you rest.

Jeremiah, the prophet, informed the Israelites of this dilemma. He said,

My people have been lost sheep. Their shepherds have led them astray; they have turned them away on the mountains. They have gone from mountain to hill; they have forgotten their resting place.
(JEREMIAH 50:6)

Jesus is our "resting place." He will provide a reprise from the struggles of life and the daily burdens we carry. As we abide in Him in love and faith, we will also discover in Him our "Resting Place."

Our Redeemer cries out to us and asks us to find rest in Him:

Come to Me, all you who labor and are heavy laden, and I will give you rest. (MATTHEW 11:28)

Chapter Fifteen

THE REDEEMER

Just as Naomi had predicted, Boaz promptly appeared at the city gate early the next morning on behalf of Ruth and herself in fulfillment of his oath to Ruth.

Boaz did not announce his presence to the elders of the city, so the ten men were surprised to see him. After exchanging pleasantries, Boaz took his place at the gate and waited. He looked to the heavens and spoke to God: *Lord, I have done all that is humanly possible; the rest is left to You.* No sooner had Boaz completed his prayer of faith and supplication, than Tov, the near kinsman to Elimelech, appeared at the city gate as if put in place by divine providence.

Boaz could not call him by his given name, which meant "good." Instead Boaz called out to him, *"Pelony Almony!"* Tov turned and acknowledged Boaz who was sitting with ten other elders near the gate. Trying to restrain from showing his displeasure toward the man who refused to do what was right for Naomi and Ruth, Boaz greeted him and asked him to sit down.

Boaz had a plan, and the Lord God of Israel helped him put his plan in motion. As if in a court of law that would decide the destiny of humanity, Boaz began his impassioned plea on behalf of the woman he loved.

THE BIBLE STUDY

Now Boaz went up to the gate and sat down there; and behold, the close relative of whom Boaz had spoken came by. So Boaz said,

"Come aside, friend, sit down here." So he came aside and sat down.

And he took ten men of the elders of the city, and said, "Sit down here." So they sat down.

Then he said to the close relative, "Naomi, who has come back from the country of Moab, sold the piece of land which belonged to our brother Elimelech. And I thought to inform you, saying, 'Buy it back in the presence of the inhabitants and the elders of my people. If you will redeem it, redeem it; but if you will not redeem it, then tell me, that I may know; for there is no one but you to redeem it, and I am next after you.'" And he said, "I will redeem it."

Then Boaz said, "On the day you buy the field from the hand of Naomi, you must also buy it from Ruth the Moabitess, the wife of the dead, to perpetuate the name of the dead through his inheritance."

And the close relative said, "I cannot redeem it for myself, lest I ruin my own inheritance. You redeem my right of redemption for yourself, for I cannot redeem it."

Now this was the custom in former times in Israel concerning redeeming and exchanging, to confirm anything: one man took off his sandal and gave it to the other, and this was a confirmation in Israel.

Therefore the close relative said to Boaz, "Buy it for yourself." So he took off his sandal. (RUTH 4:1–8)

Now Boaz went up to the gate. Boaz went to the gate himself; he did not send an emissary, for he did not want his words to be altered or misconstrued. Jewish sages believe he was holding fast to the belief, "One who performs a task himself hastens it toward its conclusion." It was also more meritorious to perform a redeeming task himself than to have an agent do it for him.[1]

And sat down there. Despite Boaz's eagerness to settle the matter, he was determined to give the other redeemer his fair chance to exercise his lawful right to redemption. Boaz did not go to the redeemer himself; instead, he went to the city gate and sat down. Boaz waited, as if to say, "I have done all I can. The rest is left to God."[2] The hidden power of God became even more visible.

It was then that God began to show off!

Behold, the close relative . . . came by. What a striking coincidence! The nearer kinsman simply came passing by at the very moment Boaz sat as an elder at the city gate. Sound impossible to you? This was not a coincidence, for Jewish scholars believe if the relative had been at the "opposite end of the world God would have caused him to fly, so to speak, to be there, in order to relieve the righteous Boaz of the anxiety of waiting."[3]

The Midrash commentary states when it came to the serendipitous order of events taking place, "Boaz played his part, Ruth played hers, Naomi played hers, whereupon the Holy One, blessed be He, said: 'I too, must play Mine.'"[4]

Scripture is orchestrating the order of events, for when Boaz said to Ruth, "In the morning it shall be" (RUTH 3:13), and indeed, the next morning, "Behold, the close relative . . . came by" (RUTH 4:1), it is believed Boaz's own confession of redemption caused divine providence to confirm it.[5]

Boaz confessed Ruth's redemption would come by morning. As a righteous man, he knew the Torah as it pertained to the Levirate marriage (DEUT. 25:5). He confessed God's Word and had faith it would come to pass. The language of the New Testament has within it the phrase *to confess.* Confession means "to say the same as." This means as believers we say the same with our mouths as God has said in His Word! We align our speech to agree with the Word of God. Our High Priest's authority and blessing are released over our words when we confess the Word of the living God.[6]

Boaz was more honorable than other men, therefore, God heard his prayers and answered them, just as Scripture described in this verse from Job.

> *Yes, the Almighty will be your gold and your precious silver. . . . You will make your prayer to Him, He will hear you, and you will pay your vows. You will also declare a thing, and it will be established for you; so light will shine on your ways.* (JOB 22:25, 27–28)

"Come aside, friend." The relative's name was Tov, as recorded in genealogical records. Yet Boaz did not call him by his name, which means "good" in Hebrew; commentaries say that the relative did not deserve to be called by his given name. Instead he was addressed in the Hebrew as *Pelony Almony,* which means "such a one" or "You there" or in common simpler terms "Mr. So and So." This less-than-dignified form of salutation implied the relative had insulted Naomi and Ruth by not coming forward sooner.[7] His name implied a faceless statistic. He could have made a difference; Tov could have mattered, but he chose not to.

Ten men . . . sat down. Boaz assembled ten men, a *minyan,* which is a quorum required to publicly discuss the *halacha,* the oral regulations of the law, which permitted a Moabite convert to marry a Jew. These same ten men would also serve as the official body, witnessing the marriage ceremony if indeed the union were to take place.

"Redeem it." . . . "I will redeem it." Boaz presented his case convincingly. The near kinsman heard the facts concerning Elimelech's land, which Naomi had sold in order to provide for herself and Ruth. Tov agreed to redeem the land to add to his own inheritance, but he was unaware of the additional condition concerning Ruth.[8]

"You must also buy it from Ruth." Boaz set the trap! When he heard the relative was willing to buy Naomi's field, Boaz informed Tov of the condition attached to the buyback: The near kinsman must also marry Ruth.

Boaz, great advocate that he was, began to explain to Tov and the elders that the near kinsman did not fulfill his full obligation when he agreed to buy back Naomi's field, for Naomi only owned three-fourths of the land.

When Ruth became a convert, she automatically inherited what belonged to her husband, Mahlon; therefore, one-fourth of the field belonged to her with the other fourth belonging to the estate of Chilion. Chilion was dead, and his widow, Orpha did not convert to Judaism but returned to Moab and could not marry into the chosen line; her inheritance was lost, and consequently, Chilion's portion of the estate defaulted to Naomi.

Boaz legally divided the estate and informed the relative that it was essential to redeem Ruth's portion of the estate when he redeemed Naomi's.

Moreover, Boaz continued to reveal that Ruth was not willing to sell her portion of the field unless the near kinsman married her. You can feel the tension at the gate! There was Boaz, a fine orator, pleading the case of the woman he loved and that of Naomi, his relative. There was the near kinsman, pale with shock over the proposition set before him. There were the elders, ready to witness the next step. And there was the crowd of townspeople who now gathered around the twelve men, curiously awaiting the outcome. Many of those in the crowd were Naomi's old friends. We can only imagine what was going through their minds.

Boaz continued with his final summation. He made it clear to Tov that the main purpose of this entire transaction was to perpetuate the name of the deceased; the acquisition of the field itself was secondary.[9]

With the facts presented, Boaz sat back and waited for the close relative to reply. By this time, all of Bethlehem was waiting for his decision.

"I cannot redeem it." The close relative gave several reasons why he could not go any further with the transaction. First, he did not want to take on a second wife who would destroy the harmony of his home. Second, he was concerned that if he took the young Moabite as his wife and had fathered children with her, he would contaminate his own line and compromise his own children's inheritance. The offspring he produced with Ruth would legally be considered Ruth's and Mahlon's, not his.[10] All of Tov's reasons to decline his right to Naomi and Ruth were risks. Tov could have chosen to try to redeem the women and risk failure, but instead, he failed to try.

Consequently, if Tov chose not to redeem Ruth, he must relinquish the right to redeem the field.

"You redeem my right." The closer relative knew the Levirate marriage would be an obstacle to his soul, for if he participated without the selfless purpose of perpetuating the name of the deceased, the Law, which was a commandment when done with good motive (*yibum*) might then be interpreted as the sin of incest.[11]

The close relative knew Boaz was a powerful and highly respected man whose noble character and actions would be upheld by future courts. Tov, on the other hand, was a common man. He believed his decision to marry a Moabite would be contested, and he and his descendants might run the risk of being cut off from Jewish society. Therefore, he made his choice to relinquish his position and asked Boaz to take his right of redemption.

Took off his sandal. Samuel, the author of this poignant story, takes time to inform us that the act of affirmation using the article of clothing was not of biblical origin but an ancient custom (RUTH 4:7), which attained the force of Torah law.[12]

The custom under discussion was that of the sale (redemption) or barter (exchange) of an item, where the seller removed his shoe and gave it to the buyer to symbolize the transfer of goods. Beyond its symbolism, the act had legal force: with it, the transaction in question took effect. "This was a confirmation in Israel"—the act witnesses observed and to which they testified in order to confirm the transaction was now legal and permanent.[13]

The near kinsman verbally and publicly gave up his right to redeem the land as well as Ruth by removing his shoe and giving it to Boaz. He said, "I cannot redeem it . . . Buy it for yourself." The transaction Boaz had hoped and prayed for was now sealed.

LIFE LESSONS

LIFE LESSON ONE:
OUR KINSMAN-REDEEMER IS RELATED

Boaz was the only kinsman-redeemer who chose to redeem Ruth and Naomi. He qualified because he was Elimelech's blood relation, and he was the kinsman-redeemer by exclusion since the presence of Ruth in the transaction excluded the other kinsman.

We have a Redeemer who is greater than Boaz, the Lord Jesus Christ of whom Job said:

> *For I know that my Redeemer lives, and He shall stand at last on the earth.* (**JOB 19:25**)

Because Boaz is the only kinsman-redeemer who is a type of Christ, our Kinsman-Redeemer, he occupied a position significant to Naomi and Ruth as Christ occupies a position significant to man. When the redemption of man engaged the attention of God, He sent His Son:

> *But when the fullness of the time had come, God sent forth His Son, born of a woman, born under the law, to redeem those who were under the law, that we might receive the adoption as sons.* (**GALATIANS 4:4–5**)

The answer to the question, "Why did God become a man?" is defined by one word—*redemption*. The Word was made flesh in order to pay the ransom for man's sin. Jesus, who is the Word, is also the:

- **Redeemer—"As for our Redeemer, the LORD of hosts is His name, the Holy One of Israel" (ISAIAH 47:4).**

- **Lamb of the world—"Behold! The Lamb of God, who takes away the sin of the world!" (JOHN 1:29).**

- **Ransom for all—"For there is one God and one Mediator between God and men, the Man Christ Jesus, who gave Himself a ransom for all" (1 TIMOTHY 2:5–6).**

When His creation sinned, God, the Father, did not distance Himself from the sinner; to the contrary, He came down as the portrait of sinful flesh to redeem the sinner. Christ became a man and inhabited the tent of human flesh, which was the initiation of the work of redemption. Man attempted to be like God in the Garden and failed; Christ sought to become like man and succeeded. He became related to us so that He might redeem us:[14]

> *The Spirit Himself bears witness with our spirit that we are children of God, and if children, then heirs—heirs of God and joint heirs with Christ, if indeed we suffer with Him, that we may also be glorified together.* (ROMANS 8:16–17)

By our faith in Christ, we become the adopted sons and daughters of God whom He loves as much as His own Son.

Two young brothers came to Sunday school for the first time. While registering for class, their teacher asked their ages and birthdays. One of the boys answered, "We are both seven. My birthday is April 8, 1998, and my brother's birthday is April 14, 1998."

"That's impossible!" answered the teacher.

"Oh, no, it's not!" the young boy said. "One of us is adopted!"

"Which one?" asked the teacher.

The two young brothers looked at each other and smiled. Then one of them proudly responded, "We don't know. We asked our daddy, and he told us he loved us both so much he just couldn't remember which one of us was adopted!"[15]

As fully adopted and fully redeemed children of God the Father, we share the same inheritance as His Son, Jesus Christ. In order to qualify as our kinsman-redeemer, He must be related. Our Redeemer is related—by blood.

The kinsman-redeemer must be related, and the kinsman-redeemer must be willing.

LIFE LESSON TWO:
OUR REDEEMER IS WILLING

One of the many noteworthy traits Boaz possessed was the impressive desire and willingness to redeem Ruth at any price. The Mosaic statute did not place a mandatory responsibility on the redeemer: he could, or could not, decide to redeem. The only constraint was the blood tie.

If love for the lost relative did not motivate a redeemer, no law could force him to redeem. The "other redeemer" was perfectly willing to redeem the land, but not the woman. While Ruth was the element of redemption that provoked the "other redeemer" to abstain from redeeming, Ruth was also the component that motivated Boaz into action.

Boaz loved Ruth from the first time he caught a glimpse of her in his field. As her true kinsman-redeemer, he chose to set his act of redemption in motion. Boaz was more than willing to become Ruth's liberator; he was eager to deliver her from her poverty and loneliness. His love for her motivated his actions.

We have a Redeemer who is greater than Boaz, a Redeemer who was willing and able to redeem humanity. Christ, our Kinsman-Redeemer, was not forced into His sacrificial position; He freely accepted the commission. Jesus told the Pharisees:

> *Therefore My Father loves Me, because I lay down My life that I may take it again. No one takes it from Me, but I lay it down of Myself. I have power to lay it down, and I have power to take it again. This command I have received from My Father.*
> (JOHN 10:17–18)

In order to successfully achieve redemption, Boaz needed to buy back the land that belonged to Naomi and Ruth, and he had to marry Ruth and provide for her and her household. For Christ to achieve redemption for us, He had to endure the Cross. He did not seek to avoid the Cross; He willingly gave Himself to it:

> *Looking unto Jesus, the author and finisher of our faith, who for the joy that was set before Him endured the cross, despising the shame, and has sat down at the right hand of the throne of God.*
> (HEBREWS 12:2)

Christ knew that His death would provide the payment of redemption for the sinner and liberate him from the penalties of his transgressions. Jesus told James and John, the sons of Zebedee:

> *Just as the Son of Man did not come to be served, but to serve, and to give His life a ransom for many.* (MATTHEW 20:28)

The prophet Isaiah depicted the death of Christ with great detail:

He was oppressed and He was afflicted, yet He opened not His mouth; He was led as a lamb to the slaughter, and as a sheep before its shearers is silent, so He opened not His mouth.
(ISAIAH 53:7)

The four Gospels affirm Isaiah's account of Christ's death (MATT. 27:13–14; MARK 15:3; Luke 23:8–9; JOHN 19:8–9).

Christ did not protest at His own trial. He did not try to escape the penalty, which His enemies sought to inflict upon Him. Our Kinsman-Redeemer faced His accusers, accepted their verdict, made no appeal for help, and bore the unjust punishment enforced upon Him. He indeed was the "Lamb of God that takes away the sin of the world" and was a willing sacrifice, as "a sheep before her shearers is silent."

Christ is our Kinsman-Redeemer, willingly paying the price of redemption. He deliberately drank the cup, eagerly endured the Cross, and joyfully accepted His Passion for the sake of those He loved.[16]

My Redeemer gave up His life because of His love for me.

During the Second World War, a young soldier asked his officer for permission to go out into the "No Man's Land" between the trenches of heated battle to bring in one of his friends who lay seriously wounded. "You can go," said the officer, "but it's not worth it. Your friend is probably dead, and you will throw your own life away."

Nevertheless, the young soldier willingly chose to go. Somehow, he managed to get to his friend, hoist him onto his shoulder, and bring him back to the trenches. The young man stumbled into the hole and fell beside his friend who lay at the trench bottom.

The officer ran to the aid of the two young soldiers and examined them both. He then looked tenderly on the rescuer and said, "I told you it wouldn't be worth it. Your friend is dead, and now you are mortally wounded."

Breathing his last, the fatally injured friend said, "It was worth it, sir."

"How do you mean, 'worth it'? I tell you, your friend is dead!" answered the confused officer.

"Yes, sir," the young man answered, "but it *was* worth it, because when I got to my friend, he was still alive, and he said to me, 'Jim, I knew you would come.'" And with that, the young soldier died.[17]

We have been wounded by our sin, yet we are still alive, and our Redeemer sacrificed His life to save us.

As the kinsman-redeemer, Boaz had to be related, he had to be willing, and he had to be able to redeem.

LIFE LESSON THREE:
OUR REDEEMER IS ABLE

Boaz was called a "mighty man of wealth." As a man of wealth, he could pay the price needed to redeem the land. As a man of valor, he possessed the morals to redeem Ruth. As a judge, he was prepared to meet both legal requirements.

The "other redeemer" possessed the advantage over Boaz in that he was a closer relative, but he lacked the willingness and ability to redeem both the land and Ruth.

The law of Deuteronomy kept Ruth out of the commonwealth of Israel, but Boaz used his ability to redeem her from the power of the law. She was seen as a stranger, outside of the privileges granted to God's people, but a "mighty man of wealth" paid the price and brought her into the nation, into his home, into his heart, and into her destiny.

We have a Redeemer who is greater than Boaz, and His name is Jesus Christ. Christ was known as Rabbi, who taught His followers (JOHN 3:2).

Christ was known as Master. The ten lepers testified to this in Luke 17:13. Christ is known as the King of kings and Lord of lords (REV. 19:16).

However, of all the many titles Christ possesses, the one most powerful is that of Redeemer, which enhances the meaning of all the other titles. Job used it: "For I know that my Redeemer lives" (JOB 19:25) and so did Isaiah: "The Redeemer will come to Zion" (ISAIAH 59:20). Yet nowhere in the New Testament is Christ given the title of Redeemer. However, He has a name that profoundly defines the title of Redeemer. That name is Jesus. The name in Hebrew is *Joshua,* which means "The salvation of Jehovah" or "Jehovah is a Savior."

Joseph, Christ's earthly father, received a prophecy from the angel that said:

> *And she will bring forth a Son, and you shall call his name JESUS, for He will save His people from their sins.* (MATTHEW 1:21)

Only through the name of Jesus Christ did the title of Redeemer find adequate fulfillment. The name of Jesus is reserved for the One who hung on the cross for the redemption of our sins. He is our Redeemer today because of his redemptive work, which was accomplished on the cross two thousand years ago. The Son of God took this name because He came to earth to redeem. The human name implied all that the term *Kinsman-Redeemer* implied.

Jesus is mightier than Boaz, because he is able to redeem lost sinners. He is able, because He was God embodied by human flesh, and He can do all that God can do. Jesus was the Omnipotent Redeemer, who brought to the work of redemption all the wisdom and power of God, His Father.

Two passages of Scripture manifest Jesus' ability to redeem lost sinners. The first is found in John:

> *And other sheep I have which are not of this fold; them also I must bring, and they will hear My voice; and there will be one flock and one shepherd. Therefore My Father loves Me, because I lay down My life that I may take it again. . . . My sheep hear My voice, and I know them, and they follow Me. And I give them eternal life, and they shall*

never perish; neither shall anyone snatch them out of My hand. My Father, who has given them to Me, is greater than all; and no one is able to snatch them out of My Father's hand. I and My Father are one. (JOHN 10:16–17, 27–30)

The second passage of Scripture reveals more of our Redeemer's ability to redeem:

Therefore He is also able to save to the uttermost those who come to God through Him, since He always lives to make intercession for them. (HEBREWS 7:25)

The apostle Paul tells us that Christ will go to the far end of the world to retrieve a sinner from destruction. We are lost, possessing no hope, and without God. God then lifts His mighty arm of redemption and begins to move on behalf of the sinner, and the blood of Christ, which was willingly shed on the cross, makes us one with Him. Hence the word *atonement,* which when broken down means "at-one-ment" with Christ.

When Jesus Christ, our Redeemer, our Boaz, first laid His eyes on us, we were covered with the stench of sin and were outside the covenants of Israel. As Gentiles, we were cut off from God and without hope. Our sin and alien status prevented us from entering into the presence of the Lord:

That at that time you were without Christ, being aliens from the commonwealth of Israel and strangers from the covenants of promise, having no hope and without God in the world. But now in Christ Jesus you who once were far off have been brought near by the blood of Christ. (EPHESIANS 2:12–13)

Moreover, like Ruth, there was the opportunity for "another kinsman" to redeem us. The Law becomes the "other redeemer" in this plan of salvation. The Law is a "closer relative" to humanity as Tov was a closer relative to Naomi than Boaz.

However, the two closer relatives could not redeem humanity or Ruth without endangering their own inheritance. The Law cannot redeem man unless it lowers its standards to conform to man's weak capability to maintain it. If the Law did compromise itself so man could live under its mandates, then it would no longer be the Law, but merely a system of concessions with low standards:

> *For as many as are of the works of the law are under the curse; for it is written, "Cursed is everyone who does not continue in all things which are written in the book of the law, to do them."*
>
> *But that no one is justified by the law in the sight of God is evident, for "the just shall live by faith." Yet the law is not of faith, but "the man who does them shall live by them."* (GALATIANS 3:10–12)

Salvation by works is a plan for redemption, but it is not God's plan of redemption because the Law cannot forgive sin:

> *Therefore by the deeds of the law no flesh will be justified in His sight, for by the law is the knowledge of sin.* (ROMANS 3:20)

Had Naomi and Ruth relied on the ability of the nearer kinsman to redeem them, they would have been lost forever, for he had no ability or desire to redeem. It was only in Boaz that they found their rest. Salvation by works is a feeble attempt to save a lost soul, and it is foolish to trust such a redeemer. Works cannot forgive man; only God, who promises never to leave or forsake us, even after all we have done, can forgive our transgressions:

> *For He Himself has said, "I will never leave you nor forsake you."* (HEBREWS 13:5)

Salvation by faith in Christ Jesus is the only redemption plan that is able to redeem:

> *Knowing that a man is not justified by the works of the law but by faith in Jesus Christ, even we have believed in Christ Jesus, that we might be justified by faith in Christ and not by the works of the law; for by the works of the law no flesh shall be justified.* (GALATIANS 2:16)

Faith in our Kinsman-Redeemer is the only plan of salvation which is effective, for we have a Redeemer who is able to save the last, the least, and the lost.[18]

During the Second World War, a man died in battle near a small village in France. His two friends wanted to give him a proper burial and managed to find a small Roman Catholic cemetery at the outskirts of the village. When the friends found the clerk in charge of the burial grounds, they told him their deceased friend was a Protestant and requested special permission to bury him in the cemetery.

The clerk refused their request, because it violated the law governing the church. However, the clerk, moved by the disappointment the two friends showed at the news of his refusal, allowed them to bury their comrade outside the fence of the cemetery. Grateful, the two men buried their beloved friend.

Several months later, the two men passed through the French village once again and decided to visit their friend's grave. They searched for the grave but could not find it. Confused, they finally went in search of the clerk who had given them permission to bury their friend outside the gate. They could not find the clerk; instead, they found the priest in charge of the parish. The two men explained their dilemma. The priest smiled and took them within the gates of the Catholic cemetery, where he showed them the grave of their Protestant friend. The men were puzzled; someone had moved the grave!

Continuing to display a smile of compassion, the priest explained that he was in his office several months prior when he overheard the two friends petition the clerk for permission to bury their dear brother within the gates of the cemetery. Knowing the clerk would not compromise the law of the church, he said nothing. Nevertheless, later that same evening, long after everyone was asleep, the priest, who had the power and ability, moved the fence of the cemetery to include the dead soldier.[19]

Our Redeemer is also able to move the "fence of the law" and redeem the undeserving.

According to Jewish law, the kinsman-redeemer had to be related, he had to be willing, he had to be able to redeem, and he had to be free to redeem.

LIFE LESSON FOUR:
OUR REDEEMER IS FREE

The kinsman-redeemer must be free from the curses that make redemption necessary for another. Boaz could not have acted in the capacity of a redeemer had he sold himself into slavery or had he been a Moabite.

Boaz was a "mighty man of the law." He observed the law and performed the proper sacrifices required of him. Therefore, no claim prevented him from being a redeemer. Boaz was of the chosen line. His redemption of Ruth would bring her into the genealogy of David, which linked David to the tribe of Judah. This same genealogy was Christ's, which gave Him the legal right to the throne of David. This genealogy was also Boaz's, and it afforded him everything that belonged to David and Christ:

Who are Israelites, to whom pertain the adoption, the glory, the covenants, the giving of the law, the service of God, and the promises; of whom are the fathers and from whom, according to the flesh, Christ came, who is over all, the eternally blessed God.
(ROMANS 9:4–5)

There could be no objection to Boaz as a redeemer for he belonged to the chosen line. He was also a rich man who did not owe another man anything and
never had to sell his property to another to repay any debt.

However, we have a Redeemer who is greater than Boaz, and he fully met
this requirement since He was free from the curse of sin. Jesus told His disciples:

> *I will no longer talk much with you, for the ruler of this world is
> coming, and he has nothing in Me.* (JOHN 14:30)

The law was not able to silence Jesus, for He did not break it; to the contrary,
He kept it in all its mandates. He made sure that the disciples understood this.
He said:

> *Do not think that I came to destroy the Law or the Prophets. I did
> not come to destroy but to fulfill.* (MATTHEW 5:17)

Christ was not a Gentile who never attempted to keep the law's instruction;
He was "made under the law" and kept Himself within its guidelines:

> *But when the fullness of the time had come, God sent forth His Son,
> born of a woman, born under the law, to redeem those who were
> under the law, that we might receive the adoption as sons.*
> (GALATIANS 4:4–5)

Christ was a sinless Savior. He was the impeccable Christ. He possessed no
inherent sin and, therefore, had no sinful nature:

> *For such a High Priest was fitting for us, who is holy, harmless, unde-
> filed, separate from sinners, and has become higher than the heavens;
> who does not need daily, as those high priests, to offer up sacrifices,*

first for His own sins and then for the people's, for this He did once for all when He offered up Himself. For the law appoints as high priests men who have weakness, but the word of the oath, which came after the law, appoints the Son who has been perfected forever. (**HEBREWS 7:26–28**)

Jesus Christ, our Redeemer, was free to redeem us because He was not implicated in man's sin. Christ owed sin nothing. We see the power of the "great exchange," for when He went to the cross, our sin became His, and He "was made sin" so we might become righteous:

For He made Him who knew no sin to be sin for us, that we might become the righteousness of God in Him. (**2 CORINTHIANS 5:21**)

Jesus Christ presented all the credentials of a kinsman-redeemer when He came to earth, just as Boaz presented all his credentials to the elders at the city gate. Like Boaz, He was a free man. Christ was not born under the slavery of sin. He was able to pay the penalty of sin because He was not subject to it.[20]

At the turn of the last century there was a one-room schoolhouse where pupils were kept in check through severe discipline. The noon recess ended, and the teacher interrogated the class about the disappearance of a little girl's lunch. After a few minutes of verbal threats and demands, a sob was heard in the back of the room. It was little Billy—a thin, frail, undernourished child whose family was the poorest of the poor.

"Did you take Mary's lunch?" demanded the teacher.

"Yes, sir," quivered Billy through his tears. "I was hungry."

Unmoved, the teacher declared legalistically, "Nevertheless, you did wrong to steal, and you must be punished!"

As the teacher removed the thick punishing strap from its place on the wall, he ordered Billy to the front of the room and told him to remove his shirt.

The teacher raised his arm, ready to inflict the reprimand over the bent and trembling body of little Billy.

Suddenly, a loud, husky voice shouted from the back of the room, "Hold it! Teacher!" Big Jim strode down the aisle, removing his shirt as he came. "Let me take his whipp'n," begged the giant of a young man.

The teacher was aghast, but believing that justice must be demonstrated, he consented to the strange request and thrashed his thick belt on Big Jim's back with such force that blood poured from the young man's flesh. As the stronger boy winced in racking pain and his eyes filled with tears, little Billy cried for the love he was witnessing. Billy never forgot the day that Big Jim took his place.[21]

My Redeemer was not paying a penalty for Himself. He died for my sin. He died for your sin.

The kinsman-redeemer had to be related, he had to be willing, he had to be able to redeem, he had to be free to redeem, and he had to have the legal tender for redemption.

LIFE LESSON FIVE:
OUR REDEEMER PAID THE PRICE

The kinsman-redeemer must have the price that is the acceptable amount agreed upon by the two parties to accomplish the deliverance.

There was no difficulty for Boaz, the rich kinsman, to redeem the small estate of Elimelech. He simply went into his coffers, secured Elimelech's land, and expressed his willingness to marry Ruth. However, we have a Redeemer who is greater than Boaz, and the price He paid for our redemption at Calvary was that of precious blood:

Knowing that you were not redeemed with corruptible things, like silver or gold, from your aimless conduct received by tradition from

*your fathers, but with the precious blood of Christ, as of a lamb with-
out blemish and without spot.* (1 PETER 1:18–19)

In order to better comprehend the legal tender Christ used to accomplish the redemption of man, we must first understand what happened the night of the first Passover, which also marked the time of Israel's redemption. The night of Israel's redemption was also the birthday of a nation.

God told the Jews to take an unblemished male lamb in its first year from each household and slay it. Moses then directed them to take the blood of this lamb and place it on, above, and over the doorposts of the home of every Jew. In a sense, each Jewish home was sealed in lamb's blood.

Then, as promised, on the fourteenth day of the month of Nisan (also called Abib, sometime in March or April),[22] God executed His final statement of power over all the gods of Egypt. As He passed through the land of Egypt, He struck all the firstborn of the Egyptian families, both man and beast, with death. However, when God saw the blood of the unblemished lamb on the doorposts of the homes of the Jews, He "passed over" them and spared the firstborn of that household. The sign of the Passover was blood. The acceptable, legal tender of redemption of the Jews on the first Passover night was the blood of spotless lambs.

Why does blood have such great prominence in the act of redemption? Because blood represents life:

*For the life of the flesh is in the blood, and I have given it to you upon
the altar to make atonement for your souls; for it is the blood that
makes atonement for the soul.* (LEVITICUS 17:11)

The shedding of the blood of animals sets forth a sacrificing of life in substitution for the one making the sacrifice. Why should it be necessary for man to have a substitute to shed blood for him?

Humanity stood in disobedience to the will of God, stood in rebellion to

His authority, stood in treason to the government of God, and stood in ingratitude to the love of God. Humanity sinned against God:

> *For all have sinned and fall short of the glory of God, being justified freely by His grace through the redemption that is in Christ Jesus.* (ROMANS 3:23–24)

If God is the Moral Ruler of the universe, there must be a penalty for this sin.

> *Behold, all souls are Mine; the soul of the father as well as the soul of the son is Mine; the soul who sins shall die.* (EZEKIEL 18:4)

If every man is a sinner and every soul that sins shall die, then all humanity must experience physical death.

> *And as it is appointed for men to die once, but after this the judgment . . .* (HEBREWS 9:27)

But what of spiritual death, which is the eternal separation from God?

The only hope for the sinner to avoid spiritual death and have eternal life in Christ is for someone to pay the penalty for the sinner, which is satisfactory to God. Now we must agree on the legal acceptable tender. It is reasonable to assume that the death of animals could not atone for the sinner:

> *For it is not possible that the blood of bulls and goats could take away sins.* (HEBREWS 10:4)

If not animal sacrifice, then we must conclude that a man must be willing to pay with his blood the price of redemption for the penalty of man's sin. Now we must find someone who is satisfactory to God.

We have already stated that the redeemer must be related by blood, but if he has the blood of Adam in him, he is corrupt. He too would need a redeemer. In his own strength, man is hopelessly lost, for no man can provide the incorruptible legal tender that is acceptable to God.

This is where God steps into the picture of redemption with the price that is the only acceptable, legal tender of heaven. God personally issued the currency that redeemed man:

Therefore, when He came into the world, He said: "Sacrifice and offering You did not desire, but a body You have prepared for Me. In burnt offerings and sacrifices for sin You had no pleasure. Then I said, 'Behold, I have come—in the volume of the book it is written of Me—to do Your will, O God.' . . . He takes away the first that He may establish the second. By that will we have been sanctified through the offering of the body of Jesus Christ once for all. (HEBREWS 10:5–10)

The blood of bulls and goats could not redeem man—for it was tainted. The blood of man could not redeem man—for it was tainted. It required the blood of *the unique God-Man* to redeem mankind.

The only legal tender that was the acceptable price for redemption was the blood of Jesus Christ, God incarnate, our Redeemer. We measure the value of any currency by what it can purchase. An old saying expresses this: "I am not interested in money, only what money can buy."

The legal tender of heaven, the precious blood of Jesus Christ, has bought eternal life for the sinner through the redemption of sin. Literally millions of martyrs have died for the faith, but only one Redeemer lives, who has died for the sinner and paid the penalty for sin with His blood.[23]

A renowned Bible scholar had a dream in which he stood on the day of judgment before God himself—and Satan was there to accuse him. Satan opened his books full of accusations, pointing to transgression after transgression of which this man was guilty. As the proceedings went on and on, the man's heart sank in despair.

Then he remembered the cross of Christ—and turning upon Satan, he said, "There is one entry in your book which you have not made, Satan."

The devil retorted, "What is that?"

"It is this—the blood of Jesus Christ, His Son, cleanses us all from sin!" And with that the devil walked away.[24]

Once the blood of Christ has been entered against your sin, there is no balance due, for the price has been paid in full.

What can wash away my sin? Nothing but the blood of Jesus![25]

Chapter Sixteen

THE COVENANT

Boaz dreamed of the meeting at the city gate for months, and now he held the fruit of it in his hand: Tov's shoe. One of the Torah foundations was to clarify the facts precisely so there would be no room for confusion. He had presented his case to the elders and the witnesses with great detail to make certain he was the sole owner of all Elimelech's property.

With the land transaction behind him, Boaz now concentrated on the real reason he was at the city gate: to acquire Ruth as his wife. He presented his motives passionately before the elders: "I know many of you may find fault in me for taking such a young and beautiful woman as my wife, for I am much older than she. I want to vow before you and these witnesses that my motives are pure. I have come this day to fulfill a *mitzvah* of the Torah and perpetuate the name of the deceased."

All those present knew Boaz's heart was chaste, so his sincere intent was met with the joint approval of the elders and the witnesses. Boaz smiled as he summoned Ruth to his side. Taking her hand in his, they took their place under the marriage canopy. There they solemnly proclaimed their vows, and the seven blessings of marriage were spoken over them by the witnesses and the ten elders.

The people were so moved by the union of this righteous redeemer to the beautiful Gentile convert that they spoke additional blessings over them.[1]

"We are witnesses before God and all future generations that this deed is as virtuous as those involving Jacob and Rachel. We bless you with the same blessings. May you and your wife continue to build the house of Israel and may royalty come out of the tribe of Judah through your sacred union."

Ruth stood by her new husband in amazement of *Hashem* and His goodness. First, she was born a Moabite, a stranger from the covenants of promise, without hope and without God. Next, providence brought her into the chosen people on the road of repentance where she accepted the God of Abraham, Isaac, and Jacob and Naomi as her own—she became a Jew.

Then, it "happened" that she had been brought to Boaz's field and put under the wings of the God of Israel. Later she found herself on the threshing floor where she asserted her claim for redemption. Now she stood before the city gates in front of the elders and the witnesses as the bride of her redeemer. Ruth wept tears of joy, for *Hashem* had truly been good to her.

THE BIBLE STUDY

And Boaz said to the elders and all the people, "You are witnesses this day that I have bought all that was Elimelech's, and all that was Chilion's and Mahlon's, from the hand of Naomi. Moreover, Ruth the Moabitess, the widow of Mahlon, I have acquired as my wife, to perpetuate the name of the dead through his inheritance, that the name of the dead may not be cut off from among his brethren and from his position at the gate. You are witnesses this day."

And all the people who were at the gate, and the elders, said, "We are witnesses. The Lord make the woman who is coming to your house like Rachel and Leah, the two who built the house of Israel; and may you prosper in Ephrathah and be famous in Bethlehem. May your house be like the house of Perez, whom Tamar bore to Judah, because of the offspring which the Lord will give you from this young woman." (RUTH 4:9–12)

"You are witnesses." This phrase is repeated twice, once in verse nine and once in verse ten. Jewish scholars believe that Boaz summoned two sets of witnesses, one for the land transaction and one for the marriage covenant. In doing so Boaz took every possible precaution to ensure the legality of the proceedings. His detailed accuracy would also rebut any question that would later arise regarding the validity of David's genealogy.[2]

Chilion and Mahlon. Their names are recorded in reverse order from the other places they were mentioned. In this verse Chilion and Mahlon are listed in the order of their death and the succession of their inheritance. Scholars believe Boaz mentioned Chilion's property first to stress that his property had also been redeemed; therefore, no descendant of his widow, Orpah, would ever be able to dispute Boaz's absolute ownership of Elimelech's estate.[3]

"Ruth . . . my wife." Boaz mentioned Ruth separately because a Jewish wife is a respected and beloved partner in the sacred commandment of building a Jewish home. Therefore, Boaz mentioned his marriage covenant separately to make it clear to the witnesses that he does not associate Ruth and his land acquisition in the same transaction.[4]

"Ruth the Moabitess." Boaz stressed that Ruth was a Moabitess to make sure the witnesses understood that the Oral Law permitted female Moabite converts to enter into the household of Israel.

Boaz also emphasized Ruth as "the Moabite," which means "of the father," a tribute to Abraham, the father of a multitude of nations (GEN. 17:5). It was Lot, Abraham's nephew, and Lot's daughters who conceived the seed of the nation of Moab, and that same seed would eventually conceive King David.

Abraham had been distressed by the revelation in the "Covenant of the Parts," which stated that his descendants would suffer exile and enslavement (GEN. 15:13). God then promised that just as He would scatter them so He would gather them, and just as He would enslave them so He would redeem them:

> *Therefore say, "Thus says the Lord God: 'I will gather you from the peoples, assemble you from the countries where you have been scattered, and I will give you the land of Israel.'"* (EZEKIEL 11:17)

Ruth was the fruit of this promise to Abraham: from her, the house of David would arise, culminating in the Redeemer, our Messiah.[5]

"Widow of Mahlon." Ruth was still considered Mahlon's wife, because it was believed that her husband's spirit lived within her. Boaz forgave Mahlon's sin against Israel when he married Ruth, therefore exonerating Ruth as well.[6]

"We are witnesses." Verses eleven and twelve hold within them a series of spontaneous blessings that were offered in unison by all present. The elders and the witnesses observed the proceedings and blessed Boaz in three ways:

First, the blessing over the woman: "The LORD make the woman who is coming to your house like Rachel and Leah, the two who built the house of Israel" (RUTH 4:11). The blessing emphasized that despite the fact that Ruth came from foreign stock and upbringing, by virtue of coming to a righteous man such as Boaz, she would become like Rachel and Leah—also foreigners, daughters of Laban, the Aramean—who married Jacob and built the house of Israel. The blessing stated that Ruth would merit righteous descendants, just as these foreign women gave birth to the Twelve Tribes of Israel.

Second, the blessing over Boaz: "May you prosper in Ephrathah and be famous in Bethlehem" (v. 11). This blessing was spoken over Boaz's family name and the future glory of his family, which would bring praise to Bethlehem.

Third, the blessing over Boaz's house: "May your house be like the house of Perez, whom Tamar bore to Judah" (v.12). Just as the home of Perez, the son of Tamar, was ascribed to Judah. so may Boaz's house be honored and distinguished through the offspring that *Hashem* would give Boaz through this young woman.[7]

"Be famous in Bethlehem." This blessing extended to Ruth. "May she no longer be known as Ruth of Moab, but Ruth of Bethlehem."[8]

"Like Rachel and Leah." Ruth is compared to these two women because they too came from non-righteous parents. Ruth, like Rachel and Leah, left her parents to cleave to the God of a righteous husband.

The elders also called forth a blessing over the future descendants of the union of Ruth and Boaz. Rachel had been barren and was later granted conception; Ruth had also been barren during her ten-year marriage to Mahlon. How miraculous that she should conceive at the age of forty by a husband of eighty![9]

"Like the house of Perez." The elders and the witnesses wanted to share in the *mitzvah,* the good deed Boaz had performed in marrying Ruth. They did so by bestowing their blessing upon Boaz and his future household, and therefore, blessing the royal posterity of the Messiah.

As the blessings were uttered over Boaz and Ruth, it was as if the spirit of holiness was hovering over the marriage covenant that was taking place in Bethlehem. Ruth had entered the community of Israel from the field of Moab, and she was set as a precious pearl in the Crown of Israel. One day she would be called "the Mother of Royalty."

Jewish scholars believe that while the fathers of our faith were distracted with life—the tribal ancestors were engaged in selling Joseph; Joseph and Jacob were troubled with sackcloth and ashes; and Judah was preoccupied with finding a wife—the Holy One, blessed be He, was engaged in creating the light of the Messiah. All of these events led to the birth of our Redeemer, even though they seem unrelated.[10]

If Jewish scholars asked me why Boaz married Ruth, I would answer, "For one simple reason: so my Redeemer could enter the world and take me from an existence of sin and shame to everlasting life!" If these same men asked why the light of the Messiah came, I would answer, "So that Jesus Christ the Light of the world, my Messiah, would lead me from darkness and into His light."

Then Jesus spoke to them again, saying, "I am the light of the world. He who follows Me shall not walk in darkness, but have the light of life." (JOHN 8:12)

LIFE LESSONS

LIFE LESSON ONE:
A THREE-FOLD CORD WILL NOT EASILY BE BROKEN

God first appeared on the scene of human history as a *shadkhan,* a matchmaker:

Then the rib which the LORD God had taken from man He made into a woman, and He brought her to the man. (GENESIS 2:22)

In the theater of my mind, I see the great Creator, the Master Architect of the world and mankind, bringing Eve to Adam on His arm and placing both of them under His wedding canopy made of the lush green leaves of the trees He had formed with His hands. What a scene!

Moses, who is merely the human recorder of the Book of Genesis, would never have begun the first book of the Bible with such an amazing act of intimacy—the intimacy between God and man and then between man and woman. No, this account was supernaturally inspired.[11]

We must note that God is not a spectator in the covenant of marriage. He initiates the concept of marriage, and He concludes it. When Jesus came to earth, He mirrored God's passion and support for marriage; so much so, that He performed his first miracle at a wedding. What prompted Jesus to carry out His first miracle at such a setting?

He wanted the wedding to be a success. If the wedding celebration ran out of wine, the bride and groom would suffer humiliation, and the wedding would not have been a festive celebration but a greatly disappointing embarrassment to all present. Instead, Christ chose to create the finest wine out of water. Jesus kept His miracle from the guests in order to keep the attention on the bride and the groom, as it should be.

Jesus brought controversy to His earthly ministry, in part because of His stand on marriage. The Law allowed men to divorce women for any reason. Yet Christ stood on God's Word:

> *Have you not read that He who made them at the beginning made them male and female, and said, "For this reason a man shall leave his father and mother and be joined to his wife, and the two shall become one flesh"? So then, they are no longer two but one flesh. Therefore what God has joined together, let not man separate.* (MATTHEW 19:4–6)

Jesus Christ upheld the plan of marriage that God, His Father, had established in the Garden:

> *Then the rib which the LORD God had taken from man He made into a woman, and He brought her to the man.*
>
> *And Adam said: "This is now bone of my bones and flesh of my flesh; she shall be called Woman, because she was taken out of Man." Therefore a man shall leave his father and mother and be joined to his wife, and they shall become one flesh.* (GENESIS 2:22–24)

Jesus wanted to ensure that the concept of marriage, which was divinely ordained by the Father, was still the only standard in place. This concept of marriage in the Genesis account reveals four important truths:

First, marriage originated with God; marriage was His idea. Second, God knew exactly what kind of mate Adam would need, which is why and how He formed Eve. Third, Adam did not have to go in search of Eve; God presented her to him. Fourth, God determined how Adam and Eve would relate to one another: in perfect unity.[12]

God does not change, and neither does His Word, therefore these four truths are still in place today. As a result, when a Christian enters into marriage it should not be because it is his or her decision, but because it is God's. Christians should trust God to choose their perfect mate—their *basherte* or destined one; the one who was meant to be.

Christians who walk in the will of God have faith that God will bring the "destined one" that He has chosen into their lives—they don't have to go in search of their marriage partner. Finally, Christians must know that the purpose of marriage is still what God ordained it to be for Adam and Eve: perfect unity.[13]

The decline or restoration of any culture is accompanied by the decline or restoration of its perception of marriage. God warned the Jews about this through His prophet Jeremiah:

> *Moreover I will take from them the voice of mirth and the voice of gladness, the voice of the bridegroom and the voice of the bride, the sound of the millstones and the light of the lamp. And this whole land shall be a desolation.* (JEREMIAH 25:10–11)

A culture that no longer cherishes the covenant of marriage is either doomed or on its way to doom.[14] Yet, Jeremiah also prophesies that the generation that honors the sanctity and restoration of marriage will be restored:

Thus says the LORD: "Again there shall be heard in this place—of which you say, 'It is desolate, without man and without beast'—in the cities of Judah, in the streets of Jerusalem that are desolate, without man and without inhabitant and without beast, the voice of joy and the voice of gladness, the voice of the bridegroom and the voice of the bride, the voice of those who will say:

*   'Praise the LORD of hosts,*

*   For the LORD is good,*

*   For His mercy endures forever'—*

and those who will bring the sacrifice of praise into the house of the LORD. For I will cause the captives of the land to return as at the first," says the LORD.

(JEREMIAH 33:10–11)

By the standards of Scripture, the restoration of a people is incomplete unless accompanied by the "voices of the bride and bridegroom."[15]

Yet, we must have more than regulations to accompany a beautiful union, for without the grace of God there can be an equally harmful affect on the sacrament of marriage. The Word of God also includes romance and passion as an integral part of marriage. We witness this truth throughout the Song of Songs. A marriage that lacks passion ends in frustration, and one that lacks romance is merely lust of the flesh.[16]

God ordained marriage to have as its foundation the love of one man for one woman, the love of one woman for one man, and the love of both man and woman for God. This kind of love has the strength of a threefold cord:

And a threefold cord is not quickly broken. (ECCLESIASTES 4:12)

The Hebrew word for love is *ahavah,* which comes from the root word *hav* (to give). The meaning of the word implies that to love is to give. In the study of

Hebrew *gematria* (numerology), each letter in the Hebrew alphabet has a numerical value. The value of the word *ahavah* is thirteen, and the word *echod*, which means "one," is also thirteen. Therefore, from this correlation, we learn that true love means to give and to feel oneness and unity with your spouse and with God.[17]

God, the Great Matchmaker, esteems marriage so much that He not only opens human history with a marriage, He also brings human history as we know it to a pinnacle with a marriage:

> *"Let us be glad and rejoice and give Him glory, for the marriage of the Lamb has come, and His wife has made herself ready." And to her it was granted to be arrayed in fine linen, clean and bright, for the fine linen is the righteous acts of the saints. Then he said to me, "Write: 'Blessed are those who are called to the marriage supper of the Lamb!'"* (REVELATION 19:7–9)

Just as almighty God, the Creator and Ruler of the universe, presided over the first marriage of Adam and Eve, He too will preside over the marriage of His Son and His redeemed—the church.

Just as the bride prepares for her groom, so must the church prepare for the coming Messiah. We must adorn ourselves with the garments of our righteous deeds, which are the fruit of being justified by faith in our Redeemer. Without this preparation, we will have a very lonely existence, and no anticipation for the future rest and security that can only be found in unity with our Redeemer. We must make space in our hearts for the presence of our Redeemer, for He is the living manifestation of Hashem, the Name above every other name. We, the bride of the Redeemer, will then be part of the threefold cord with the Groom and the ultimate Matchmaker.

LIFE LESSON TWO:
GOD CALLS US TO PURITY IN MARRIAGE

The book of Ruth sanctifies the home and emphasizes the importance of vows of loyalty. Throughout the Bible, God makes it clear that we are to stay pure in the marriage covenant.

Boaz knew that Ruth had stayed pure in the days she spent in his fields, and he promised to be her kinsman-redeemer. He said, "for all the people of my town know that you are a virtuous woman" (RUTH 3:11).

God calls all of us to purity in marriage. Paul tells the early Christians, "Marriage is honorable among all, and the bed undefiled; but fornicators and adulterers God will judge" (HEBREWS 13:4).

Naomi instructed Ruth to "wash herself" in order to cleanse herself from the impurities of her past. What safeguards have you put in place to protect the sanctity of your marriage? Do you make sure that you are not alone in a private place with a man who is not your husband? Do you refrain from a close relationship with another man? Are you careful to avoid a flirtatious spirit? When Eve merely spoke to the serpent, she was being disloyal to Adam, her husband, and to God, her Creator.

As our Redeemer is faithful to us, then we must emulate our Redeemer and be loyal to our spouse. In doing so, we will remain loyal to His Word:

> *Therefore know that the LORD your God, He is God, the faithful God who keeps covenant and mercy for a thousand generations with those who love Him and keep His commandments.* (DEUTERONOMY 7:9)

God promises that if we are pure in our marriages, we will have peace in our homes. The writer of Psalms says:

Great peace have those who love Your law, and nothing causes them to stumble. (PSALM 119:165)

Once we become a part of the sacred marriage covenant, our homes should become sanctuaries where the love of our Lord Jesus Christ can be felt the moment our husbands and families walk through the door. They should feel safe and secure; they should feel the harmony and protection of their Kinsman-Redeemer. They should feel the presence and anointing of the Holy Spirit. Even the stranger who walks into our homes should feel peace within its portals. This is a great responsibility and also a great opportunity to share the gift of salvation that God has so freely given us.

Chapter Seventeen

THE RESTORATION

*I*t was a beautiful morning. The sun shone brilliantly as if to announce more than the dawn of a new day—also the beginning of a new hope. Naomi prepared to receive her guests this morning. She busied herself with their arrival, making sure that her honey cakes were ready to present to the women who had bid her good-bye more than twelve years before.

Naomi was a bit apprehensive. The same women who wept when she left had also resented her return to Judah with the Gentile from Moab. Yet today would be different; today they were coming to bless her—and bless Ruth of Bethlehem and Obed, Naomi's grandson. Today they would console her for the death of Boaz and maybe—just maybe—even forgive her for leaving Bethlehem.

For a moment Naomi rested in a chair and looked out the large window of the beautiful home she shared with Ruth, her grandson, and many, many servants. Boaz had been good to them; before his passing, he had taken care of the future needs of his new family.

As Naomi anticipated the arrival of her guests, she began to remember. She remembered the day she left her beloved Bethlehem. She remembered the death of her cherished husband and sons in the spiritual wasteland of Moab. She remembered how the Spirit of the living God had compelled her to return to the land she loved so much. She remembered the look in Ruth's eyes when she received the God of Abraham, Isaac, and Jacob as her own. Oh, how vividly clear she remembered that precious moment!

Tears flowed from her eyes as she remembered her shameful walk back into the city—what a difficult day that had been. She remembered the pangs of hunger and the desolation she had felt once back in her deserted home.

Then hope miraculously rekindled within her when Ruth returned from the gleaning fields with more than enough food for both of them. What a good recollection that was! Naomi remembered that very special day with fondness, for that was the day she knew the hand of God was still upon her.

She smiled as she recalled the wedding that was even more beautiful than her own: the wedding of Ruth and Boaz. Oh, what a day that was! It was a day of love and celebration. The people of Bethlehem rejoiced with blessings on their lips for the union of the righteous kinsman-redeemer and his beautiful Gentile convert. Naomi laughed aloud as if sharing a secret with the Lord, for she had partnered with Him in bringing the two together.

Suddenly, she was stirred out of her daydream by the cry of her precious grandchild. She walked over to Obed's cradle, took him in her arms, and held him close to her bosom. Naomi felt the spirit of motherhood quicken within her. This nurturing spirit had not died when her precious sons died. It is a spirit no mother can quench. As she looked upon the face of this beautiful gift, she praised her God for His goodness. All the pain of the last twelve years was erased from her memory as she observed his innocent countenance. Only hope remained in her heart for the future this child would bring.

Naomi began to sing a song of thanksgiving unto God. "Blessed be Your Name from this time forth and forevermore! From the rising of the sun to the setting of the same, I will praise Your name continually! Lord, You have raised me out of the dust and ash. You have replaced what the locust has eaten, and You have placed me with royalty. You have granted the barren woman the home of a joyful woman of children, blessed by Your Holy Name!"

Her song calmed Obed, who was lying in her arms. As Naomi stared at her grandson's sweet and peaceful expression, she could almost see the face of Mahlon—her beloved son.

THE BIBLE STUDY

So Boaz took Ruth and she became his wife; and when he went in to her, the LORD gave her conception, and she bore a son. Then the women said to Naomi, "Blessed be the LORD, who has not left you this day without a close relative; and may his name be famous in Israel! And may he be to you a restorer of life and a nourisher of your old age; for your daughter-in-law, who loves you, who is better to you than seven sons, has borne him."

Then Naomi took the child and laid him on her bosom, and became a nurse to him. (RUTH 4:13–16)

Boaz took Ruth. Ruth became Boaz's wife. The two stood under the marriage canopy or *chupah,* which was designed by God and symbolized the couple's new home, open to the community in which they will now be included and will want to include into their new lives together. The *chupah* can be no more than a talit or prayer shawl that is supported by four poles. The Jewish marriage ceremony consists of *kiddushin,* a contracting bond of consecration, symbolized by the giving of a ring, for example, and the nesuin, the seven blessings which are recited by the witnesses present at the wedding.

The LORD gave her conception. Neither Boaz nor Ruth had offspring from their previous marriages. Yet together, with the divine intervention of *Hashem,* they established a dynasty that will last as long as mankind.

Since the marriage was to fulfill God's will and was consummated out of the purest motives, the Scripture does not say, "she conceived and bore a son." Instead, the words are, "the Lord gave her conception." Boaz was old, and Ruth was barren from a ten-year marriage, so they needed divine assistance and *Hashem* provided that assistance.[1]

The Book of Ruth does not mention the name of Boaz again. Jewish historians and religious scholars believe that Boaz died on the night of his wedding, and therefore, Boaz performed his *mitzvah,* his good deed, in accordance to God's timetable. Had he waited one day to redeem Ruth, the root of the house of David and the Messiah would not have come into being. Scripture asserts the importance of acting at the proper time:

> **To everything there is a season, a time for every purpose under heaven: A time to be born, and a time to die.** (ECCLESIASTES 3:1–2)

Those who defer doing a *mitzvah,* a good deed, by saying, "There is yet time," do not fulfill the Torah. Had Boaz delayed in redeeming Ruth even one day, he would have died without an heir.[2]

And she bore a son. These words are another verification that Boaz was dead at the time of his son's birth, for had he been alive, the Scripture would read, "she bore a son unto him."[3]

Boaz was an honorable man, recognized for accomplishing many great deeds, such as aiding the end of the famine in Judah through his prayers of intercession to Jehovah, leading Israel as a righteous judge, and conquering Israel's enemies. But his greatest achievement was planting the seed of the house of David. Once Ruth conceived, the sages believe that Boaz's soul had completed its mission, and Boaz died, for Divine Providence directs the destiny of every human being.[4]

Like Boaz, no mention of Ruth's name is made after verse thirteen; however, Jewish sages believe that Ruth lived to see her great-great-grandson, Solomon, take the throne of Israel after the death of his father, David. Therefore, it is concluded that her mission—marrying Boaz and giving birth to a son who would lead to the royal throne of the Messiah—was also accomplished.[5]

"Who has not left you this day without a close relative." The women are bestowing blessings on Naomi, Ruth, and Obed. They are saying to Naomi,

"The child that Ruth birthed will redeem you in your old age since he carries the soul of your son Mahlon." In other words, if this baby had not been born to Ruth, then Naomi would be destitute now and in her old age.[6]

"May his name be famous in Israel." The women prayed that the newborn child would become a great man like his father, Boaz, whose name would constantly be on the lips of the people of Israel. The people would heed his counsel and judgment as they did his father's, and they would name their children after him, for he would be known as a *tzaddik,* a righteous one.[7]

In Hebrew this final blessing over the child referred to the word *king* to suggest that just as Boaz had redeemed Ruth, so their descendant would redeem Israel.

Moreover, just as "this day" the sun rules the sky, so would Ruth's seed rule Israel forever.

Generations later, the queen mother Athaliah destroyed all the royal seed, except one child—Joash—who escaped to continue the royal dynasty (2 KINGS 11). To this day Jewish sages declare that it was the women's blessing—"Who has not left you this day without a close relative"—that saved David's seed from annihilation.[8]

"A restorer of life and a nourisher of your old age." Blessings continued to flow from the women's hearts. They prayed that the child born to Ruth would bring joy to Naomi's heart and restore her spirit. They prayed that Obed would care for Naomi when she became old and be the one to bury her when she died. Furthermore, if Naomi educated him to walk in righteousness to God, her soul would find reward in eternity:[9]

> ***As one whom his mother comforts, so I will comfort you; and you shall be comforted in Jerusalem.*** (ISAIAH 66:13)

Even more, the Hebrew word for restorer literally translates "soul restorer," which alludes to the resurrection of the dead that will take place during the reign of David's descendant, the Redeemer of all redeemers—the Messiah![10] Yes, we have good news—we will all one day be restored:

> *The Lord Himself will descend from heaven with a shout, with the voice of an archangel, and with the trumpet of God. And the dead in Christ will rise first. Then we who are alive and remain shall be caught up together with them in the clouds to meet the Lord in the air. And thus we shall always be with the Lord. Therefore comfort one another with these words.* **(1 THESSALONIANS 4:16–18)**

"Who is better than seven sons." It was well known by all of Bethlehem that Ruth loved Naomi with a love that few could equal. The women were emphasizing this point by telling Naomi that Ruth's love was better than the love of seven sons, and the child she bore would love her as her daughter-in-law loved her.[11]

In addition, the women were noting that the child would be righteous, because he was the product of seven generations of righteous men, or *tzaddikim*, who preceded him: Perez, Hezron, Amminadab, Ram, Nahshon, Salmon, and Boaz. The seventh in line is known as "saintly," but the eighth even more so . . . "who is better than seven sons."[12]

Became a nurse to him. Unlike other noblewomen of means, who gave their children over to a nursemaid, Ruth gave her baby to Naomi to nurse, guide, and care for. Ruth trusted Naomi and knew she would show this baby the ways of *Hashem*. And Naomi did so: She taught her grandson what she had taught her children and her daughters-in-law—to walk in righteousness and to serve God.[13]

Naomi had the privilege of nurturing her grandson physically, emotionally, and spiritually. God had restored everything the enemy had taken from her.

LIFE LESSONS

LIFE LESSON:
OUR REDEEMER WILL RESTORE EVERYTHING
THE ENEMY HAS TAKEN, AND MORE

Many of you reading this book have lost much in your lifetime. Some of you may have lost a parent or a husband, maybe even a child. Others of you have lost your marriages to divorce, either because of infidelity or due to neglect. Still others of you have lost your home and most of your possessions because of financial reversal. You may have lost your health and are battling disease. Some of your children have been overcome by the demons of drugs and alcohol. You are overwhelmed and caught in despair; you have simply lost your hope and are drowning in a sea of depression. Whatever your problem, there is an answer for you in the Word of God.

The Holy Scripture makes God's promise of restoration very clear. He reiterates this promise throughout the Old Testament:

So I will restore to you the years that the swarming locust has eaten. (JOEL 2:25)

Return to the stronghold, you prisoners of hope. Even today I declare that I will restore double to you. (ZECHARIAH 9:12)

As you claim God's promise of restoration, remember three spiritual truths: First, once you have been redeemed, you no longer have to pay the penalty of your sin. Jesus is speaking directly to you with these words:

Most assuredly, I say to you, he who hears My word and believes in Him who sent Me has everlasting life, and shall not come into judgment. (JOHN 5:24)

Unfortunately, many of us keep paying a self-imposed penalty for our sin even after we have repented and our sins have been forgiven and forgotten. We have been held captive long enough. We must begin a new season in our lives—a season of fresh beginnings and hope.

We must learn to proclaim the Word of God over our lives in order to find strength and direction for a new day.

In the Latin the word *proclaim* means "to shout forth." It is a strong word. To proclaim God's Word is to confess what He promises in an aggressive manner—in a confident manner. When we proclaim God's Word, we release the authority of His powerful Word into any situation in our lives.[14]

> *For as the rain comes down, and the snow from heaven, and do not return there, but water the earth, and make it bring forth and bud, that it may give seed to the sower and bread to the eater, so shall My word be that goes forth from My mouth; it shall not return to Me void, but it shall accomplish what I please, and it shall prosper in the thing for which I sent it.* (ISAIAH 55:10–11)

The time to proclaim God's Word over your life is now! Pray the proclamation below, which is taken directly from God's Word, to help you find direction and a renewed hope for your life.

PROCLAMATION OF FREEDOM
FROM THE PENALTY OF SIN

My God has redeemed me from the hand of the enemy. I have been cleansed and sanctified by the blood of my Redeemer. I owe the enemy nothing, for God has forgiven me and Jesus Christ has paid full price for the penalty of my sin. The enemy has no power over me, for Christ died for me and makes intercession on my behalf. (Taken from PSALM 107:2; 1 JOHN 1:7; HEBREWS 13:12; ROMANS 3:23–25; *and* ROMANS 8:34.)

The second spiritual truth is: Once you have been redeemed, you have been delivered from the power of sin. Satan no longer has claim to you. Hear Jesus speaking directly to you:

Behold, I give you the authority to trample on serpents and scorpions, and over all the power of the enemy, and nothing shall by any means hurt you. (LUKE 10:19)

The apostle John also reassured Christians of their power over sin. I'm sure he also claimed this deliverance from sin's power for himself:

But if we walk in the light as He is in the light, we have fellowship with one another, and the blood of Jesus Christ His Son cleanses us from all sin. (1 JOHN 1:7)

Our Redeemer is not a slave trader in the marketplace of sin, and we are no longer slaves to worldly desires either. We cannot be sold to the world again, for we have been bought with a price so great, no one else can equal it. Because of this great sacrifice we must learn to walk in the fruits of the Spirit and not walk in the works of the flesh, for there is no middle ground for the believer.[15]

Claim this position for yourself or for someone you love as you declare the proclamation below:

PROCLAMATION OF DELIVERANCE FROM SIN

I am delivered from my transgressions. I am washed, sanctified, and justified in the Name of the Lord Jesus and by the Spirit of God who dwells in me. I have been redeemed out of the hand of the devil by the blood of the Lamb, and by the word of my testimony. The Lord will always deliver me from evil work and preserve me for His purposes.

I will not walk in the flesh, but in the Spirit, because the Spirit of God dwells in me! (*Taken from* **PSALM 39:8; 1 CORINTHIANS 6:11; EPHESIANS 1:7; REVELATION 12:11; 2 TIMOTHY 4:18;** *and* **ROMANS 8:9**)

Finally, the third spiritual truth is: Once you have been redeemed, sin has no power over you. Sin is the provoking of God's justice, the violation of His mercy, the abuse of His grace, the mockery of His patience, the ridicule of His power, and the condescension of His love. We cannot exist in God and exist in sin—it is impossible—we must be redeemed from the presence of sin. Again listen to the Word of the Lord:

> *Therefore if the Son makes you free, you shall be free indeed.*
> (**JOHN 8:36**)

Now assert this freedom, just as Paul did:

> *For the law of the Spirit of life in Christ Jesus has made me free from the law of sin and death.* (**ROMANS 8:2**)

McGee defines *redemption* as the "Proclamation of Emancipation" for sinners, which is written in the blood of Christ.[16] Not only have we been bought and delivered by the blood of the spotless Lamb, we have been transformed! We have been moved from the position of "slave to sin" and placed as an heir and joint heir in God's kingdom. Take a moment now to proclaim your freedom or the freedom of someone you love:

PROCLAMATION OF FREEDOM
FROM THE PRESENCE OF SIN

Whatever I do in word or deed, I will do in the name of Jesus, my Lord. Through the sacrifice of Jesus on the cross, I have been set free from the curse and have entered into the blessing of Abraham.

I am a child of God. I shall be like Him, and I will purify myself just as He is pure, because I have this hope. God is love, and as I abide in love, I abide in Him and God abides in Me. My spirit bears witness to the Spirit of God, and I am an heir and joint heir with Christ! (Taken from COLOSSIANS 3:17; GALATIANS 3:13–14; GENESIS 24:1; 1 JOHN 3:2–3; 1 JOHN 4:16; *and* ROMANS 8:16–17.)

Once you have been redeemed, you must go beyond the cross and go to the empty tomb of the Redeemer. The cross represents our sin and His suffering—the empty tomb represents our promise of everlasting life and His victory over death, hell, and the grave!

You have a purpose in Christ, and He has a purpose for you. Naomi accomplished her purpose: She showed unconditional love for Ruth in her sinful state and patiently introduced her to *Hashem* and His laws. Naomi's love gave Ruth a desire to follow her to her birthplace: the land of Judah. Because of the pure outpouring of love Naomi showed Ruth, God restored everything the enemy had taken from her.

Just as with Naomi, God will restore in your life what you have lost to sin and its penalties. You must praise your Redeemer for all He has done and is doing and will do, just as David did:

> *You have turned for me my mourning into dancing; you have put off my sackcloth and clothed me with gladness, to the end that my glory may sing praise to You and not be silent. O LORD, my God, I will give thanks to You forever.* (PSALM 30:11–12)

Take the advice of Pastor James, who encouraged his church:

> *My brethren, count it all joy when you fall into various trials, knowing that the testing of your faith produces patience. But let patience have its perfect work, that you may be perfect and complete, lacking nothing.* (JAMES 1:2–4)

The Lord promises that you will be "lacking nothing"! Stand and dance for joy! Our Redeemer cannot lie. All He has promised you will come to you when you have faith in His Word and in His power to do what His Word says He will do. His Word will accomplish marvelous works in your life! You must only believe, and as Naomi, you will accomplish your divine purpose.

Ruth accomplished her purpose. Her solemn desire to know the God of Naomi caused her to denounce her idols and walk into the promises of Abraham. Ruth's destiny did not begin when she married Mahlon. It did not begin when he died, and it did not even begin when she married Boaz. No, Ruth's destiny was determined before time was recorded; it began before creation was accomplished, for her destiny was ordained by the God who ordains all our destinies. They all began in His heart before time was born.

But Ruth had to choose to be submissive and obedient and allow God to create a rest and security for her future as well as produce within her part of the Scarlet Thread that would bring forth not only her own destiny but the divine destiny of an entire nation.

Boaz accomplished his purpose. Because of his love for God and His Righteousness, God was able to use him as Ruth's redeemer. He loved Ruth with a purity that few men possessed for a woman, and God rewarded him. His willingness to obey God's mandate and accomplish His will enabled the God of all creation to give Boaz an heir who would produce the royal throne of the Messiah.

What is your purpose? You are redeemed. You have been bought with a precious price. You have been made new, free from sin and shame. Everything the thief has taken from you will be restored, and you have a destiny in Christ, your Redeemer! Rejoice in your redemption and know God knows you intimately—He knows your strengths and your weaknesses—He knows your potential, and He has a divine purpose for your life.

God is not merely an observer—your judge, who is constantly keeping track of all your indiscretions to determine whether you merit heaven or hell as a just reward. He is the Higher Power in your life who has designed your destiny. God knows every fiber of your being and every thought and desire you possess. As God does His part you must do yours, which is to let Him lead you in the paths He has chosen for you.

Someone described their relationship with God as similar to a ride on a tandem bicycle. They were in the front seat directing their course, and God was in the back helping pedal the bicycle.

From time to time, I have imagined this journey. I tried my very best to find my own way, depending on God to pedal from behind, hoping He would support all the choices I was making along life's path. I can almost remember the day I finally exchanged places with Him and let Him take the lead. Life has been so much better for me since I let that exchange take place.

Since I let Him take the lead in our journey, it has been all I can do to hang on! He knew delightful trails, up steep, narrow mountain roads and through deep, winding, rocky valleys—trails I would never have chosen on my own. He navigates these paths with incredible skill and at breakneck speed, I might add. Even though it seemed uncertain at times, I could hear His voice encourage me along our path: "Keep pedaling, don't stop, Diana—just trust Me, I know the way!"

Many times through our journey together, I have asked Him, "Where are you taking me? I think You may have made a mistake. Are You sure this is the way You want me to travel? There aren't many people on this road, You know. They are all going the other direction! I think you should have turned right, instead of left! Are You listening to me? Are You even paying *attention*?"

Somehow I can see His smile as He looks back at me. Then I trust Him even more, for not to trust Him is more frightening than the journey.

There were days when my eyes were so filled with tears I couldn't see the road—I was so relieved He was navigating then. I remember yet another time when I got so scared I thought I would have to jump off the bicycle. He leaned back, took my hand, and squeezed it until He felt certain I was secure in Him once more. Then off we went again!

At first, I didn't trust Him to take control of my life. I guess somehow I thought He didn't care about me—maybe because I believed I wasn't good enough or pretty enough or special enough. I felt He was too busy, or even look-ing the other way, and somehow would wreck the bicycle and take me with it. But I was wrong.

He knows all the bicycle secrets—He knows how to take sharp turns around corners that suddenly creep up on our journey. He dodges big boulders on life's highway and even masters "slippery when wet" conditions. Somehow these hindrances don't seem to bother Him at all. He knows how to pedal through the dark, scary passages, just slowly enough so I won't fall off but will overcome these dips in the road with sufficient hope and confidence to con-front the next obstacle in our path. I finally believed He loved me enough to stay with me, no matter how difficult the course.

I have learned to stay quiet and listen as I sit behind Him and pedal through life. He has taken me to wonderful places—beautiful places, strange places, lonely places, scary places, and divine places—but never to a place He has not gone before. I so take pleasure in the journey now that I have let Him lead. I worry less. I have confidence in Him, and I am secure about my future, for fear does not control my direction anymore. I can feel the cool breeze on my face, and I am actually enjoying the view.

Even now there are times I feel I can't do any more or go any further. Then my constant Companion and Guide simply leans back and lovingly whispers, "I know you can do more, and I know you can go further, Diana. I have confidence in you; I know what I have put in you. I know your destiny. Keep pedaling!"[17]

Remember, God is too wise to make a mistake and too loving to be unkind. He knew the paths you would travel long before you began your journey. He knows everything about you; He knows your limitations and your potentials. I suggest that you read through Psalm 139 and imagine yourself on God's tandem bicycle—with Him in the lead. He is looking back at you, hoping you will trust Him for the rest of your journey together.

> *O Lord, You have searched me and known me,*
> *You know my sitting down and my rising up;*
> *You understand my thought afar off.*
> *You comprehend my path and my lying down,*
> *And are acquainted with all my ways.*
> *For there is not a word on my tongue,*
> *But behold, O Lord, You know it altogether.*
> *You have hedged me behind and before,*
> *And laid Your hand upon me.*
> *Such knowledge is too wonderful for me;*
> *It is high, I cannot attain it.*
> *Where can I go from Your Spirit?*
> *Or where can I flee from Your presence?*
> *If I ascend into heaven, You are there;*
> *If I make my bed in hell, behold, You are there.*
> *If I take the wings of the morning,*
> *And dwell in the uttermost parts of the sea,*

Even there Your hand shall lead me.
And Your right hand shall hold me.
If I say, "Surely the darkness shall fall on me,"
Even the night shall be light about me;
Indeed, the darkness shall not hide from You,
But the night shines as the day;
The darkness and the light are both alike to You.
For You formed my inward parts;
You covered me in my mother's womb.
I will praise You, for I am fearfully and wonderfully made;
Marvelous are Your works,
And that my soul knows very well.
My frame was not hidden from You,
When I was made in secret,
And skillfully wrought in the lowest parts of the earth.
Your eyes saw my substance, being yet unformed.
And in Your book they all were written,
The days fashioned for me,
When as yet there were none of them.
How precious also are Your thoughts to me, O God!
How great is the sum of them!
If I should count them, they would be more in number than the sand;
When I am awake, I am still with You . . .
Search me, O God, and know my heart;
Try me, and know my anxieties;
And see if there is any wicked way in me,
And lead me in the way everlasting.

(PSALM 139:1–18, 23, 24)

Chapter Eighteen

THE LOVE STORY

aomi waved good-bye to her friends, and as was her custom, she sent them all away with the last of her honey cakes. She closed the door and admired the fine home she was in. She felt the linen robe she was wearing, the colors so bright and vivid—they were the colors of the spirit that leaped within her.

Naomi was so happy. Her friends had bestowed blessing after blessing upon her daughter-in-law Ruth and her grandson Obed—and they had blessed Naomi as well. Many of them had come to her through the course of the morning and asked her forgiveness for being judgmental and distant. Their visit was much more than Naomi could have hoped or imagined.

She felt complete for the first time in years. Naomi raised her hands and began to praise *Hashem* for the blessings and prophecies the women had spoken over her and her grandson.

"Oh Lord, what wonderful works You have done! You have shown Your infinite mercy to me and restored all I lost when I sinned against You and Your people by leaving Your promised land. I exalt You, for You were with me in my time of trouble, and now You rejoice with me in my time of plenty.

"Oh Lord, You are very great, and You are clothed with honor and majesty. My grandson will live according to his name—he will be a servant of God! Blessed is Your name, Jehovah God, for you are good! I shout praises unto You, O Lord, for the children of Your covenant live and their descendants will be established before You forever more! Blessed be Your mighty name!"

Naomi spent most of her time praising the Lord these days; this was a practice she cherished. She walked over to her grandson as he lay sleeping, smiled, and softly called out the name her friends had given him. "Obed, what a fitting name you have. Servant of God . . . Yes, a wonderful name it is."

Many questions arose within her as she looked into his face: *What will you look like, my little Obed? Who will be your wife? What descendants will come from you? Could it be, my little angel . . . could it be as my friends have prophesied . . . that one day the Redeemer of mankind will come from you? Could you be the forefather of our much-awaited Messiah?*

Obed continued to sleep, oblivious to what his loving grandmother was thinking. It would be years before anyone realized that the love story that began in the gleaning fields of Bethlehem would lead to the birth of a baby in a lonely manger—shaping the destiny of the world.

THE BIBLE STUDY

Also the neighbor women gave him a name, saying, "There is a son born to Naomi." And they called his name Obed. He is the father of Jesse, the father of David.

Now this is the genealogy of Perez:
Perez begot Hezron;
Hezron begot Ram, and Ram begot Amminadab;
Amminadab begot Nahshon, and Nahshon begot Salmon;
Salmon begot Boaz, and Boaz begot Obed;
Obed begot Jesse, and Jesse begot David.
(RUTH 4:17–22)

"Son born to Naomi." Naomi's friends could see God's hand in her restoration. He had brought many miracles to Naomi's life, including raising the child that

was born to Ruth and Boaz. It was as if the baby were Naomi's. Even though Ruth bore him, Naomi raised him.[1]

Called his name Obed. The name *Obed* meant "one who serves God with a full heart." The line of David is traced directly to Obed, the son of Ruth, the Moabitess. A manmade story would have linked David's lineage to an aristocratic Israelite mother, but divine prophecy linked David to a Gentile convert, for the voice of prophecy speaks without fear of man.[2]

Now this is the genealogy of Perez. Perez was the son of a relationship between Judah and his daughter-in-law, Tamar. To avoid embarrassment over this incident, the name of Judah is avoided in the text and the genealogy begins with his son, Perez.[3]

Hezron. His name is mentioned in Genesis 46:12.[4]

Ram. Ram was the second son born to Hezron (1 CHRON. 2:9). However, the Midrash records that the first son, Jerahmeel, married a Canaanite woman, and therefore was considered unworthy to be an ancestor of the house of David.[5]

Amminadab. One of the greatest personalities of the tribe of Judah. During Israel's slavery in Egypt, his daughter became the wife of Aaron (the Kohen, and the high priest of Israel) (EXODUS 6:23).[6]

Nahshon. He was the leader of the tribe of Judah.[7]

Salmon. He was the brother of Elimelech and Tov and the father of Boaz.[8]

Boaz begot Obed. As stated earlier there are eighty-five verses in the Book of Ruth. The number eighty-five corresponds to the numerical value of the name of Boaz. Oh how our mighty God orchestrates every detail of creation! Obed was known as the man who served the Master of the Universe with a perfect heart fulfilling God's essential demand of a king.[9] Could it be because of what his beloved grandmother, Naomi, planted in his soul?

Jewish scholars believe the Book of Ruth is written for Israel, which circumcises its infants at the age of eight days. For the Jews circumcision begins in Genesis 17 when the Lord speaks to Abraham and instructs him to circumcise himself and the male members of his household as "My covenant between Me and you and your descendants after you." According to Jewish tradition, Obed was born circumcised, symbolizing the fact that he was born obedient and part of the covenant.[10]

Jesse begot David. The sages record, "So said the Holy One blessed be He to David: 'What need have I to record the genealogy of Perez, Hezron, Ram, Amminadab, Nahshon, Salmon, Boaz, Obed, and Jesse? Only on account of you; I have found my servant David.'"[11]

THE FOUR GENTILE WOMEN

The story of the chosen line is one of the themes of Scripture. The line, which leads from Adam to Christ, is the line that is followed in the Word of God. It is known as the "chosen line," and Israel is the elect nation.[12]

> ***For you are a holy people to the Lord your God, and the Lord has chosen you to be a people for Himself, a special treasure above all the peoples who are on the face of the earth.*** (DEUTERONOMY 14:2)

The Old Testament lists the generations of the chosen family. The majority of the generations are listed in Genesis, with the offspring of the chosen line recorded and the rejected line omitted. For example, Abraham had other children besides Isaac, but only Isaac is followed in Scripture. Isaac had another son besides Jacob, but only Jacob's line is listed.[13]

The Book of Ruth provides a link between the tribe of Judah and David and consequently to Jesus Christ, our Redeemer. Because of this significant connection, this beautiful book becomes one of the most vital manuscripts in Scripture.

Of the fourteen generations that are listed in the Old Testament, eleven are in the Book of Genesis, the generations of Aaron and Moses are recorded in Numbers 3, and the last generation is listed in the Book of Ruth.

Two genealogical tables are given in the New Testament that link Jesus to King David—one in Matthew, the other in Luke. We will briefly follow the link between the Book of Ruth and the genealogical account in Matthew:

The book of the genealogy of Jesus Christ, the Son of David, the Son of Abraham . . . (MATTHEW 1:1)

Please trust me. I know the "begets" are usually something most of us ignore when reading Scripture. They seem to have a tranquilizing effect—they put us to sleep. Yet there is something very inspiring about the accounts we are about to review.

Earlier in our journey I said that the Gospel of Matthew had four additions to the genealogy mentioned in the Book of Ruth. These inclusions are the names of four women. Yet these are not merely women; they are Gentile women.

The question arises: why are these four Gentiles, who were outside the covenant, included in the genealogy of Christ when women were never included in biblical genealogy? The incidents surrounding these exceptional women help us answer this very important question.

The Bible is not a boring book; we find within its pages adultery, murder, deception, love, mercy, grace, and redemption. For example, in Genesis 38, we encounter the first incident, the story of illicit fornication, involving the first Gentile woman of the chosen family tree in the Gospel of Matthew. She was a Canaanite, and her name was Tamar.

Tamar used unorthodox means to ensure the succession of her descendants. She was doubly widowed by two of Judah's sons. Judah, Tamar's father-in-law, promised her his third son in order to continue the lineage but never fulfilled his word.

After waiting for years to marry and have a descendant, Tamar took matters into her own hands. She disguised herself as a prostitute and waited for Judah on his journey to Timnah. Tamar bargained a fee with Judah for her services, and her father-in-law agreed to her conditions and had intercourse with her. Consequently, Tamar conceived and gave birth to twin sons.

Because of the sin she committed with her father-in-law Judah, Tamar was included into the royal line of the Messiah. From their union came Perez, a direct ancestor of David. The first Gentile woman was included into the Scarlet Thread leading to the Messiah because of sin.[14]

The second woman was Rahab, the mother of Boaz. Rahab's account can be found in Joshua 2. She was also a Canaanite and a prostitute. She was one of the many Canaanites who showed support for the Israelites who left Egypt and traveled in the wilderness to the Promised Land.

Rahab faithfully believed in the supernatural power of the God of the Israelites. She hid the spies and bargained with Joshua's messengers for the safety of her family. Rahab's courageous deeds and great faith are also recorded in the letter to the Hebrews (11:31), and in the Book of James (2:25). The second Gentile woman in the genealogy of Christ entered into the Covenant by faith.[15]

The third woman was Bathsheba, the wife of Joab's armor bearer. Her story is told in 2 Samuel 11–12, and 1 Kings 1–2. David set eyes on this beautiful woman while she bathed on her balcony, and he desired her. So David sent for Bathsheba, took her, and sent her home without mention of love or affection—instead this king was driven by power, lust, and self-gratification. Bathsheba became pregnant with David's son and, to hide his sin, David premeditatedly killed Bathsheba's husband, Uriah, by sending him to the front lines of battle and certain death.

The Lord was greatly displeased with David's actions, so God exposed David's sin through Nathan, the prophet. When confronted, David admitted his sin; he repented before God and begged His forgiveness. David did not want anything to separate his soul from the God he loved.

The transgression was David's, yet both Bathsheba and David suffered sin's harvest—the death of their firstborn son. But because of the covenant love God had for David, and His acknowledgment of Bathsheba's innocence, He gave them a second son—Solomon. Solomon was beloved of the Lord, and he became the king of Israel after David's death and entered into the line of the Scarlet Thread.

Our Redeemer was a direct descendant of King David. This entitled Jesus to the right of dominion over David's land—*Eretz Israel.* While Christ was on earth, there was no other claimant to the throne of David, and Bathsheba was part of that lineage. The third Gentile woman walked into the genealogy of Christ on the road called repentance.

The fourth Gentile woman in the genealogy of Christ was Ruth. By this point in our journey, we all know and love Ruth. Two of the four women were great sinners and the third participated in great sin, but not Ruth. She was a rose among the thorns. She had no flaws—only love, devotion, and faithfulness.

She was a Moabitess, and the law kept her out of Israel. She needed a redeemer, and Boaz was the willing redeemer. Boaz extended grace to Ruth as he put his robe of righteousness over her and allowed her to walk the path to the promises of Abraham, Isaac, and Jacob. Ruth entered the genealogy of Christ through the amazing grace of God.[16]

Indeed, we are all sinners in need of repentance, and we all come short of the glory of God. We receive salvation through faith, and by grace, we are redeemed:

Being justified freely by His grace through the redemption that is in Christ Jesus. (ROMANS 3:24)

THE LOVE STORY OF GRACE

Grace is the gift of God that can be easily misinterpreted and often abused. Grace is not a voyage into the world of dreams. Grace is not magic that transforms life to our desires. Grace is not a cure-all for disease or a formula for perfection. Grace is not even euphoria for romance or a miracle pill for success. Grace is certainly not a free ticket to sin. Grace does not make everything right.

Instead, grace is the courage to live every day while everything around us is falling apart. Grace is the power that redeems us from our sin and sets us on the right path. Grace inspires us to believe. Grace affords us the strength to hope for tomorrow, even when we have failed today. Grace is our freedom from condemnation. Grace is the eyes through which God sees us:

> *But by the grace of God I am what I am, and His grace toward me was not in vain; but I labored more abundantly than they all, yet not I, but the grace of God which was with me.* (1 CORINTHIANS 15:10)

Grace is the unmerited favor of God.

THE LOVE STORY OF REDEMPTION

I divided the Book of Ruth into eighteen sections, which are the number of scenes I encountered when reading this beautiful manuscript. The number eighteen in Hebrew *gemetria,* corresponds to the word *life.* Life in Hebrew is *chai,* made of two letters; the first is *chet,* which is equal to the number 8, and the second is *yud,* which is equal to the number 10. Together, these letters equal 18, which stands for life.

This book is about love and life—the love and life of a family, the love and life of a Moabite convert and a righteous judge. This book is also about eternal life, which can only be obtained through redemption—redemption that can only be accomplished through love:

> *But when the kindness and the love of God our Savior toward man appeared, not by works of righteousness which we have done, but according to His mercy He saved us, through the washing of regeneration and renewing of the Holy Spirit, whom He poured out on us abundantly through Jesus Christ our Savior, that having been justified by His grace we should become heirs according to the hope of eternal life.* (TITUS 3:4–7)

The Book of Ruth is a love story about redemption. Redemption is defined as love—the kind of love that inspired our Kinsman-Redeemer to pay the price of His own precious blood for the release of His beloved bride's scourge of sin. This same love brings the bride into the house of the Redeemer, and this same love brings His bride (you and me) into His heart—now and forevermore:

> *He has sent redemption to His people; He has commanded His covenant forever: holy and awesome is His name.*
> (PSALM 111:9)

God's Word no longer intimidates me—I embrace it—I welcome it into my life. I am enriched by its message and continually changed by its power. Because of my relationship with the Word and its Author, I have become aware of the incomparable value of my inheritance.

I am determined to pass on this priceless gift to my children and my grandchildren. For if I were to gain the fame of the world and become richer than the richest, I could leave no greater legacy to my children than the love I have for my Redeemer, for He is the promise of my eternal inheritance.

THE INHERITANCE

Something happened as I took my journey through the Book of Ruth: I fell in love with Naomi. Maybe it is because of the season of my life. I am blessed to be a daughter, a daughter-in-law, a mother, a grandmother, and a mother-in-law. Through my study, I realized the importance of Naomi's place in the redemption of Ruth, in the life of her grandson, Obed, and most importantly in the Scarlet Thread that leads to our Messiah.

I want to be like Naomi—forgiven, restored, and loved. I want to do what Naomi did: love my children, my daughters-in-law, my grandchildren, and any spiritual children the Father puts in my path with a love that will direct them forevermore to the One I love the most—my Redeemer.

One day a young mother set her foot on the path of life. "Is the way long?" she asked.

And God said, "Yes. Your journey will be long and beautiful and rewarding, but your way will be hard at times. And you will be old before you reach the end of it. Yet the end will be better than the beginning, and I promise to walk this way with you."

The young mother was happy, and she could not believe that anything would be better than the beginning, for nothing could be better than the years when her babies were young and so willingly dependent upon her.

So she played with her children in the brightness of day. She trained them in the way they should go. She laughed with them in times of joy and dried their tears when they tripped and fell along the path of life. She gathered flowers with them and let her children bathe in the clear streams along the way; and the sun shone on them and their days were good. And the young mother cried, "Nothing will ever be better than this."

Then night came, and storms arrived. The path was gloomy, and the children shook with fear and cold. The mother drew them close and covered them with her mantle as an eagle covers her eaglets with her wings. And the children said, "Oh, Mother, we are not afraid, for you are near, and no harm can come to us." And the mother said, "This is better than the brightness of day, for through the storms of life I am teaching my children confidence and courage and trust."

And the morning came, and there was a steep hill ahead, and the children climbed and grew weary. Even though the mother was weary as well, she encouraged her children all through their journey. "A little patience and fortitude," she said. "Don't despair for we are almost to the hill's pinnacle."

So the children continued to climb, and when they reached the top, they said, "We could not have done it without you, Mother, for we put our steps right where you put yours."

And the mother lay down that night and looked up at the stars in the heavens and said, "Lord, this is a better day than the last, for my children have learned fortitude in the face of challenge. Yesterday, I gave them courage. Today, I have shown them strength, endurance, and patience."

The next day strange clouds appeared: clouds of war and hate and evil, clouds of suffering and despair, which darkened the earth. The children fumbled in the darkness and faltered in their faith, and the mother said, "Look up. Lift your eyes to the Light and look to your Redeemer." And the children looked above the clouds and saw the Everlasting Glory, the Light of the world, and He guided them and brought them beyond the darkness into the radiance of His presence.

That night the mother said, "This is the best day of all, for today I have shown my children God."

And the days went on, and the weeks and the months and the years, and the mother grew old, and she became frail and bent. But her children were tall and strong and walked with courage, faith, patience, trust, and hope.

When the way was hard, they remembered all their mother had breathed into them, and they helped their mother. When the way was too difficult for her to travel, they lifted her, for she was light and never a burden. Because the mother had put mercy in them, mercy she received. Then she came to the end of her journey, and her children escorted her to a shining road and a golden gate that flung wide open.

The mother said, "I have reached the end of my journey. And just as my God promised, the end is better than the beginning, for my children can walk without me and their children after them, for I have taught them to put their hand in the hand of their Redeemer. I know they will never walk alone after I am gone."

And the children said, "You will always walk with us, Mother, even after you have gone through the gates, for you have shown us God." And they stood and watched her as she willingly went on without them. The gates closed after her, for this day the mother planted the last seed in their lives—this day she taught her children how to die. Just as God makes the dying leaves beautiful on the trees of fall, so does God make a mother more beautiful than ever when her wrinkled hand takes the hand of her Creator and walks into eternity with Him.

And her children said, "We cannot see her, but she is with us still. A mother like ours is more than a memory—her name is like the company of God on the lips of her children. She is a living presence."[17]

We are a constant presence in the lives of our children, whether they are our natural children or our spiritual children. The greatest gift Naomi gave Ruth was not unconditional love and acceptance, even though they were precious gifts. No, the greatest gift of all was her love for her Redeemer. What we put into our children in the way of hope and faith through this same Redeemer is like an eternal wellspring of living water. They will draw from these waters long after we are gone from their presence.

A young girl saw her aged grandmother planting a small apple tree in the garden and asked, "You don't expect to eat apples from this tree, do you Grandma?" The old woman rested on her knees and said, "No, my darling, I don't, but all my life I have enjoyed apples—never from trees I have planted—always from those planted before me. I plant this tree for you and your children, and one day you will taste of its fruit long after I am gone."[18]

Our children will enjoy the spiritual fruit we plant within them long after we are gone. We must all strive, with the help of God, to show our children strength, courage, grace, and mercy. One day they will see the face of God in our eyes; they will feel His tenderness in our touch and will long for His redemption because of His presence in us!

THE SCARLET THREAD OF REDEMPTION

I love the Book of Ruth. I love the people in this book, and I love the purpose of this book, but I love my Redeemer more. He is my Beloved in whom my soul is well pleased, and as His bride, I must prepare for His coming. My cares and trials become insignificant when my expectancy turns toward His return and the blessing I will have with Him in eternity.

God, the Father, gave His most treasured possession to prove His love for me. So willing a bridegroom was Jesus Christ, His Son, that He gave up His life so that His Word might sanctify me, His bride, with the washing of water by the Word. He wove me into the Scarlet Thread with His precious blood and adopted me into His chosen line. God, the Father, did His part. Jesus Christ, His Son, did His. Now it is my turn to do mine:

> *In Him you also trusted, after you heard the word of truth, the gospel of your salvation; in whom also, having believed, you were sealed with the Holy Spirit of promise, who is the guarantee of our inheritance until the redemption of the purchased possession, to the praise of His glory.* (EPHESIANS 1:13–14)

The Book of Ruth is a priceless portrait of redemption.

Every brush stroke details the nail-pierced hands of Christ

lovingly wrapped around me while I was yet a sinner, grafting

me into the blessings and benefits of Abraham. Because of this

self-sacrificing love, I will be with my Bridegroom in eternity,

celebrating everlasting life in a kingdom that will never end—

and this, my friends, is where the love story truly begins.

THE SCARLET THREAD OF REDEMPTION

JUDAH — TAMAR
(Gentile woman grafted in by sin)
|
PEREZ
|
HEZRON
|
RAM
|
AMMINADAB
|
―――――――――
| |
ELISHEBA   NAHSHON
|
SALMON — RAHAB
(Gentile woman grafted in by faith)
|
BOAZ — RUTH
(Gentile woman grafted in by grace)
|
OBED
|
JESSE
|
DAVID — BATHSHEBA
(Gentile woman grafted in by repentance)
|

So all the generations from Abraham to David are fourteen generations, from David until the captivity in Babylon are fourteen generations, and from the captivity in Babylon until the Christ are fourteen generations. (MATTHEW 1:17)

|

CHRIST — THE REDEEMED BRIDE
(You and I, grafted in by redemption)
ISAIAH 61:10

NOTES

CHAPTER 1

1. J. Vernon McGee, *Ruth, The Romance of Redemption* (Wheaton, IL: Van Kampen Press Inc., 1954), 8.
2. Ibid., 9.
3. Ibid.
4. *The Spirit-Filled Life Bible* (Nashville: Thomas Nelson, 1991), 389.
5. Yehoshua Bachrach, *Mother of Royalty* (Jerusalem/New York: Feldheim Publishers, 1973), 1.
6. Ibid., 6.
7. Ibid.
8. McGee, *Ruth*, 24.
9. Yehoshua Bachrach, *Mother of Royalty*, 6.

CHAPTER 2

1. Rabbis Nosson Scherman/Meir Zlotowitz, The ArtScroll Tanach Series, *The Book of Ruth* (Brooklyn: Mesorah Publications, 1989), 60.
2. Ibid., 61.
3. Elie Wiesel, *Sages and Dreamers* (New York: SummitBooks, 1991), 53.
4. McGee, *Ruth*, 15.
5. Ibid., 40.
6. Ibid., 42.
7. Bachrach, *Mother of Royalty*, 11.
8. Ibid., 15.
9. Rebbetzin Esther Jungreis, *The Committed Life* (San Francisco: HarperSanFrancisco, 1998), 62.
10. Bachrach, *Mother of Royalty*, 15.
11. *The Spirit-Filled Life Bible*, 388.
12. Ibid.
13. McGee, *Ruth*, 38.
14. Ibid.
15. Bachrach, *Mother of Royalty*, 14.
16. George Robinson, *Essential Judaism* (New York: Pocket Books, 2000), 575.
17. Scherman/Zlotowitz, *The Book of Ruth*, 79.
18. *The Woman's Study Bible* (Nashville: Thomas Nelson, 1995), 433.

19. Ibid.

20. McGee, *Ruth*, 39.

21. Bachrach, *Mother of Royalty*, 23.

22. Ibid., 21.

23. http://womensissues.about.com/cs/abortionstats/a/aaabortionstats.htm

24. James S. Hewett, *Illustrations Unlimited* (Wheaton, IL: Tyndale, 1988), 15.

Chapter 3

1. Scherman/Zlotowitz, The ArtScroll Tanach Series; *The Book of Ruth*, 69.

2. Ibid.

3. Bachrach, *Mother of Royalty*, 26.

4. Scherman/Zlotowitz, *Book of Ruth*, 70.

5. Bachrach, *Mother of Royalty*, 28.

6. Ibid., 29.

7. Ibid., 31.

8. Derek Prince, *The End of Life's Journey* (Charlotte, NC: Derek Prince Ministries-International, 2004), 162.

Chapter 4

1. Scherman/Zlotowitz, The ArtScroll Tanach Series; *The Book of Ruth*, 72.

2. Yehoshua Bachrach, *Mother of Royalty*, 35.

3. Scherman/Zlotowitz, *Book of Ruth*, 79.

4. McGee, *Ruth*, 45.

5. Ibid.

6. Ibid., 46.

7. Bachrach, *Mother of Royalty*, 143.

8. Ibid., 47.

9. *The Spirit-Filled Life Bible*, 386.

10. *The Living Nach* (New York/Jerusalem: Moznaim Publishing Corporation, 1998), 534.

11. Quoted extensively from Hewett, *Illustrations Unlimited*, 19–20.

12. Hewett, *Illustrations Unlimited*, 20.

13. Adapted from Hewett, *Illustrations Unlimited*, 186.

14. Ibid.

Chapter 5

1. Scherman/Zlotowitz, The ArtScroll Tanach Series; *The Book of Ruth*, 82.

2. Ibid.

3. Bachrach, *Mother of Royalty*, 57.

4. Scherman/Zlotowitz, *Book of Ruth*, 83.

5. Ibid., 85.

6. Ibid.

7. Hewett, *Illustrations Unlimited*, 51.

8. Shoney Alex Braun, *My Heart Is a Violin* (1st Books Library, 2002), 38, 55–58.

9. Hewett, *Illustrations Unlimited*, 411.

CHAPTER 6

1. Scherman/Zlotowitz, The ArtScroll Tanach Series; *The Book of Ruth*, 85.

2. Bachrach, *Mother of Royalty*, 63.

3. Scherman/Zlotowitz, *Book of Ruth*, 86.

4. Rabbi Yosef Ze'ev Lipowitz, *Ruth, The Scroll of Kindness* (Jerusalem/New York: Feldheim Publishers, 2001), 79.

5. McGee, *Ruth*, 90.

6. Bachrach, *Mother of Royalty*, 68.

7. Scherman/Zlotowitz, *Book of Ruth*, 88.

8. Ibid.

9. McGee, *Ruth*, 90.

10. Ibid., 92.

11. Ibid.

12. Migdal Ohr- Nourishing the Seeds of Israel's Future

CHAPTER 7

1. Scherman/Zlotowitz, The ArtScroll Tanach Series; *The Book of Ruth*, 89.

2. Ibid.

3. Ibid.

4. Bachrach, *Mother of Royalty*, 81.

5. McGee, *Ruth*, 57.

6. Scherman/Zlotowitz, *Book of Ruth*, 91.

7. Ibid.

8. *Webster's New World Dictionary of the American Language with Student Handbook* (Nashville: The Southwestern Company, 1971) 187.

9. Derek Prince, *Blessing or Curse: You Can Choose* (Grand Rapids, MI: Chosen Books, 2000), 189–97.

10. *Webster's New World Dictionary of the American Language with Student Handbook*, 79.

11. Adapted from Hewett, *Illustrations Unlimited*, 60.

CHAPTER 8

1. Scherman/Zlotowitz, The ArtScroll Tanach Series; *The Book of Ruth*, 94.

2. Ibid.

3. *The Spirit-Filled Life Bible*, 390.

4. Scherman/Zlotowitz, *Book of Ruth*, 95.

5. Lipowitz, *Ruth: The Scroll of Kindness*, 94.

6. Bachrach, *Mother of Royalty*, 88.

7. Scherman/Zlotowitz, *Book of Ruth*, 96.

8. Ibid., 98.

9. Adapted from McGee, *Ruth*, 59.

CHAPTER 9

1. Charles Haddon Spurgeon, *Spurgeon's Sermons on Old Testament Women Book Two* (Grand Rapids, MI: Kregel, 1995), 88.
2. Scherman/Zlotowitz, The ArtScroll Tanach Series; *The Book of Ruth*, 100.
3. Rabbi Shmuel Yerushalmi, The Torah Anthology, Yalkut ME'AM LO'EZ, *The Book of Ruth* (New York/Jerusalem: Moznaim Publishing Corp 1989), 81–82.
4. Ibid., 83.
5. *The Spirit-Filled Life Bible*, 391, footnote.
6. Excerpt from Derek Prince's Memorial Service, 1 November, 2003.
7. McGee, *Ruth*, 61.
8. Adapted from McGee, *Ruth*, 62.
9. Quoted extensively from Hewett, *Illustrations Unlimited*, 443.

CHAPTER 10

1. Yerushalmi, The Torah Anthology, *The Book of Ruth*, 83.
2. Scherman/Zlotowitz, The ArtScroll Tanach Series; *The Book of Ruth*, 102.
3. Ibid., 103.
4. George Robinson, *Essential Judaism* (New York: Pocket Books, 2000), 224.
5. http://www.aish.com/shavuotthemes/shavuotthemesdefault/Lively_Overview_The_Book_of_Ruth.aspShavuot–7
6. McGee, *Ruth*, 67.
7. Bachrach, *Mother of Royalty*, 99.
8. Scherman/Zlotowitz, *Book of Ruth*, 106.
9. Yerushalmi, *Book of Ruth*, 89.
10. Wiesel, *Sages and Dreamers*, 50.
11. Adapted from the *Comparative Study Bible* (Grand Rapids, MI: Zondervan, 1999), 54 Amplified.
12. Hewett, *Illustrations Unlimited*, 293.
13. Ibid., 290.

CHAPTER 11

1. Yerushalmi, The Torah Anthology, *The Book of Ruth*, 91.
2. Ibid.
3. Lipowitz, *Ruth: The Scroll of Kindness*, 104.
4. Yerushalmi, *Book of Ruth*, 92.
5. *The Living Nach*, 539.
6. McGee, *Ruth*, 69.
7. Ibid., 109.
8. Scherman/Zlotowitz, The ArtScroll Tanach Series; *The Book of Ruth*, 109.
9. Robinson, *Essential Judaism*, 246–47.
10. Scherman/Zlotowitz, *Book of Ruth*, 109.
11. Ibid.
12. Yerushalmi, *Book of Ruth*, 95.

13. Scherman/Zlotowitz, *Book of Ruth,* 110.

14. Adapted from Scherman/Zlotowitz, *Book of Ruth,* 110.

15. Lipowitz, *Ruth The Scroll of Kindness,* 111.

16. Quoted extensively from Hewett, *Illustrations Unlimited,* 74.

17. Derek Prince, *The Spirit-Filled Believer's Handbook* (Orlando, FL: Creation House, 1993), 87.

18. Ibid., 77–82.

19. Ibid., 83.

20. Ibid., 85.

CHAPTER 12

1. Scherman/Zlotowitz, *Book of Ruth,* 112.

2. Yerushalmi, *Book of Ruth,* 99.

3. Ibid.

4. Scherman/Zlotowitz, *Book of Ruth,* 113.

5. Yerushalmi, *Book of Ruth,* 103.

6. Derek Prince, *The Spirit-Filled Believer's Handbook* (Orlando, FL: Creation House, 1993), Chapter 37.

7. William T. Ligon, Sr, *Imparting the Blessing to Your Children* (Brunswick, GA: Shalom, Inc., 1989), Chapter 5.

8. Derek Prince, *The Power of Proclamation* (South Pacific: Derek Prince Ministries, 2002), 108.

9. Hewett, *Illustrations Unlimited,* 35.

10. Ibid., 35.

CHAPTER 13

1. Yerushalmi, The Torah Anthology, *The Book of Ruth,* 104.

2. Bachrach, *Mother of Royalty,* 116.

3. Yerushalmi, *Book of Ruth,* 105.

4. *The Living Nach,* 541.

5. Ibid.

6. Ibid.

7. Robinson, *Essential Judaism,* 33.

CHAPTER 14

1. Lipowitz, *Ruth: The Scroll of Kindness,* 121.

2. Bachrach, *Mother of Royalty,* 119.

3. Rabbi Shmuel Yerushalmi, The Torah Anthology, *The Book of Ruth,* 108.

4. Bachrach, *Mother of Royalty,* 119.

5. McGee, *Ruth,* 76.

6. Rebbetzin Esther Jungreis, *The Committed Life* (San Francisco: HarperSanFrancisco, 1998), 245.

7. Bachrach, *Mother of Royalty,* 30.

8. McGee, *Ruth,* 31.

9. Ibid., 76.

CHAPTER 15

1. Lipowitz, *Ruth: The Scroll of Kindness,* 124.
2. Yerushalmi, The Torah Anthology, *The Book of Ruth,* 111.
3. Scherman/Zlotowitz, The ArtScroll Tanach Series; *The Book of Ruth,* 120.
4. Ibid.
5. Lipowitz, *Ruth,* 124.
6. Bachrach, *Mother of Royalty,* 123.
7. Yerushalmi, *Book of Ruth,* 112.
8. Scherman/Zlotowitz, *Book of Ruth,* 124.
9. Yerushalmi, *Book of Ruth,* 122.
10. Scherman/Zlotowitz, *Book of Ruth,* 125.
11. Yerushalmi, *Book of Ruth,* 123.
12. Ibid., 124.
13. Ibid.
14. Adapted from McGee, *Ruth,* Chapter XI.
15. Quoted extensively from Hewett, *Illustrations Unlimited,* 250.
16. Adapted from McGee, *Ruth,* Chapter XII.
17. Quoted extensively from Hewett, *Illustrations Unlimited,* 226.
18. Adapted from McGee, *Ruth,* Chapter XIII.
19. Inspired by Hewett, *Unlimited Illustrations,* 249.
20. Quoted extensively from McGee, *Ruth,* Chapter XIV.
21. Adapted from Hewett, *Illustrations Unlimited,* 34.
22. *The Spirit-Filled Life Bible,* 98.
23. Adapted from McGee, *Ruth,* Chapter XV.
24. Inspired from Hewett, *Illustrations Unlimited,* 67.
25. Robert Lowry, Nothing But the Blood."

CHAPTER 16

1. Scherman/Zlotowitz, The ArtScroll Tanach Series; *The Book of Ruth,* 130.
2. Yerushalmi, The Torah Anthology, *The Book of Ruth,* 127.
3. Ibid., 128.
4. Ibid., 129.
5. Bachrach, *Mother of Royalty,* 130.
6. Scherman/Zlotowitz, *Book of Ruth,* 129.
7. Ibid., 130.
8. Ibid.
9. Yerushalmi, *Book of Ruth,* 130.
10. Bachrach, *Mother of Royalty,* 131.
11. Derek Prince, *God Is a Match-Maker* (Grand Rapids: Chosen Books, 1986), 13.
12. Ibid., 17.
13. Ibid., 18.
14. Ibid., 20.
15. Ibid.

16. Ibid., 21.
17. Rebbetzin Esther Jungreis, *The Committed Life* (San Francisco: HarperSanFrancisco, 1998), 250.

CHAPTER 17

1. Yerushalmi, The Torah Anthology, *The Book of Ruth,* 133.
2. Ibid.
3. Scherman/Zlotowitz, The ArtScroll Tanach Series; *The Book of Ruth,* 134.
4. Moshe Pinchas Weisblum, *Ruth Talk* (Middle Village, NY: Jonathan David Publishers, 2005), 201.
5. Ibid., 202.
6. Scherman/Zlotowitz, *Book of Ruth,* 132.
7. Yerushalmi, *The Book of Ruth,* 134.
8. Ibid.
9. Ibid., 135.
10. Ibid., 136.
11. Ibid., 135.
12. Ibid.
13. Ibid.
14. Derek Prince, *The Power of Proclamation,* 6.
15. McGee, *Ruth,* 148.
16. Ibid., 152.
17. Inspired from Hewett, *Illustrations Unlimited,* 247.

CHAPTER 18

1. Scherman/Zlotowitz, The ArtScroll Tanach Series; *The Book of Ruth,* 133.
2. Ibid., 134.
3. Ibid.
4. Ibid., 135.
5. Ibid.
6. Ibid.
7. Ibid.
8. Ibid.
9. Ibid.
10. Yerushalmi, *The Torah Anthology, The Book of Ruth,* 140.
11. Ibid.
12. McGee, *Ruth,* 19.
13. Ibid.
14. Adapted from McGee, *Ruth,* Chapter IV.
15. Ibid.
16. Ibid.
17. Adapted from *A Mother's Path* by Temple Bailey, http://legacy.bluesky40.com/authors.html
18. Adapted from Hewett, *Illustrations Unlimited,* 259.